In Search of
Parenthood

In Search of Parenthood

Coping with Infertility and High-Tech Conception

Revised and Updated

Judith N. Lasker
Susan Borg

Temple University Press
Philadelphia

Temple University Press, Philadelphia 19122
Copyright © 1994 by Temple University
All rights reserved
Published 1994

♾ The paper used in this publication meets the minimum
requirements of American National Standard for Information
Sciences—Permanence of Paper for Printed Library Materials,
ANSI Z39.48-1984

Printed in the United States of America

Library of Congress Cataloging-in-Publication Data

Lasker, Judith.
    In search of parenthood : coping with infertility and high-tech
conception / Judith N. Lasker, Susan Borg. — Rev. and updated ed.
        p.   cm.
    Includes bibliographical references and index.
    ISBN 1–56639–258–6 (cloth) — ISBN 1–56639–259–4 (pbk.)
    1. Infertility.   2. Human reproductive technology.   I. Borg,
Susan.   II. Title.
    RC889.L37   1994
    616.6′92—dc20   94–12494

To Miriam and Arnold Lasker,
Barry Siegel,
Shira and Ariella Lasker Siegel

And to Ruth and Emanuel Oransky
and Laura and Margo Borg

*With awe and gratitude
for the miracle of life
and love that connects
one generation to another*

Contents

Significant Others

Effects on the Family

Preface to New Edition

When a book is reissued in a new edition, this often means that a new preface is tacked onto the front of an unchanged text. We have chosen a very different route—a complete update with important revisions to the 1987 edition. Every chapter has been changed, some quite significantly, and many more recent references have been added.

We decided to revise the book because so many changes have occurred since it was first published. Certainly many of the technologies for conception have changed. Some, particularly *in vitro* fertilization and GIFT, have achieved better success rates over these intervening years, although the rates are still low. Some procedures, such as ovum donation, gestational surrogacy, and microinsemination, which were fairly rare in 1987, have become much more widespread. And the ovum transfer program, about which we wrote with great skepticism, no longer exists, but its story is very instructive.

New techniques are being developed constantly, so that no book can ever be totally up-to-date. We have included, however, the major trends and changes that are defining infertility practices for the foreseeable future.

The other major change of the last seven years is the greatly increased level of critical discourse about these new technologies. At the same time that alternative methods for conception have become increasingly available and accepted, concerns about their dangers to individual patients and their implications for women as a whole have been raised with great cogency. In the first edition, we discussed the early criticisms of worried feminists and ethicists; we have incorporated those worries with greater urgency in this new edition, as some of the dire predictions have been borne out by many troubling experiences.

We hope that this book will illuminate the dilemmas that new technologies create for individuals and for society. Each new technique offers hope and trauma, terrible costs, and some wonderful benefits. We hope that both the individuals who are seeking to make the best decisions for themselves and the public that is attempting to sort out the meaning and future of the momentous changes we describe will find insight in these pages.

Judith N. Lasker
Susan Borg
September 1994

Acknowledgments

Without the help of hundreds of people, this book would not have been possible. We want each one of them to know that our words of gratitude are very deeply felt.

The many women and men who were willing to share their private pain and their experiences with infertility and new techologies are the heart of this book. In addition, the surrogate mothers and sperm and embryo donors who we interviewed gave us valuable insights into the vital role of the "third parent" in many of these new methods. We have guarded the anonymity of all of these people by changing their names and combining stories, but we have also tried very hard to be true to their words and their feelings.

We are very grateful to the professionals who shared their experiences and expertise with us. They gave us insights into the excitement, the frustrations, and the doubts. In many cases, they helped us to find people who would be willing to be interviewed about their experiences as donors, surrogate mothers, or clients of fertility programs. We list their names here, the attorneys, nurses, physicians, psychiatrists, psychologists, researchers, and social workers, with a sincere thank you: Howard Adelman, Ph.D., Linda Applegarth, Ed.D., Kenneth J. Borg, Esq., Annette Brodsky, Ph.D., John Buster, M.D., Diane Clapp, R.N., Alan DeCherney, M.D., Anne Marie DeLise, R.N., Robert Echenberg, M.D., Ramon Garcia, M.D., Gale Golden, M.S.W., Dorothy Greenfield, M.S.W., Hilary Hanafin, Ph.D., Ellen Herrenkohl, Ph.D., Gary Hodgen, Ph.D., James Holman, M.D., Pat Humpries, R.N., Elaine Ishita, R.N., Noel Keane, Esq., Ekkehard Kemmann, M.D., Andrea Koch, Ph.D., Gregory Lang, M.D., Linda Lynch, Dorie McArthur, Ph.D., Hugh Melnick, M.D., Dorothy Mitchell, R.N., Fanny Nero, R.N., Samuel Pasquale, M.D., Zev Rosenwaks, M.D., Barbara Katz Rothman, Ph.D., Burton Satzberg, Esq., Marion Sokolik, M.S.W., James Twerdahl.

Our thanks to the RESOLVE organization, both nationally and in many local chapters, which published our request for people to interview and provided us with valuable information and connections.

Many friends and colleagues read and commented on selected chapters or even the entire manuscript. We thank the following people for the time and thought they gave to making the writing as clear, complete, and accurate as possible: Diane Clapp, Robert Cohen, Ann Ehrenkrantz, Joel Ehrenkrantz, Katie Griffiths, Ellen Herrenkohl, Mary Ann Hughes, Susan Lippa, Jackie Litt, Rosemary Merrill, Debby Nolan, Joan Odes, Louise Potvin, Carole Reese, Carol Selman, Jane Stein, Kandi Stinson, Susan Turkel, and Sheryl Weinstein. Barbara Katz Rothman has been a valuable colleague and friend who has contributed in many ways to this book and also gave us extensive comments on the final draft.

A number of Lehigh University students played a very important role in the research for this book, both in searching out the literature and in assisting with the data from two surveys that we conducted. Many thanks to Mary Ann Hughes, Ken Litwin, Mary Loder, Alice Mesaros, Brenda Panicchi, and Linda Wimpfheimer.

Anne Van Doren and Carol Wranovic did an excellent job of transcribing the tapes of interviews, and Judy Specht and Carol Sabo assisted a great deal with typing and word processing expertise. Tom, Suzanne, and especially Sandy Kelly made the typing, multiple revisions, and completion of the manuscript a family project. We thank them for the many lost weekends, and for being available and helpful at all times.

This has been an expensive project, including travel to infertility programs, typing and transcribing, telephone calls, equipment and supplies, and research assistance costs. We are very grateful to Lehigh University for providing the financial resources needed through several sources: the Class of 1961 Professorship; the Unsponsored Research Fund; the Science, Technology and Society Program; and the Biomedical Research Support Grant. The Department of Sociology and Anthropology and the Center for Social Research at Lehigh also provided important moral support and material assistance for the completion of this work.

Since we live in different states, we have had to find a midway point in which to meet and work. Parts of this book were written in various diners and public libraries in western New Jersey. A special note of thanks to the wonderful librarians in Washington, New Jersey, who made us feel so much at home in our search for a place to work.

Our families have contributed tremendously to this book. A special thanks to Barry Siegel and Alan Oransky for comments and suggestions and to Marcia Eskin for all of her help and support.

Our parents, as always, have taught, guided, and encouraged us. We so much appreciate their advice and their pride. Ruth and Manny Oransky have been very supportive, and Ruth's generous assistance with the children has been indispensable. Miriam and Arnold Lasker, in addition to regularly sending valuable articles, read almost every draft of every chapter. They gave enormously of their time, energy, and expertise to help us organize and present our thoughts clearly. Their wisdom has marked almost every page.

Our daughters, Shira, Laura, Margo, and Ariella, have done more than anyone else to help us appreciate the "search for parenthood." Their lives have been a miracle for us. We thank them for their inspiration and for the joy they have given us.

In Search of
Parenthood

Introduction

Many people have asked us how we came to write this book together. They wonder why two women, one a sociologist living in Pennsylvania and the other an architect and city planner living in New Jersey, drove hundreds of miles each week to write about infertility.

We met over forty years ago, in Mrs. Cosgrove's kindergarten class. We grew up together, around the corner from each other, sharing the play and dreams of childhood. In all of those years spent in each other's homes and on the phone together, we rarely talked about having children. We just assumed that one day, when the time was right, we would become mothers.

Years later we both discovered, tragically, how false that assumption had been. Within a horrible period of six months, we each watched our firstborn baby die. From our experiences we learned that pregnancy does not always occur easily and that healthy babies should not be taken for granted. We relied on each other for comfort and for support in our grief. Out of that sharing came *When Pregnancy Fails: Families Coping with Miscarriage, Ectopic Pregnancy, Stillbirth, and Infant Death*, a book we wrote about the experience of loss in pregnancy.[1]

We have spoken about miscarriage and infant loss to many groups since the book was first published. Because of our writing and speaking, we have met thousands of men and women who also grieve for the babies they have lost. Each one of them reminds us that creating a healthy baby is an intricate, miraculous process that goes wrong much too often.

Many of the people we have met are struggling with infertility as well. Their stories of grief for the children they cannot have touched us deeply. We felt their pain and frustration even more strongly because of personal encounters with infertility. We realized that there is almost no understanding from others for this kind of loss. From our awareness of the enormous impact of infertility and the many changes occurring in its treatment came the desire to write *In Search of Parenthood*.

Most people like us who have struggled to become parents started out thinking they had some control over their lives. We all grew up with the revolutionary idea of reproductive choice. With more effective birth control and abortion legalized (if not always available) we could plan when (or if) we wanted to have children. We have arrived painfully at the realization that we really have very little control. The idea of "reproductive freedom" is a cruel reminder of what we thought we were entitled to and discovered we have lost.

Becoming a parent seems as though it should be easier than ever before. There is much greater knowledge about reproduction and many new treatments for infertility. Yet the most advanced medical technologies and the best efforts of both prospective parents and health professionals cannot guarantee success. Millions of Americans are now caught up in a desperate search to have a baby.

Why do so many people have trouble conceiving? Infections, sexually transmitted diseases, environmental toxins, and occupational hazards are all important factors affecting the fertility of both men and women. As couples wait longer to begin having children, there is more time to be exposed to these hazards. In addition, medical care itself has caused some infertility. Some birth control measures, especially the Dalkon Shield I.U.D., have fostered infections that destroyed women's reproductive organs. DES, a hormone given to pregnant women several decades ago, caused infertility in many of their children years later. Even cesarean sections increase the chance of problems because of infections and scarring that may result from surgery.[2]

According to the National Center for Health Statistics's (NCHS) 1988 National Survey of Family Growth, 4.9 million women, or one in every twelve women of childbearing age in the United States, has difficulty conceiving or carrying a child. Of course not all of those who report difficulty are actually trying to or want to have another child. On the other hand, results from the 1982 National Survey of Family Growth revealed that about one-fourth of the 9.5 million women who are in couples in which one partner was sterilized for contraceptive reasons still would like to have a child. These women are often also candidates for the methods described here.[3]

The percentage of nonsterilized women who are infertile (8%) has remained constant over the course of two decades. Yet there is a widely held perception that infertility is dramatically increasing. This is due to the fact that the same percentage results in growing *numbers* of women as those in the large demographic bulge created by the baby boom generation get older, and particularly as women in their thirties begin trying to conceive for the first time. At the same time, adoption has become increasingly difficult or unavailable. Partially as a result of these changes, the demand for infertility services has grown enormously.[4]

Although infertility is almost twice as likely to affect black women as white women, particularly among those who have been pregnant before, the demand for services is especially strong among middle- and upper-middle-class educated and mostly white people in their thirties who have never had children. They are people with resources but, because of their age, not much time to wait. Medical, legal, and scientific professionals as well as corporate interests have rushed in to respond to this situation. The result has been that the number of infertility-related programs has multiplied in the past few years. Not surprisingly, therefore, the number of women who reported in the NCHS national survey that they had sought infertility services in the previous year increased 264 percent between 1982 and 1988.[5]

These programs promise alternatives that may help fulfill the dreams of people who want so much to be parents. But they also carry with them very high emotional and financial costs. In this book, we examine the new technologies—the hope they offer as well as the difficult dilemmas and personal challenges they present.

The methods we look at are artificial insemination with sperm from the husband (AIH) or from a donor (AID), *in vitro* (better known as test-tube) fertilization (IVF) and its variations such as GIFT (gamete intrafallopian transfer) and ovum donation, and surrogate motherhood. In addition we will examine the case of ovum transfer (OT) from a donor woman, a method that failed and which illustrates some of the potential problems with what many physicians call "Assisted Reproductive Technology" (ART). Although there are many possible treatments for infertility, and new procedures have been developed that may increase the chance of "natural" conception, these are the most publicized and the most controversial. Variations on each method are being developed all the time. While the alternatives are very different from each other, the attention they have received, in contrast to other infertility treatments, is largely due to their being methods of conceiving a child without sexual intercourse.

Much of the research on which the methods are based was originally intended to help cattle breeders and has been going on for decades. Only in the past decade have these methods begun to be widely available for solving problems of human infertility. The success rates continue to be low, and many couples who are concerned about infertility eventually conceive without any intervention. Yet more and more people are convinced—by advertising and media reports that often greatly exaggerate the chances of success, by the urgings of their doctors, as well as by the positive experiences of some others—that artificial insemination, IVF, surrogacy, or some combination of these, are their only avenue to parenthood. As treatments are perfected, as the concern about infertility continues to rise, and as more private companies and medical institutions seek to participate in the challenge and the profits to be made from infertility programs, the numbers of people trying these methods will continue to rise rapidly worldwide.

Infertile people now make up the greatest portion of those who are interested in the alternatives. Other situations might also lead people to consider them. One member of a couple might carry a genetic trait that he or she does not want to risk passing on to a child. There are women for whom pregnancy may be dangerous. Single heterosexual or gay women who want to become parents without sexual involvement are increasingly using AID. Although in this book we refer primarily to infertile couples, we intend for our comments to apply to anyone who has difficulty in conceiving or carrying a healthy baby and who might consider one of these methods.

Over the past few years there has been increasing concern about the use and potential of these technologies. For example, critics are very concerned that poor women are being exploited for their breeding capability by wealthy women and their husbands, and that surrogate mothers will be hired for convenience by women who simply do not wish to be pregnant. The typical practice of AID encourages parents to attempt to create superior children with selected genetic traits. Embryos created through IVF are already being genetically screened and cloned in experiments. While these methods could help reduce genetic disease, they may also lead to a narrowing of acceptable human variation and help to achieve the widespread preference for sons, which currently results in selective abortion of female fetuses.

The new methods give even greater power to scientists and physicians, who not only assist couples to conceive on their own but also actually "perform" the conception themselves in their offices or laboratories. They are storing the beginnings of life in "banks" and, in many cases, turning their practices into commercial ventures. The production of children is now a $2 billion business. All of this raises serious questions about how we think of children and of the women who give birth to them. As scientists gain more control over reproduction, many thoughtful people worry that babies have already been turned into products of a commercial process in which the parts are being bought and sold and screened and perfected, with the mother reduced to being the packaging.

These are very real worries, and the direction of research raises troubling questions. Most infertile people, however, do not worry about these issues. They would like nothing better than to conceive the "old-fashioned" way. For them, the alternatives are not a convenience or an adventure or a social problem. They are only a last resort in a personal quest. The conflict between personal choices and social consequences is one of the most important themes in any understanding of the rapid changes in infertility treatment.

A great deal has already been written about these alternatives. Important books and articles examine carefully the legal, ethical, or political problems raised by the new technologies. Some authors extol the wonders of the new discoveries and explain the technical aspects in detail. Others condemn them as ethically questionable, religiously unacceptable, or socially dangerous.

Our purpose is a different one. We examine the impact of these methods on the many people whose lives they touch—the hopeful parents and their families, the donors and surrogate mothers, the professionals, and of course the children. We look at the personal side, the emotional impact of the technology, and the social context within which families are deciding which alternatives to pursue. The technical details are changing extraordinarily fast, as almost every week brings publicity about new developments. But the feelings and concerns of the people involved, which are the focus of this book, remain basically the same.

These methods are bringing enormous benefits to many people, but they also present many emotional risks and potential physical dangers. No one knows for sure what long-term effects these new medical procedures may have on the mothers and fathers or on the children. The debate over their safety has intensified as new research both exposes hazards and brings about technical improvements.

People already feeling vulnerable because they have not been able to have children now face unprecedented dilemmas and decisions. How much are they willing to go through to try to have a child? Can they find the right resources? Can they afford it? Should they tell anyone? Can they take the added stress and physical risk? How do they feel about being part of an experiment, doing something others may condemn? How should they relate to the person who provided the semen or the egg or who carried the baby for them?

As we consider these questions, we address the differences in the ways men and women tend to respond to them. These differences often create difficult times for couples already under great stress. They may disagree on how important it is to have a biological child rather than adopt, or how much to share the news of what they are doing with friends, or on what they will later tell the child. The responses to these issues are often very different depending on whether it is the man or the woman who has been identified as infertile.

In examining these methods, we must ask how the increasing medical control over life, the transformation of babies into commodities created from parts purchased by those with money to do so, the view of surrogate mothers as incubators with a contract and no ties to the baby they carry— how does all this affect the people who are now turning to professionals, looking for emotional support as well as medical expertise? And what about the much greater number who cannot afford even to consider the possibilities? How will this medical control affect all of us in the future?

The public knows little about the people who are sperm or ovum donors or "surrogate mothers," people who are increasingly involved in these efforts to conceive. We will compare the motivations and experiences of the anonymous sperm donors to those of the women who contract to conceive and carry a baby for someone else. Is it really so easy for any of them?

The new technologies have challenged us to reconsider what we mean by a parent or by a family. For instance, donor insemination is giving single people, both homosexuals and heterosexuals, greater options for parenthood. Some parents are including surrogate mothers as part of their families, and increasingly relatives are the source for donated ova. The possibilities for control over conception raise numerous questions, concerns, and possibilities with regard to social relationships.[6]

In the heated debates that have emerged around these new alternatives, we find it impossible to join those who take a position that is unequivocally for or against. The more we have studied the experiences of people trying these methods, the more we feel torn between the two sides of this debate.

Both of us have known the anguish of not having the baby we wanted so much. Now that we are mothers with living children, who are so central to our lives, we cannot imagine anyone taking away our chance of having them. We have also seen the incredible joy of people who have finally had babies after all else failed. Because of these experiences, we feel reluctant to see options eliminated if they do in fact help people who want to become parents.

There is another side to this situation, though. We worry more and more about the abuses that have resulted from the commercialization of conception. We are disturbed by the exploitation of women hired as surrogates, many of whom grieve deeply for the babies they thought they could give up. We detest the growth of profiteering at the expense of infertile people. And we share with many critics the concern that increasing medical control over conception, pregnancy, and childbirth is leading to more restrictions on the lives of women and on the kinds of children it is acceptable to have. We have little confidence, after seeing so many abuses in the past, that scientific discoveries in the field of reproduction will be used only to help people. We have seen people pressured into trying an expensive and stressful method simply because it was there, only to meet with renewed devastation from one more failure. We have learned of patients being deceived about the likelihood of success and led on by physicians with little experience.

In spite of what we have learned, we find ourselves sometimes recommending one or another of these alternatives. We understand the desperate need of our friends to become parents. Yet we also warn them that this is not easy, that the issues are complex, that they need to know exactly what they are getting into.

———•———

Our review of the literature in medicine, sociology, psychology, law, and ethics has given us some information about the issues we considered to be important in writing this book. But we knew that the best insights would come from talking with people who had experienced the various methods. We wondered at first, since these methods were quite new when we started, if we could find men and women who would share their stories with us.

It was easier to find people than we had expected because so many lives are affected by infertility. Some people were referred to us by physicians and staff members of IVF and surrogacy programs; others were found through personal contacts. The largest single group was made up of people who responded to our requests for assistance in both national and local newsletters of RESOLVE, a support organization for infertile people. Most of the infertile people in our study had already tried one or more of the alternatives; some had considered them and decided not to go on. Some had had successful pregnancies, others were still trying to conceive. Many had adopted children.

We interviewed people from all over the country, in person and by phone, and all of these interviews were taped (with permission) and transcribed. In addition, 94 people (65 women and 29 men) completed questionnaires sent out to those who responded to our request in RESOLVE newsletters. We also visited a variety of infertility clinics and surrogacy programs of different types and sizes throughout the country, interviewing physicians, nurses, lawyers, and therapists. We also interviewed donors—surrogate mothers and sperm and embryo donors. All together, over 200 people directly contributed their experiences to this book.

The interview transcripts and the questionnaires are the sources for the quotes used in this book. The stories of specific couples whom we describe sometimes combine quotes from several interviews; they are intended to portray the issues that people involved experience while being faithful to the words of those who spoke with us.

This book is based, then, on the widely varying experiences and perceptions of a relatively large number of people, but they were not selected in a highly systematic way, and many of them volunteered to participate in response to an ad. Thus they do not represent all people who are infertile or who try alternative methods of conception. This study should be considered exploratory, one that has attempted to uncover the many important personal issues raised by the new alternatives.

We also wanted to find out more about the attitudes of people who are not directly affected by infertility. We surveyed 165 students at two colleges in Pennsylvania to obtain their views on the new alternatives. In addition, we investigated existing polls and national surveys to learn the opinions of the general public and the ways they have changed over time.

It is our hope that by reading this book, people who are considering these methods will have a clearer picture of what they are likely to face. Those who have already begun, or finished, trying an alternative should recognize that their experiences and emotions are shared by many others. Also, we want professionals to understand better their clients' experiences so that services might better meet their needs. And we hope the general public will gain a more complete idea of what these significant changes mean.

———— • ————

Since our personal tragedies, we have between us given birth to three healthy babies and adopted an infant. We have been through the travails of fertility treatment, the anxieties of prenatal testing, and the struggle for successful birth uncomplicated by excessive intervention. We feel like survivors, attuned to the fragility of birth and life by our personal experiences.

We look at our kindergarten class picture now and see two curly haired smiling girls for whom the world was so simple. We would never have believed then, nor even understood, the joys and tragedies of childbirth that would join our lives and our work so many years later.

The Trauma of Infertility

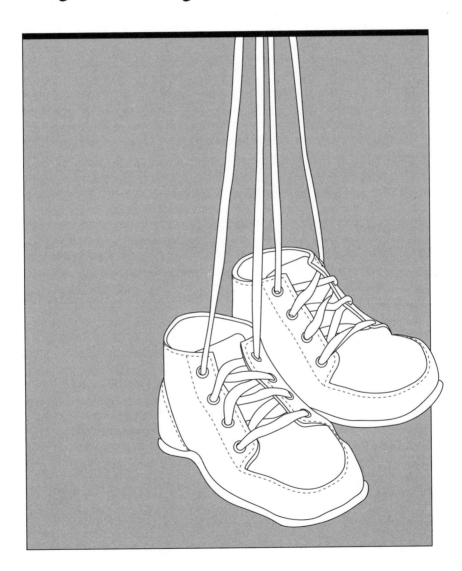

CHAPTER 1

The Drive to Have Children

We'll sell the car, the house even, if it comes to it. . . . There was nothing I wouldn't give up if it meant we could have a child.

—JOHN BROWN
Our Miracle Called Louise[1]

Over and over we have heard such words of desperation, of willingness to endure any pain or expense, even to risk one's life, all in order to have a child. The search for parenthood by infertile people has been compared to terminal cancer victims' quest for a cure. But infertility, though painful, is not life-threatening. Why are some people so driven in their efforts?

Personal and Social Pressures

Gail is a thirty-four-year-old woman we interviewed who has been through eight cycles of AIH (artificial insemination with her husband's sperm) and four attempts at IVF (test-tube fertilization) in the past five years, all without success. Gail is a calm, good-natured person, but she describes herself as "driven" to keep trying to get pregnant:

> It's worth it all to know you've done everything that you can do. I don't want to always be wondering if we should have pushed a little harder or tried something else. At least I know my inability to conceive is not from lack of trying.

What is it about conceiving and bearing children that is so crucial to infertile people like Gail, that makes them willing to try almost anything?

11

Some scientists, agreeing with Harvard sociobiologist Edward O. Wilson's theories, claim that people's desire to reproduce is innate, perhaps even programmed into their genes. Although there may be a biological component to wanting to bear children, no one has yet been able to prove or measure it. On the contrary, a great deal of evidence shows that social and psychological pressures to have children are at least as powerful, if not more so, than the biological pressures.[2]

Gail's desire for children is like that of many other people. She talks about the feeling of emptiness, the sense that her family is not yet complete. She and her husband Bill have been married for nine years, and they are eager to share their love with children. They yearn for the pleasure of cuddling babies and playing with them as they grow. They want to pass on their values, to see themselves as living on in the future through the lives of their children.

Gail and Bill fear that they are losing not only the fantasy of their ideal family but a part of themselves. Will they ever see themselves in the face of a young child? Will there be someone for them to teach, to play with, someone who will miss them when they're gone? Or, will their lives, like their bodies, be "sterile," "barren"?

Gail and Bill's own internal drive to be parents is strongly reinforced by external pressures. They feel that they have made their own choice to have children, but it is also obvious that this choice would be greatly approved by others. Gail described the pressures from her family and friends:

> When I was little, my parents talked a lot about what it would be like when I grew up and became a mother. "Growing up" and "becoming a mother" seemed like the same thing. After I got married, the comments started coming in from my friends as well as my parents—"Well, when are you going to have a family?" they kept asking us. They were all having kids, and we felt very left out. I'm sure this all had an impact on our wish for children.
>
> It isn't just my relatives and friends. I think it's in the air, almost like an epidemic. Everywhere I go there are pregnant women and babies, in the stores, on TV, just walking along the street. It makes you feel abnormal not to be pushing a stroller or buying the newest kind of diaper.

The pressures to have children go beyond comments from others and commercials on television. They are deeply imbedded in the culture, supported by powerful social norms.

Every culture has its ideal image of what a man and a woman should be like, and for the woman, the cultural ideal is almost always focused on motherhood. People who do not have children are generally considered to be selfish and maladjusted, a harsh judgment from society.[3]

The influence of social pressures becomes most obvious when there is a shift in fertility trends. In the United States, for example, there have been a number of dramatic changes over the past few decades in the number of children per family. In the aftermath of World War II, women were encouraged to have large families, and the birth rate rose sharply. Then, in the late 1960s and early 1970s, fertility dropped steadily. Childlessness became more acceptable, and small families were preferred. In the 1980s, social forces began to move us in the opposite direction once again. The media increased their focus on childbearing and women's roles as mothers, the number of births increased every year, and big business responded eagerly with new products and services. Many young women are now, in the 1990s, feeling particularly pressured to become mothers early in order to avoid the much-publicized fertility problems that might arise later.[4]

These changes are responses to the economic and political climate of the time, not simply the accumulation of millions of individual decisions. We all like to think that such important decisions as whether to have children and how many to have are made by ourselves, independently. Yet our behavior, consciously or unconsciously, is often strongly influenced by prevailing social trends.

The pressures to have children affect not only married couples. A growing number of single women, both lesbian and heterosexual, are turning to technological means of conception because of their desire to have children.[5]

The demands of others also affect those who already have one child. If having no children is selfish, having one and denying him or her the chance to have siblings is said to be cruel. "Only" children are stereotyped as spoiled and maladjusted, despite considerable evidence to the contrary. A study by sociologist Nancy Russo found that the plan to have one child is almost as unpopular among Americans as the goal of having none. This attitude makes the frequent situation of secondary infertility even more difficult for people who are trying so hard to have another child.[6]

Why should it be necessary to pressure people to have children? If the notion that children bring the ultimate fulfillment (especially for women) were true, then no one would need encouragement. But having children can be a very risky business.

National surveys generally agree that couples without children are happier with their marriages than those who do have children. Women, paradoxically, suffer the most from having children. Mothers are more likely to be depressed than non-mothers. And women who, without children, are equal to their husbands in almost every way in their marriage, quickly discover that the arrival of a child sharply reduces their power in marital decision making. Even women who continue working outside of the home lose power as they become defined as primary caretaker and homemaker.[7]

Of course there is another very different reality—that children *can* be wonderful, that parenting can be the most satisfying experience in one's life. Having children is neither pure heaven nor total hell but some incredible combination of both. The vast majority of people keep their eyes fixed on the positive, the beautiful, and take the risk. They count on the miracle of new life and the love that children bring. They cannot imagine going through life without them.

It is understandable why many people like Gail who cannot have children are so desperate. They have failed to fulfill their own desires, their expectations of what their lives should be like. They have also failed to fulfill the powerful mandate of society, but not by any choice of their own. And they feel the stigma that is attached to anyone who deviates from the most central norms of society.[8] It is no wonder that some people are willing to undergo enormous stress and risk to become parents.

Why Not Adopt?

If the goal were primarily to be parents, it should not matter so much where the children come from. Gail told us she is asked by some of her friends, "Why not just adopt?"

> They don't seem to understand why, for me, adoption is still a last resort. It just is not the same as having a biological child.

The social norm is not only to be a parent; it is to be a biological parent. We are urged to create new life, to perpetuate the species.

Most of the people who responded to our questionnaires and interviews indicated that they had indeed considered adoption or were already on a waiting list. The fact remains, however, that almost all of them (including some who had already adopted one child) were still pursuing other alternatives. Why don't they give up on trying to conceive, especially after repeated failures? Why do they reject adoption or turn to it only as a last resort?

Adoption is risky and difficult. Waiting lists for healthy infants are long. The costs are exorbitant. Adoption agency caseworkers ask a lot of personal questions, make judgments, and have excessive control over one's life. Some people simply are not eligible. These are the reasons people gave us for not wanting to pursue adoption.

But infertility procedures are often described in exactly the same terms. Programs are impersonal; waiting for results is unbearable. Failure rates are high, and costs are prohibitive for many. Even so, most people prefer to try infertility treatments, with all their problems, rather than face the difficulties of adoption. There is one very basic reason for this choice: Most people want a biological child.

All those people who filled out our questionnaire and said they had rejected adoption as an alternative cited the desire for a biological child as the reason. Those who try the reproductive alternatives are going through all of this trouble and stress not only to be parents but also to create their "own" children.[9]

Becoming parents is very closely tied, in the minds of many, to the proper functioning of their bodies. A man sees a biological child as proof of his virility. For a woman, a biological child means being able to experience pregnancy, birth, and breast-feeding. For both, the inability to produce a child is a threat to their sexual identity.

For many people, genes are the key issue. As Bill said:

> Gail is really smart and pretty, and I feel good about myself. It would be neat to see our qualities passed on to a child. And we worry about how healthy or intelligent an adopted child would be. At least with our own, we think we'd have a pretty good idea of what we'd be getting.

Some people worry about the effects of adoption on children, especially foreign-born or biracial children. Having "one's own" seems so much less complicated. It is certainly more acceptable to the world around us.

A child is the most visible demonstration of a couple's love for each other, a miraculous creation out of the union of two intimate people. One woman expressed her regret at losing this possibility:

> The hardest part of all of this has been dealing with the idea of our lovemaking not producing a little part of ourselves, melted together. I still miss my husband's smile or his eyes in our adopted son, although I love him dearly.

Men usually appear to be the driving force behind the preference for a biological child.[10] Many women told us that they would be happy to adopt, but that their husbands wanted a genetic connection. The men agreed. Why the difference?

Genes are obviously the biggest contribution men make to the creation of a child. They cannot carry, birth, or nurse a baby. In addition, they are rarely the major caregiver. Women can "mother" in many ways. Many men, especially those who have not yet experienced the daily caring and loving that fathering can entail, focus on the biological connection.

Gail explained her husband's reluctance to adopt:

Bill thought he would feel more comfortable with a child that was ours biologically. He says he just couldn't accept an adopted child as his own.

Men may also be more concerned with carrying on the family name and heritage. One man who learned he was infertile explained:

The hardest part was telling my father. I felt like I had failed him. I had broken the chain, the idea of continuity from the past to the future, which still seems so important in some primitive part of ourselves.

When adoption was easier, it may have been a more acceptable solution. In any case, it was often the only alternative to childlessness. Today, the situation is dramatically different. People keep trying for biological children not only because they want them and not only because of social pressures but also because infertility specialists are promising new alternatives. It has become increasingly difficult for infertile people to say no to this new set of pressures.[11]

The Pressure to Keep Trying

An individual's desire to keep trying to have a baby is powerfully reinforced from the outside—from media accounts of miracle babies, from acquaintances who have been successful, and from friends who encourage one to try a new method they have heard about. One woman told us how she felt overly pressured by optimistic news reports:

If I see one more article or book that says, "You *Can* Have a Baby," or "New Hope for Childless Couples," I think I'll scream. Sure it's good for the public to know, but the message seems to be that if you just try hard enough or go to the right doctor you're sure to get pregnant. I wish it were so easy!

The most direct pressure, and the hardest for many to resist, comes from physicians. Almost everyone we surveyed who attempted conception through AIH or AID (artificial insemination with a donor's sperm) cited a doctor's recommendation as the reason. The choice of *in vitro* fertilization was explained as "our last hope," "our only choice," a message that is strongly reinforced by the medical community.

A staff member of an IVF program described the pressure to try alternatives:

More and more it has become a matter of 'all roads lead to *in vitro*.' More and more physicians around the country are saying to couples, 'Well there's always IVF.'

People who do decide to try a new method must first of all have the financial resources required; poor women who are infertile have very few options. Second, they are usually very persistent people, very driven to succeed.[12] They are people, like Gail, who feel compelled to keep going:

> For someone who doesn't gamble and hates the idea of getting on a roller coaster, it was quite an effort to decide to try IVF. But at the same time, I found the idea of quitting most frightening. It was as if all the tests, operations, and medication through the years would have been for nothing. I just could not face the idea of failure.

Gail is very accurate in describing her decision as a gamble, a high-risk venture into the unknown. Gamblers make pacts with themselves (pacts that are often broken) about how much longer they will try to win or how much more money they will spend on each game. Infertile people do the same. They often "hedge their bets" by getting on adoption lists while trying to conceive. They promise themselves that they will try just "one more time," or "one more year," or until the money runs out.

Every new technique creates new options and new pressures, added possibilities, and increased risks. It is hard to decide whether it is worth all the risks one has to take to pursue another alternative. Is it worth the problems of having a child who is biologically related to only one parent? Is it worth the money? Is it worth the personal stress and physical pain? And most of all, is it worth taking the risk of failing once again?

Many people, despite all of the pressures, decide that they have had enough. It is not worth it to them to keep trying, to keep hurting and hoping. They discover that their lives can be very fulfilling in other ways than parenting, or that adopted children bring them every joy that they had hoped for.

Others decide that it is worth the risk, the trouble, the stress of the treatment. Their commitment to having a biological child compels them to go on, overshadowing other goals. Not being able to have children makes them feel so unhappy that some are willing to try anything that might help. Theirs is a grief that is often overwhelming, a sense of loss that only success, it seems, can erase.

CHAPTER 2

The Feelings of Grief

Once again pregnancy has eluded us. I awake with moderate cramps and lower back pain. No flow. Resisting the urge to take Motrin since maybe this is a false alarm and I might really be pregnant, I endure several hours of increasingly more severe pain. Finally, the blood comes. Right on time, my period has started. And so begins another cycle, a pattern that has repeated itself again and again over the past two and a half years.

As I have done a countless number of times in the past two weeks, I run to look at my chart. My cervix was right, my cervical mucus was right, my basal body temperature was right, and our timing of intercourse was right. What more could we have done? Clearly, infertility listens not to fact or reason. It must have greater weapons in its arsenal.

I picture endometriosis down there looking smug and very certain that it will continue to defeat our every attempt at pregnancy. And there are my diseased tubes and ovaries, weak and powerless against this enemy, that thus far has not been beaten by Danazol or major surgery.

Hope and courage and optimism line up facing despair and hopelessness and depression, prepared to do battle. Maybe this cycle pregnancy will be the victor; endometriosis and infertility, the losers.

Probably not.

—KATHLEEN S. MCGINNIS-CRAFT
in *RESOLVE Newsletter* [1]

The image of fighting against an unseen enemy captures the feelings of many who struggle with infertility. They feel as if they have been struck by a natural disaster, an unexpected and uncontrollable devastation of their lives. Of course not all infertile people respond in the same way, and many do not consider the inability to conceive to be a major disaster. But for those who do, the emotions they may experience are as those of people who grieve for the death of a loved one.

Yet this is a different kind of grief. A death has finality to it, but infertility seems to go on indefinitely. It is like having a chronic illness; there is the continuing reminder of loss coupled with continued hope for a cure. Each month there is a new hope, the fantasy of being pregnant, the conviction that *this* time it just has to work. Then, once again, the crushing evidence of failure. One woman who wrote an article in the *RESOLVE Newsletter* described it this way:

> Being infertile has been compared to having a loved one missing in action; I hope and grieve simultaneously, a delicate tension.[2]

A death is not only final, it is also a public event, a rallying point for family and friends to offer sympathy and help. Infertility, in contrast, is a very private trauma, unrecognized and misunderstood by others. Deaths are marked by ceremony and gravestones. Other life crises also have their rituals. But the loss each month of the possibility of a desperately wanted child goes unnoticed, marked only by the purchase of more sanitary napkins. As one woman told us:

> A lot of people don't understand that infertility is very much like having a child die. You grieve for the baby who wasn't conceived this month, and for all the babies you'll never have.

The devastation brought by infertility is hardly a new phenomenon. The Bible, for example, contains a number of stories about women who could not bear children. The book of Samuel opens with one such story, about Hannah. Her grief, like that of so many people, was also misunderstood.

Hannah's husband Elkanah, who loved her very much, could not understand why she was so upset, asking if he was not good enough for her: "Hannah, why do you weep? And why do you not eat? And why is your heart sad? Am I not more to you than ten sons?"

Elkanah's other wife Peninah had children, and she taunted Hannah constantly. Even Eli, the priest in the temple where Hannah went to pray for a child, scorned her. He took her obvious distress to be a sign of drunkenness, until Hannah explained that she was "a woman sorely troubled," filled with "great anxiety and vexation" (1 Sam. 1).

The Grief Process

The grief that Hannah felt is a normal response to loss. It is hard to imagine how so much pain and bitterness can be normal and even necessary for coping. But grief has been aptly described to us by a social worker as a circle of fire around a bereaved person. One must walk through and be burned in order to get to the outside, or else stay trapped inside forever. The "burns" of grief wound us in many ways that are common to almost all losses. They are the now widely recognized reactions of shock, denial, anger, guilt, depression, and resolution.[3]

Most couples are shocked when they find out they have infertility or genetic problems. They had thought that they were largely in control of their future, that surely having children would be part of the natural progression of their lives. They are stunned, disbelieving, when it turns out otherwise. Feeling vulnerable, they are frightened to discover how little control they have over what happens to them. Since infertility is so uncertain, many people find it easy to deny it. "This isn't happening to me," they say. Some denial helps a person to adjust to an overwhelming situation. Total denial can be destructive, however, if a couple delays seeking help until it is almost too late to do anything. One man told us about his experience:

> My wife and I were trying hard to have a baby. After a year, my wife's physician didn't seem worried; so we didn't even suspect anything could be wrong. After another year, he thought we should have some tests, but I was sure it was just our timing. How could anything be wrong with us?
>
> It took another year to get me to go get my sperm tested, and I went only because of my wife's insistence. I just didn't want to believe anything could be wrong. Now I wish we hadn't wasted all that time.

Sometimes the grief over being infertile goes underground, unacknowledged. This can happen when a diagnosis of male infertility is followed immediately by successful AID (artificial insemination with donor sperm) or when a baby becomes unexpectedly available for adoption soon after the detection of blocked tubes. The feelings do not necessarily disappear. They may reemerge without warning later on, still demanding attention.

Men are more likely than women to deny the problem or their feelings. Women, on the other hand, often deny the incredible rage that is part of the grief of infertility. According to studies, women have a harder time showing their anger than men. One woman quoted by psychologist Patricia P. Mahlstedt said:

My husband told me he hated what the past few years had done to me. He said he watched me turn into an angry, bitter, hateful person. It was a long time before I realized how angry I was. I was consumed with anger before I understood what was eating me up inside. Then my problem was finding what to do with my anger—how at least to channel it, if not resolve it.[4]

Anger and frustration can be all-too-constant companions. Anger at insensitive friends or relatives who say "just relax," "go on vacation," or "adopt and then you'll get pregnant." How could so-called friends be so ignorant, so impatient with the depression and preoccupation infertility causes? Some may find that they no longer can stay in contact with these "friends" who fail to understand. They find themselves feeling isolated and lonely. Family parties become too painful, especially as new nieces, nephews, and cousins appear each year.

Friends and relatives are not the only targets of anger. Doctors, nurses and hospitals are often high on the list. Infertile people feel very vulnerable to the doctors' control over their lives. They are tired of the endless painful procedures they must endure. They are angry at physicians who have no infertility expertise yet assure that they can help. They are angry at the specialists who have no time for them or who are condescending and insensitive.

One man's comment reveals a common sentiment:

We foolishly believed everything the various doctors told us. We learned the hard way that we had to cut through the "we know best" garbage to get accurate information. We had to find the person who really knew what he was doing, instead of wasting so much time with inexperienced gynecologists who claimed to be specialists but really were not.

A woman who was going through AIH (artificial insemination with her husband's sperm) reflected one frequent source of anger at physicians:

I know their time is precious. I know I am only one of many patients. But when they can offer me only one block of time and expect that I should rearrange my whole day on one day's notice and then pay dearly for their time, and this happens over and over every 28 days, it is a source of repeated frustration.

The anger may extend to doctors in general, especially if it is suspected that a medical intervention caused the problem to begin with. DES daughters and women whose fertility was destroyed by IUDs are furious that they must turn for help to the medical system that they hold responsible for their trauma.

Many infertile people are upset about the cost and time that they spend trying to get pregnant. Many give up their jobs to be available for the tests and procedures. Others may have to mortgage their homes to obtain the thousands of dollars needed for many treatments. One woman wrote to us to share her feelings:

> One thing about being infertile, you'd better have a large income and good insurance because everything you do to diagnose infertility and to achieve a pregnancy is very expensive and not for the average couple. Maybe someone should sell infertility insurance so when you get married and can't have children, it'll pay for treatment or adoption.

After experiencing a loss or tragedy, at some point people ask themselves, "What could I have done to avoid it?" Even if it is an event totally out of their control, they wonder if God or fate is punishing them. Guilt, for real or imagined offenses, is inevitable. But the constant search for a cause, the preoccupation with possible faults can poison one's life.

The media help fuel the guilt. News reports cite the rise in sexually transmitted diseases as causing the increase in infertility problems, and people begin to wonder about their past relationships. The guilt is even greater if one links infertility to a past abortion. In reality, abortions have not been shown to cause infertility, but it is hard to forget them, especially in the current political environment.[5]

Many decisions we've made in our lives may come back to haunt us, even though they may have been the best decisions at the time. The choice of birth control methods or the decision to wait to have children may have increased the likelihood of infertility. How ironic, how tragic that our efforts to control fertility, to control the course of our lives, may have led directly to our loss of the ability to conceive.

Psychiatrists have long claimed that emotional distress or neurosis can cause infertility. According to such theories, relaxation or therapy is what is needed to achieve a successful pregnancy. This viewpoint only adds to the burden of guilt. Fortunately it is now possible to identify organic causes for over 90 percent of infertility. Hard medical evidence has made psychological theories much less convincing. Also, more therapists have recognized that distress is usually a result, not a cause, of infertility.[6]

An exact diagnosis can cause renewed guilt and more questions: "How did my tubes get so scarred?" "Why are my sperm so slow?" "What did I do to make this happen?" But a diagnosis is also an answer and the basis for a treatment strategy. A diagnosis can make it easier to accept the situation, to decide what to do next. The fewer than 10 percent of infertile people who find no cause are therefore doubly frustrated. For example, we interviewed a woman who was undergoing AIH for unexplained infertility. She described her feelings:

> As a woman you just expect to have a baby; so you say to yourself, "What did I do wrong, what's happening inside my body that's not right?" I have an image in my mind of Pac Man. Maybe I have these little things like antibodies eating the sperm, chubba, chubba, chubba. You can get really crazy.

The feelings of guilt, anger, and frustration can turn into serious depression. Depression is a frequent response to infertility.

> At this time in my life I wanted a house, I wanted a career. I wanted the kids and everything. And I wind up renting an apartment from my mother, staying home and cleaning, and being very domestic. I haven't been able to work for three years because I have to be on call, going back and forth to the hospital, monitoring urines. And Sometimes I feel that there's nothing left in my life.

It is hard to make decisions when one is feeling depressed. It is hard to muster the energy needed to investigate all the alternatives, to keep going back for more and more procedures. As one woman said:

> Sometimes I feel so low, all I want is to lie in bed. I have to drag myself to the doctor. I know if I don't, I'll have no chance at all.

These feelings of grief—shock, denial, anger, guilt, and depression—are common to all kinds of losses. There are other painful emotions that most discussions of grief neglect, but which can affect infertile people very powerfully. They may have a strong sense of failure. Their bodies have failed to perform a very basic function, and their sense of themselves as a man or woman is challenged. One woman said:

> Intellectually, I know that this doesn't mean I'm a failure as a wife or a woman or that I'm not feminine. But, as many times as you go through this, your emotions take over and you do feel like a total failure.

Infertile people cannot help but feel jealous of others who have had no problems in bearing children. Wherever they go, they feel surrounded by babies and pregnant women. Whenever they watch television, pick up a magazine, or read a paper, they are reminded that they live in a fertile, unsympathetic world. Some people are especially furious at those parents who neglect and abuse their children. One woman told us bitterly:

I can't even control my own damn body. Other women
have babies so easily and just take it for granted. They even plan
exactly when they want the baby to arrive—those are the ones
that drive me crazy.

Jealousy appears even in groups intended to help infertile people.
Psychiatrist Miriam Mazor observes:

Women who have had a series of miscarriages are viewed
as "more fortunate" by those who have never conceived; those
who ovulate regularly are seen as "more normal" by those who
do not. . . . Rarely will they tolerate a member with a secondary infertility problem (one who has borne a living child), and
they have difficulty in dealing with the issue of what to do about
group members who become pregnant, with the initial impulse
being to expel the offending member.[7]

Grief with Secondary Infertility and Pregnancy Loss

Becoming pregnant is a major achievement. But for some people it
may not, unfortunately, end the grief. Many people have one child and
then can have no more. Others experience the terrible loss of a baby.

We tend to think of infertility as being the same as childlessness. It
is surprising to realize, then, that of all infertile couples, more than half
already have one or more children.[8] If they have been trying unsuccessfully to conceive for a year or more, they are considered infertile, no
matter how many other children they have.

Those who experience secondary infertility are especially shocked,
for their experience makes them feel certain that they can be successful
again. They also feel even more isolated; others tell them to feel grateful for the child or children they already have. Gjerde Dausch, writing
in the *RESOLVE Newsletter*, describes how she hid the existence of her
son from her RESOLVE friends. Although she very much wanted another
child, people trying to have their first did not consider her infertile. Her
response:

Yes, we have a child, but our problems and feelings are the
same. Just because we have one child does not mean we can't
or don't mourn the loss of the unborn child.

There is a great deal of guilt with secondary infertility. Dausch writes:

I spent a great deal of time reflecting back on my life to see
where I had gone wrong to merit only one child. . . . My emo-

tional state, I believe, suffered even more as a result of having a child. I could never tell myself that my infertility was an act of fate or something possessed from birth. Since it was so easy the first time, I felt that I must have done something after his birth to cause my infertility. . . . I had had the ability to have children, and I kept looking for what I did to destroy this.[9]

A new trauma may confront those who actually do conceive. Miscarriage and ectopic (tubal) pregnancy are common early in pregnancy, especially for those with fertility problems. The chances of losing a pregnancy appear to be particularly high with *in vitro* fertilization. Some women will experience a successful first trimester only to face the heartbreaking news of a genetic problem discovered by a prenatal test such as amniocentesis. They will have to decide whether to end this much-wanted pregnancy, whether to abort the child whose obvious movements and growth had already brought such joy. Increasingly, as a result of fertility drugs, women who conceive are carrying triplets, quadruplets, or more, and they are confronted with the possibility of having to abort one or more fetuses in order to improve the chances of survival for the others.[10]

As in any other group of pregnant women, some infertile people who finally conceive will experience premature labor, stillbirth, or newborn death.[11] So close to their goal, they feel betrayed and cheated when they have to bear another loss. One woman who conceived after having infertility problems wrote to us about her feelings about the baby's death:

> When I became pregnant, I really thought that we had won the battle, and would somehow be protected from more problems because we had "paid our dues" with infertility.

Ironically, those who experience such tragedies may find themselves isolated in their bereavement. Their infertile friends may tell them, "At least you got pregnant." In IVF programs, a pregnancy—no matter how brief—is counted as a "success." And they may discover what most others who have lost babies have found: that the rest of the world does not understand how disastrous these losses are.

Resolution

Resolution should be the last stage of grief. However, without a recognized loss, with no obvious end to the struggle, with little support from others, resolution may be especially hard for many people to achieve.

Grief over the loss of a loved one follows a usual course, as described by psychologists. As the loss recedes into the past, the sharp edges of the pain become a little duller. The memories are more manageable, and life begins to feel more normal.

The grief of infertility does not conform to this pattern, however. Throughout the months and years of diagnostic tests and fertility treatments and failed efforts to adopt or give birth, the disturbing emotions do not go away; instead they may gain in intensity. There may be off times, "vacations" that couples take from their efforts. ("I put my 'Do not Disturb' sign up," one woman told us.) Hope for an answer and optimism about success may ease the grief. But as time goes by, it is harder to sustain this optimism. After five years of trying to conceive, a woman wrote to us:

> Infertility is an emotionally devastating disease, which rears its ugly head over and over again. With each month that goes by, the stakes get higher, and the failure is more painful.

Each month without a pregnancy represents less time left to conceive and more evidence of a problem that is not going away. Couples who begin their efforts to have a child in their thirties and are unsuccessful may begin to panic as they see deadlines looming up ahead. Many adoption agencies and IVF programs will not accept women over forty. And there is that internal deadline—the fear of increased risk of birth defects and pregnancy complications, the recognition that time for conceiving may be running out.

Resolution may be particularly difficult to obtain for people whose infertility is "unexplained." The frustration can be seen in the following comments:

> It wouldn't be so difficult if I had an answer. I could cope, I could come to terms with myself. Now I can't decide whether I should go another two months for the inseminations, or another six months. What if I don't go? Maybe I would have become pregnant. If I knew, I think I could resign myself to the fact that that's the way things are and look for another option, maybe adoption or child-free living. It hurts deep down inside because I feel like I'm going to live fifty or sixty years and still never know why I never became pregnant. It will always be a mystery.

At each step along the way, couples must ask themselves if it is worth continuing. Some are strengthened in their desire to conceive, more committed than ever. Some parents, even after adopting, are still not ready to stop trying to have a biological child. They are still waiting for a new technique to be developed, still trying an alternative. They love their adopted children, but a resolution of their longing eludes them.

The publicity about new technologies can open the old wounds of those who truly felt they were done with trying to conceive, who have been satisfied for years with their adoptive family. News of IVF babies, tubal transplants, even postmenopausal pregnancy, may reawaken old yearnings. Once again they are faced with the uncertainty, with the "what ifs?"

It is difficult to shut the door firmly on biological parenthood. The availability of new technologies makes it a great deal harder. Such technologies are almost impossible to ignore. They offer new hope and what appear to be more choices. But choices such as these can be difficult, shattering the carefully nurtured peace of a family.

Even those who feel whole again after a birth or adoption report some residue of sadness. Life is so much better, but it is never the same again.

> I am always aware that my son was conceived with AID and wish he were a joint biological child. But the feeling is not painful and does not hurt my relationship with him or my husband. I feel I have accepted my husband's infertility and our alternatives to it. But I believe I will never forget the situation or stop feeling a little sad.

The struggle does end eventually, one way or another. For many, it ends with a successful birth or births, or it ends with adoption. It may end with a decision that living without children is truly acceptable. The important issue is not how it ends, but how satisfied and comfortable one is with the resolution.

Resolution does not depend on a child or children. It is very difficult to "give up" the battle and believe that it is a positive move, but many couples arrive at a point where they can accept that there will be no child. They decide they must stop torturing themselves, that their lives can be just as fulfilling in other ways. They are ready to move on. Finally there is peace in their lives.

Whether a couple adopts a child or decides to remain child-free, it takes great strength to decide to stop trying to conceive. Those who consider stopping have to withstand the urging of their physicians to take the next step. They may have to convince their spouse that they have been through enough. They must repress the "what ifs" in their own minds. When they do finally decide to stop, however, they often experience tremendous relief:

> I knew that there was a point when I had to quit. There are just so many times I could allow this kind of invasion, not only into my body, but also into my psyche. I don't know how long

you can hang on to the word "hopeful." You have to come to a time when you say it's over. It was such a relief to put it behind me and get on with my life.

When we asked people if they had any regrets about trying an alternative method of conceiving, 85 percent said no. Yet two major themes emerged again and again in comments about what they wish they had done differently. They regretted, often vehemently, not having sought a fertility specialist earlier. And in many cases, they were sorry they had not tried to adopt sooner:

> I always believed surgery or IVF would work eventually, and I felt I could only do one thing at a time. Now I wish I would have explored adoption earlier, because time is running out.

People who are able to adopt despite the many obstacles usually discover that the biological connection was not so important after all. As any child grows and develops his or her own independent personality, memories of conception, pregnancy, and birth recede and have little to do with the life of a family. A woman writes:

> It was very important to me to have our own child. But once we adopted a baby, I fell in love with her. All of a sudden I wasn't interested in pursuing *in vitro* anymore.

The birth or adoption of a child does bring resolution for many couples. They have achieved their goal of parenthood. Their grief can, at last, be put behind them. If they have a child conceived with the help of an alternative method, the anger they had felt about cost and stress usually disappears. "It was worth every penny" they say. "Anything that important is worth doing whatever you have to do." For many people, adoption brings a happy end to their infertility:

> My husband and I have adopted two terrific girls from Korea. I cannot imagine life without the children I have now. They are so much mine that sometimes I can't remember why I was so upset about infertility in the first place.

The Methods

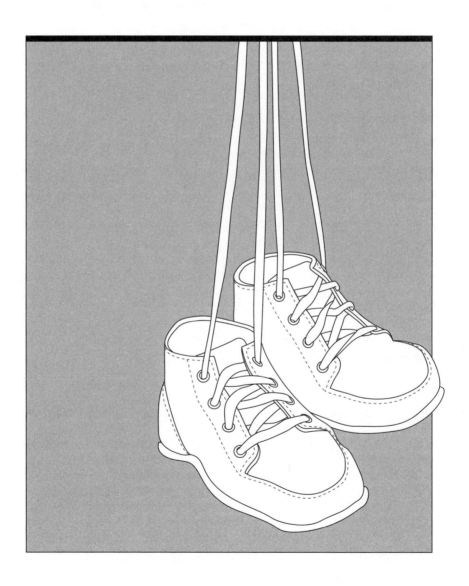

CHAPTER 3

Artificial Insemination

Monday morning, ten o'clock. This was by no means a typical day for Cathy and Mark. Each of them had arranged to take the morning off and meet the doctor before his regular office hours. Tense and excited, they hoped that this day would finally mark the successful end of their years of effort and frustration. They felt uncomfortable entering the building, looking over their shoulders and hoping no one would see them. They were surprised to see others in the waiting room—another young couple and several women sitting alone, staring at their magazines. Everyone knew that they were all there for the same reason—for artificial insemination.

Mark and Cathy are part of a growing phenomenon, one that has already produced hundreds of thousands of babies in the United States. Although artificial insemination has been performed for a long time, until recently it was still rare. There are two kinds of artificial insemination. The semen that is deposited in a woman, usually with a syringe, may have come from her husband (AIH) or from a donor (AID). Both methods can be used when a man has fertility problems. AID, because of the involvement of a donor other than the husband, has been much more controversial.[1]

In some ways, donor insemination is a combination of adoption and typical pregnancy, since a couple "adopts" half of the genetic makeup of their child but the woman is still able to have a normal pregnancy and birth. Either kind of insemination allows the man to be present at both the conception and birth, and to share the experience of pregnancy just like any other father. It is also the simplest and least expensive form of alternative conception. Because of these advantages and the growing difficulties and higher costs associated with adoption, insemination has become increasingly popular among many infertile couples.

However, one of its advantages—that the child is to all appearances the natural offspring of both parents—may also be the most troublesome aspect. The secrecy that surrounds artificial insemination can be a major source of difficulty for the parents. Because of the secrecy, artificial insemination is rarely discussed, and most people are unaware of its availability. When Cathy's physician first suggested it, she was surprised and hesitant; she had never heard of anyone using insemination before.

Mark and Cathy had been married for several years when they decided they were ready to have children. They had been very careful about birth control, wanting to get their careers started before becoming parents. It never occurred to them that they would have any difficulty once they decided to conceive. Yet, after three years of trying, they were beginning to wonder if they would ever have a child. When they both turned thirty, they finally sought a physician's advice.

The first thing the doctor did was to test Mark's sperm. It took only a simple test to determine the likely cause of the problem—Mark's sperm count was very low. Both were shocked by the news. They described their feelings:

> *Cathy:* By the time we first went to the doctor, things were already getting bad between us. We were trying so hard to have a baby that our sex life was awful after a while. I didn't want to have anything to do with him—it's not making love, it's just having sex. Then when we learned about his sperm count, well I thought that might finish us altogether. It was really hard for him to accept. But the doctor suggested we try artificial insemination using Mark's sperm, and that gave us both hope that I could get pregnant. I liked the idea because it would still be our baby.

> *Mark:* When the doctor called with the test results, I just didn't want to believe it. I never thought that not getting pregnant could be my fault. When I first found out about it, I didn't come home for two days. I had to let some steam off so I just went off by myself. I couldn't face Cathy or talk to anyone. It's hard for someone like me to try to explain this to anyone—you know, they'll think you're a deadhead, you can't do anything, you're not really a man. You know every guy looks to have a son. I didn't care so much about my job and making money anymore; I just really wanted to have a family.

> I kept asking myself how this could have happened to me. Was it genetic? Maybe I caught VD from someone I had slept with before I met Cathy. Sometimes people say if you masturbate a lot, you'll use it all up. I knew that wasn't true, but I couldn't stop wondering.

AIH and AID: Responses to Infertility

Traditionally, infertility has been viewed as a woman's problem, with most of the research and tests and treatments directed at the female partner. Yet it is now recognized that abnormalities of the semen such as in the number, shape, or speed of the sperm are present in 40 to 50 percent of the men in infertile couples. In fact, male sperm count in general has been declining recently, most likely due to environmental causes. Medical conditions that cause male infertility such as varicocele (enlargement of a vein in the scrotum) can sometimes be treated. In many cases, however, there is nothing that can be done to correct the abnormalities that interfere with conception.[2]

Increasingly, physicians are recommending some form of *in vitro* fertilization for couples with male infertility. A more common treatment for many couples, however, is found in artificial insemination. AIH (insemination with the husband's sperm) may help when the male's sperm count is low or when his sperm have poor motility. In addition, AIH is used for female infertility factors such as poor cervical mucus. It is also possible for either the man or woman to have antibodies that counteract the fertility of otherwise normal sperm; AIH may be used to circumvent this problem. AIH may also be used when a couple has experienced difficulties with intercourse for emotional or physical reasons, or when there has not been a conception for some unknown reason.[3]

The pregnancy rate with AIH varies greatly from one study to another, depending on the diagnosis, method, and number of attempts. Most studies are not well controlled to determine if pregnancy was achieved by AIH or by the couple having normal intercourse. When AIH is performed primarily for a problem with male fertility, there appears to be a much lower than average success rate and a greater likelihood of miscarriage. The Ethics Committee of the American Fertility Society, reflecting on the uncertainty of success in cases of poor sperm count or motility, antibodies, and cervical mucus abnormalities, recommended in 1986 that AIH for these conditions be carried out only in a carefully controlled research setting.[4]

In the past, the husband's sperm was usually deposited in the woman's vagina. Increasingly, doctors now put the sperm directly into the uterus. This technique (known as IUI—intrauterine insemination) is particularly effective when infertility is due to cervical factors. It is more expensive, and there is a small chance of infection.[5]

In the past few years, many fertility centers have introduced the use of superovulation through hormonal treatment of the woman before intrauterine insemination. Because of the greater likelihood of pregnancy after hormone injections (with or without insemination), the combination of superovulation and IUI is becoming increasingly routine for a variety of fertility problems, including unexplained infertility. The pregnancy rate appears to be about 20 percent, making this procedure an attractive alternative for some couples considering IVF.

In some cases, eggs are retrieved after superovulation, mixed with the husband's (or donor's) prepared sperm, and introduced either into the uterus or into the peritoneal cavity. These methods draw heavily on the techniques used in *in vitro* fertilization and are intended to avoid failure which might be due to the improper timing of insemination during natural ovulation. They also share some of the problems of IVF, however, since superovulation can have serious side effects, and there is a higher rate of miscarriage, ectopic pregnancy, and multiple births. Thus in recent years, artificial insemination has become more complicated, expensive, and possibly riskier, in an effort to improve previously low pregnancy rates.[6]

Donor insemination (referred to either as AID or DI) is used when the husband has no sperm at all, when there is a severe problem with the number, quality, or motility of the husband's sperm, or when AIH has not worked. If the husband has had a vasectomy, was exposed to toxic materials, or has a history of genetic disease in his family, a couple may turn to AID.[7]

As was true in Mark's case, AIH is often used first, before trying a donor, even though the success rate is fairly low for male factor infertility. For many men, it offers a transition time before the difficult move to the use of a donor. As Mark said:

> I began to think about the doctor's suggestion that we collect my sperm and inseminate Cathy with it. I realized it didn't matter so much to me that the method was unusual, as long as we could still have our baby together. But after five months and still no pregnancy, we were both starting to panic. Having to accept finally that my sperm were useless was the hardest thing I've ever had to do.

Cathy and Mark's physician commented on his approach:

> Husbands using AIH are usually not far along in the process of resolving their feelings. I do AIH many times in preparation for AID because a man might say for instance, "I'll never use another guy's sperm." This way I put the idea in their mind that if you have a lousy sperm count, perhaps you're going to need AID, and even if you don't think it is a reasonable thing, at least you ought to talk about it.

Experts who have studied the impact of insemination on couples oftenrecommend that they wait until they have resolved their feelings about the man's infertility before starting AID.[8] For the husband, there is the blow to his sense of himself as a man and a feeling of deficiency in his body. He may feel ashamed that he cannot father a child and regret that he is letting his wife down. Men who think they should be superior and in charge in a relationship may feel deprived and inferior—a source of terrible frustration.

For the wife, there may be anger at her husband, guilt for feeling angry, and guilt that she is fertile when her husband is not. The stress occasionally causes an ordinarily fertile woman to stop ovulating when AID is begun. With both husband and wife feeling angry with themselves and with each other, it is not surprising that conflict and sexual difficulties frequently develop between them. Couples who wait at least a few months after the diagnosis to work through their feelings before starting AID tend to be able to handle the procedure more successfully.

When their doctor suggested donor insemination, Mark and Cathy at first felt they couldn't go through with it. In desperation, they decided to see a counselor to talk through the problems they were facing. Mark said:

> I wanted to have a child so badly, and I also wanted Cathy to be able to experience a pregnancy. But I couldn't stand the idea of my wife carrying somebody else's baby. When the doctor first mentioned it, all I could think was that it would be like another man screwing my wife. I had a hard time explaining my feelings to Cathy, since I was so ambivalent and she seemed eager to try using a donor.
>
> Fortunately, the therapist helped us realize that being a biological father is very different from parenting a child. You leave your mark on the world by the way you parent your child, not by the genes you give him. I still have moments of regret, but I remind myself that AID is just a procedure. Once you have that child, it's yours and you'll love it like it has always been yours.

Not every couple needs a therapist to help them share with each other the feelings they are having. For Mark and Cathy, however, it was helpful. They are now glad that they could finally talk together about all of their painful thoughts and emotions before starting insemination. It made it much easier for them to endure the stress of the procedure and to feel that they were working together as a team to reach their goal. Mark is better able to accept his infertility, knowing that Cathy does not love him any less.

The Donor

In addition to having to deal with their grief over Mark's infertility, Mark and Cathy were both concerned about who the donor would be. Just as Mark feared that AID would be like adultery, some people assume that the woman finds a suitable man outside of the marriage and has intercourse with him. One man called a physician known to specialize in artificial insemination in order to volunteer his services—he thought he would be paid for having sex with a woman! When told he could only give a specimen anonymously, he quickly lost interest.

Usually the donor is not known to the couple at all unless they seek him out themselves. In most cases, the physician finds a donor, either through personal contacts or through a sperm bank, and the identity is carefully guarded. It has been suggested, in fact, that the term "donor" is misleading, since the man is paid for his sperm.

Mark and Cathy were especially concerned about the health of the donor because they knew nothing about him. As Cathy said:

> I was a little leery about the whole thing because you don't really know whose sperm it is. And then I worried a lot about catching AIDS. I know they usually use residents, who I'm sure are in good health, but you just don't know. The doctor said he tries to use people who have already had healthy children, and he screens for VD before every insemination.
>
> I think the time I really worried about it the most was when I was pregnant. We both knew a baby is a baby once it's conceived. But you really wonder what the baby is going to be like. You really don't know. We were both shocked when the baby was born healthy.

Who are the donors for artificial insemination? Until recently, most donors in the United States were medical students or residents recruited by private physicians for the immediate use of fresh sperm. However, reports of possible transmission of the AIDS virus and other diseases through AID led to the rapid increase in use of frozen semen in the late 1980s.

Sperm banks, which tend to recruit students and young professionals from a variety of fields, freeze the sperm for future use. In the 1970s, as few as 5 percent of all artificial inseminations involved the use of frozen sperm; by 1987, that figure increased to about 50 percent. In 1988, the Centers for Disease Control and Prevention, the American Fertility Society, and the Food and Drug Administration all recommended that only frozen donor semen be used, and that it be quarantined for at least six months until the donor could be retested for HIV infection. However, many doctors are unaware or, or do not follow, these recommendations.[9]

Freezing sperm was reported as far back as 1776 in Italy. Ninety years later, an Italian pathologist suggested starting a sperm bank so that a woman could produce "legitimate" children in case her husband died on the battlefield. (The possibility of banking sperm before battle was in fact highlighted in the American media during the time that soldiers were being sent to the Persian Gulf in advance of the 1991 war.) It was not until 1953, however, when new storage techniques were developed, that scientists could thaw sperm without changing its molecular structure. This made it possible to achieve fertilization.[10]

Fresh sperm continues to be preferred by many physicians and couples because it is less expensive and is believed to have a higher success rate—about 10 to 15 percent higher than for frozen. Yet recent studies suggest that there is no longer a difference between the two in their effectiveness, and there are many advantages in using frozen sperm. The doctor does not have the problem of finding fresh sperm from a suitable donor within a few hours of the time it is needed. Also, other samples of sperm from the same donor can be used for additional inseminations and can even be used for future pregnancies. Perhaps most important, donors of frozen sperm are much more likely to be carefully screened, and there is time to test and retest both the donor and the sperm to detect infectious disease or abnormalities.[11]

The greatest objection voiced by researchers to the system of sperm donation has been the lack of adequate screening. Even though babies born by donor insemination have fewer birth defects than the typical newborn population, there is still great concern about the potential for introducing infections and defective sperm. Most physicians who recruit donors of fresh semen question them only superficially about health and family history, and a donor who is a carrier of a genetic disease may be unaware of this fact.

One physician told an especially tragic story of a couple who turned to AID because they were both carriers of Tay-Sachs disease. They had watched their first child die a slow and awful death and did not want to take the chance that another baby would be affected in the same way. What no one knew was that the donor was also a carrier, and the baby born after insemination also died from Tay-Sachs.

As attorney Lori Andrews, author of *New Conceptions*, writes: "It is ironic that the screening of donor sperm for human AID is much less stringent than that of bull sperm in the cattle industry." The American Fertility Society and the American Association of Tissue Banks have established guidelines for screening donors, and government health officials in some areas have begun to establish regulations for more rigorous screening. Yet for the most part the practice of artificial insemination is unregulated.[12]

Another concern about the donors besides their health is the possibility that one man's sperm could be used to inseminate many women, increasing the chance of unwitting marriage between siblings. Although in reality the risks of sibling marriage are still low, it has been estimated that, theoretically, one man could donate enough semen in a year to produce 20,000 children.[13] In fact the pool of donors is usually quite small. One woman commented:

> They asked what characteristics we wanted from the donor but warned that special requests might mean a delay since there were so few donors. We often joked that it was probably one guy who went behind a screen and put on a different wig each time depending upon the request.

Such joking reflects considerable anxiety on the part of many couples about the donor's identity. Several prospective parents expressed worries about a racial mix-up, and the suspicion of some that a doctor might himself be the donor was unfortunately confirmed by the arrest and conviction of an American physician who had used his own semen in many cases without informing the patients.

Because of the potential problems with choosing donors, some couples decide to select their own. A relative of the husband or close friend may be asked, which could allow them to avoid doctors altogether. For the majority of people who prefer not to know the donor or who cannot find a willing man, experts recommend that people question a physician about the extent of screening and the number of pregnancies that have already resulted from the donor's sperm.

Other experts have also urged the keeping of detailed records of donors. Law professor George Annas argues forcefully that the current practice of discarding all records of the donor's identity ignores the best interests of the child. He calls for sealed records on all AID children and their genetic fathers that would be available to the children when they grow up. Without these records, important information on the medical history of a child in unavailable. Baran and Pannor, based on their studies of adoption and AID, firmly believe that the identity of the genetic father should be available to his children.[14]

Only about a dozen states now require some form of record keeping; in one survey reported in 1979, 83 percent of physicians opposed any such legislation. Opposition to releasing information about the donor, even without identifying information, continues to be very strong. In Congress's 1987 survey, almost half of physicians responded that they do not even keep records that would allow them to match a donor to the pregnancies resulting from his sperm. Of those who *do* keep records, approximately three-fourths insist that they would not release the information to anyone under any circumstances, even if the donor's name is kept anonymous. Physicians prefer to control their own practices and not have to respond to legislative requirements. In addition, they seek to protect the confidentiality of donors, many of whom are their colleagues and students, or to shield the infertile husband from the stigma they fear he might suffer if his condition should become known.[15]

Many practitioners of AID fear that the requirement of records will scare off potential donors as well as open up a host of possible legal problems. They gain support from the example of Sweden, which passed a law requiring that the donor's identity be recorded and available to children when they turn eighteen. The number of donors dropped dramatically for a while, and couples had to go to other countries for AID. However, the number of donors did increase again, with older married men replacing many of the students who had formerly provided most semen for insemination. And a number of studies indicate that there are donors who do wish to have their names or at least information about them available to the children.[16]

An Experience of Donor Insemination

In addition to their worry about the donor, Mark and Cathy were very apprehensive about the procedure itself. She described what happened:

> Once we decided to try AID, our doctor referred us to a specialist. The first visit was scary. You wonder if people are looking at you because they know what you're there for, especially the nurses. No one ever said anything, of course, but you just wonder what goes on in their heads.
>
> When we met the doctor, he interviewed us both and took a medical history. He asked us if we had any personal preferences and gave us a form to fill out with a lot of personal information, things like the color of our eyes, our hair. He tried to match Mark's height, weight, everything. Then I was told to take my temperature every morning before getting out of bed. When it started to go down, I was to call and get two appointments— one for that day and then one for two days later.
>
> I was really nervous the first time we went for an insemination. Thank God it went more easily than I expected. Mark came with me into the exam room although they didn't really invite him. I was glad he asserted himself because I wanted him there with me. The doctor explained that he was putting a cap over my cervix that had a tube attached to it. It felt a little uncomfortable as he did it. He went in his office for a minute and brought back a container of sperm that had just been delivered

by the resident. Then he put a syringe filled with the sperm into the tube that was sticking out of the cap. He folded up the tube so that the sperm would be pushed into the cap. He asked me to stay still for twenty minutes. Then I was instructed how to take out the cap after eight hours.

The procedure for artificial insemination is quite simple, although it varies somewhat from one physician to another. Some, for example, do not use a cervical cap as Cathy's doctor did, especially when using frozen sperm. Some use a drug to stimulate ovulation, but many do not. Physicians may inseminate twice or three times a month. Some couples pick up frozen sperm from their physician and perform the insemination at home by themselves.

Many couples who have been through AIH or AID now wish they had done it at home, if possible. In that way they could have avoided some of the tremendous difficulties that arise when coordinating with the physician's schedule. More important, it would have been less impersonal, and the husband could be actively involved. By using a syringe bought in a drugstore, semen is transferred from a container to the vagina. Some physicians teach couples how to do this if they ask for instruction.

Many times couples request that the husband's sperm be mixed with the donor's or decide to have intercoure just before or after the insemination. They hope in this way to maintain the possibility that any child conceived could be the husband's. Many physicians, however, recommend against the mixing of sperm and urge couples to refrain from intercourse prior to insemination. Sperm from different men can sometimes negate each other's effectiveness, and the success rate seems to be higher when there is no mixing.[17]

Cathy went home after the first insemination feeling very excited. She felt sure she must be pregnant. She said:

> It felt like magic—the electricity in my belly. I was so sure I was pregnant that it was like losing a baby when I found out I wasn't. Because it didn't work the first time, I would protect myself and say "No, I'm not pregnant" and just feel it's not going to happen. I thought that this is something I'm going to do every month for the rest of my life and I'm never going to get pregnant. One month I broke the thermometer, partly on purpose. I was starting to get very depressed about this.

It is not unusual for a couple to experience frustration and depression when insemination fails to produce a pregnancy quickly. Particularly after so many years of difficulty in achieving a pregnancy, AID may be seen as a last resort. If it does not succeed, despair can set in, and many couples abandon the effort after a few months.

Studies of AID report an average success rate of 60 percent, although in different studies they range from 37 to 84 percent. Martin Curie-Cohen and colleagues found that those physicians who did the most inseminations also had the highest success rate.[18]

After seven months of inseminations, Cathy and Mark were discouraged and upset. The costs of the procedure were becoming harder to bear. Although artificial insemination usually costs far less than IVF (*in vitro* fertilization) or hiring a surrogate mother, the monthly expenses mount up quickly. Each time a woman is inseminated, there is the charge for the office visit and the fee for the sperm sample. In addition, she may be taking expensive fertility drugs to stimulate her ovulation. If a couple uses intrauterine insemination, the visit is more expensive, and there is often a charge for washing and preparing the sperm. The people we interviewed said they were spending anywhere from $100 to $600 a month for artificial insemination. The Congressional Office of Technology Assessments's 1987 survey of practitioners of artificial insemination concluded that the average patient cost for four cycles was about $1,000, with physicians who carry out the most inseminations reporting considerably higher charges. Approximately three-fourths of the total costs are paid by the patients themselves.[19]

The emotional strain was even more difficult for Mark and Cathy than the financial burden. Cathy said:

> It was very hard on us. The fear that it might not work was always there. I felt the emptiness would be endless and all this effort would be futile. All the waiting each month was so hard. Another problem for both of us was the hassle of leaving work and making up enough excuses so that there would not be too many questions and then pray that I had chosen the right day.

The next month Cathy became pregnant. Mark was very excited and involved in the pregnancy. They both worried though about what the baby was going to look like. Cathy tried not to think about the donor, but sometimes she dreamed it was the doctor. Other times she had moments of panic that the donor was really totally different from Mark, and maybe even from another nationality or race. Most of the time, though, she felt overwhelmed with gratitude to this unknown person who had made it possible for her to become a mother.

People who have used AID report widely differing feelings toward the donor. Some wish they could meet him and see what he looks like or thank him for his help. Others dismiss the donor, saying they have purchased a product and the person behind it is irrelevant to them. Most people know that they will never be able to find out who the donor is and prefer to try to forget about him. Some fathers are plagued by feelings of inferiority when they compare themselves to the bright and accomplished type of man who is selected to be a donor.

When Cathy and Mark's baby Michael was born, they were both ecstatic to be parents at last. All of the worries they had had seemed insignificant. When asked if they have any sense of how the method of conception might affect their relationship to Michael, who is now five years old, they explained:

> *Cathy:* When Michael was very young, I stepped back and let Mark do things more than I would have otherwise, because I feel I have this genetic claim on him and Mark is going to need to have something special to make up for that. Over the years this has changed, and I feel we are more equal about everything.

> *Mark:* I am his father—there is no doubt in my mind. As he's growing and his features are getting more definite, I wonder who else has a nose like that. But these feelings are minor compared to the joy and gratitude of having him.

Keeping AID Secret

For most parents, the joy of having and raising a healthy child far outweighs any problems that might accompany AID. However, there are some problems faced by parents. One of these is the feeling they have done something deviant, something not really accepted by others. According to Bernard Rubin, who reviewed the history of artificial insemination, it has been discussed as far back as the second century and practiced since at least 1793. He reports, however, that it has always been opposed from many sides.[20]

In the past, some physicians called it "socially monstrous," "an offense against society." Courts ruled that AID is a form of adultery and the children born from it "illegitimate." Leaders of many religious groups have forbidden its use, claiming that it would endanger the family and violate religious precepts. Pope Pius XII, in voicing the Catholic Church's opposition in 1949, claimed that AID would "convert the domestic hearth, sanctuary of the family, into nothing more than a biological laboratory."[21]

This opposition has mostly disappeared. The medical profession now openly accepts and endorses donor insemination, and the courts and legislatures in most states have passed laws to ensure that the children have the same status as any other child born to a married couple. Sperm banks have multiplied, and infertility is a subject openly discussed in the media and among many couples. AID is increasingly available to single hetero-sexual and lesbian women as well as to married couples. Apparently many of the legal, medical, and psychological obstacles have been overcome in the past two decades.

But that does not mean going through with the procedure is easy, that there are not a host of emotional as well as medical and legal prob-lems that remain. The Catholic Church as well as the most conservative of Jewish and Protestant leaders are still opposed.[22] The general public is largely uninformed and unsupportive.

Secrecy is a key issue for those involved in insemination. Artificial insemination is almost always surrounded by secrecy—secrecy about the identity of the donor, secrecy between the couple and their friends and family about what they are doing, and secrecy from the child conceived about his or her true origins. The first recorded case of successful AID, in 1884, was done during an examination of the woman without even telling the couple involved. Since then, according to sociologist Robert Snowden and colleagues, some physicians have advocated, if possible, not telling the husband of his infertility or that a donor is going to be used.[23]

Most physicians and other staff members of AID programs strongly encourage their patients to keep AID a secret from everyone. They even suggest not telling the obstetrician who delivers the baby, so that the hus-band's name will be put on the birth certificate without hesitation. As one woman said:

> The doctor told us it's nobody else's business, that it's just between the two of us and him, and no one else has to know. That was a hard thing, you know, because so many times you want to say it. It's a hard thing to explain, and people seem to think that if you can't have your own, you shouldn't have any or you should adopt. I have a feeling his parents wouldn't accept the baby if they knew. They wouldn't think she was a part of him.

The secrecy inevitably produces some awkwardness at times, espe-cially when family members and friends speculate, as they always do, about which parent a child resembles. One father recalled:

> When he was little, everyone said he looked just like me. My mother has a picture of me when I was little and she held it up against him and she said they looked identical, like twins. I used to say, "No, look how different he looks," but now I just play along with it—I know what really happened.

Most couples feel very torn between a desire to keep the information private and a strong need to talk to others about it. They are fearful of others' reactions. Yet they also talk about the stress of "living a lie" and the wish to share such an important event with those to whom they are close. Some wish they could meet other people who have also used AID so they could compare their feelings and experiences with each other.

No matter how strongly they express a commitment to secrecy, most of the people in our study and in others had told at least one or two others. They are selective, often telling one set of parents but not the other, or certain friends they assumed would be sympathetic. But they have found it very difficult not to tell anyone at all.

The central dilemma for parents who use donor insemination is whether to tell their children. The great majority of parents who use AID insist that they will never reveal the circumstances of the conception to their children.[24] By not informing the child, the parents believe that they need never worry about a later search for the identity of the biological father. More important, they feel they will avoid any stigma that they or the child might suffer for seeming "abnormal." After all, they reason, why create unnecessary problems, particularly if friends and relatives also do not know and therefore the risk of a child's hearing from other sources is minimal?

Certainly most parents who conceive "naturally" do not tell children about the circumstances of their conception. Unlike the adopted child, where others know and neither of the parents is involved genetically, the child born of AID appears to be the product of the parents' normal pregnancy and birth. As one father said:

> I couldn't tell him. You know, I will have raised him all his life and I just wouldn't have the heart to tell him. I'm afraid he'd be ashamed of me. It might break my heart as well as his.

Then why tell the children? Some experts claim that it is essential that children know their medical history and not assume they may share any medical problems experienced by the fathers who raise them. Some also fear that maintaining a secret about the child's origin is ultimately unhealthy for the family. Aphrodite Clamar, writing in the *American Journal of Psychoanalysis*, emphasizes this possibility: "By its very nature, a secret is a potent force, assuming undue proportion and power within the family—an existential fact that remains unspoken, yet controls and colors the lives of the people involved." Baran and Pannor, who began their study of donor insemination (DI) with a belief in the value of secrecy, were led by their findings to the opposite conclusion. They found that secrecy is "lethal and destructive to the families involved. . . . We are convinced that in all DI families, the need to maintain secrecy and anonymity has had an adverse effect upon all of the members."[25] Children may sense that something is being hidden from them. Those who are eventually told often feel relieved because they had guessed that there was something different, or bad, about themselves.

The physicians who provide donor insemination usually counsel silence; social scientists who have studied AID almost always encourage openness. With the experts disagreeing and what seem to be compelling arguments on both sides, parents are faced once more with a dilemma created by the benefits of technology. (See chapter 11 for further discussion.)

Single Heterosexual and Lesbian Women

Single heterosexual and lesbian women who want very much to have children are turning more and more to AID as a solution. According to one estimate, 10,000 children conceived with AID in the United States have been born to lesbian mothers. Single women, straight or lesbian, may not want intimacy with a man in order to conceive, or they may prefer to avoid problems by not knowing the identity of the father.[26] As one lesbian woman said:

> Sex with somebody that I'm not involved with otherwise would seem so mercenary. It wasn't anything I ever considered. I kind of liked the idea of having a virgin birth. And anyway, conception is conception—it's just a matter of how the sperm gets there.

Many single heterosexual women who seek out donor insemination hope to get married but cannot wait any longer to find the right man before having children. As difficult as it is for married couples to adopt, it is even more so for unmarried women. AID is then an attractive alternative. A single mother of a four-year-old son born by AID talked about her situation:

> It's hard raising a child by yourself. But my family has been wonderful. My parents were concerned at first about the man and what he does and what he looks like. But they loved the baby from the moment he was born—it just doesn't matter anymore where the sperm came from. It's also helpful that I have friends who did the same thing, and our kids will be friends with each other and not feel so unusual.

The most difficult problem faced by unmarried women is obtaining AID. Many physicians and clinics refuse to inseminate anyone who is not in a stable marriage; others insist on first having a psychological evaluation.[27] Public attitudes are changing but are still unsympathetic. It is necessary, therefore, for single heterosexual and lesbian women to seek out a physician or a sperm bank willing to help them, or simply to do the insemination themselves.

A lesbian couple who had used a turkey baster to inseminate one partner received a great deal of media attention when they split up and the other partner sued for visitation rights. While the story created a sensation in the press, it is not an isolated case. In fact, information regarding techniques of home insemination is widely available in networks of lesbianwomen seeking to avoid the difficulties (and expense) of approaching physicians.

The outcome of that case and others like it indicates the obstacles facing lesbian parents. Courts in New York and California have ruled that even if a woman was equally involved in raising a child conceived by donor insemination, she has no rights to that child if she is not the biological mother.[28] This is particularly ironic in light of the decision of the first judge in the famous Baby M case, who ruled that being a biological mother gave Mary Beth Whitehead no rights at all to her child. In a few cases, the sperm donor has won visitation rights over the objection of the lesbian mother. These rulings demonstrate the tremendous difference between AID used by married couples and by unmarried women. In the case of a heterosexual marriage, the sperm donor has no legal rights, and the birth mother's husband is usually considered to be the parent by law.

Despite the growing number of children conceived by the artificial insemination of unmarried women, they still comprise a very small percentage of all inseminations. This proportion is certain to increase, but the obstacles point to the control that many physicians have over access to this technology. It is an example of the medical and legalprofessions' enforcement of social biases in relation to technologies for conception.[29]

———— • ————

Studies of families who have undergone artificial insemination have uncovered relatively few significant problems as a result, and some studies even found that AID couples have a much lower divorce rate than average, althought the validity of these results has been challenged.[30] Perhapsthe process of working through the conflicts of infertility leads to stronger relationships in those who have had AID. Most families are very positive about the results, and many return to be inseminated for a second child. These results have contributed to a more open-minded attitude on the part of those physicians and lawmakers who recognize the benefits for infertile families.

Not everyone is as fortunate as Mark and Cathy, who did finally have a child with AID. Those people for whom AIH or AID does not work are confronted with new decisions. What should they do next? Depending on the nature of the problem, they may try another method. Many couples, for example, who used AIH for female or unexplained infertility and for whom, therefore, AID is not appropriate, consider whether to try IVF or other treatments. Many others look into adopting a child.

For those who do succeed, artificial insemination, like many of the new technologies, creates dilemmas for individual families to resolve. It is certain to become increasingly common and more successful and therefore probably more public. Even so, it is likely to remain a secretive process, one producing a very private, but troubling, joy for parents. As Cathy said:

> I don't really think about it anymore. Just once in a while I wonder what other people would think if they knew and what Michael would think if he knew. I wonder how other parents who have had AID deal with it. And then I forget about it again, and we're just like any other family.

CHAPTER 4

In Vitro *Fertilization*

We flew into the Norfolk, Virginia airport, coming in low over the ocean with its persistent, lapping waves. It was a beautiful warm day, a day we had looked forward to for two years. I was one determined lady to get pregnant, even if it meant a long wait to get into what we considered the best in vitro program in the country. I was going to force a baby out of my body; it meant so much to me. As we rode in a cab to the Medical Tower, I wondered how many thousands of others had already made this same trip, this "pilgrimage to Mecca." Were they all as filled with nervous excitement as I was, as desperate and as hopeful? How many had left again by the same route, their dreams destroyed in sunny Norfolk? I prayed that I would be one of the lucky ones.

Hundreds of thousands of people, like this woman, are now considering or have already attempted *in vitro* fertilization (IVF). The birth of Louise Brown, the first "test-tube baby" in England in 1978, represented a major breakthrough in fertility treatment, drawing the attention of the world to the miracle of IVF. The first American program opened in Norfolk, Virginia, in 1981, and approximately two hundred more have followed. Worldwide, tens of thousands of babies have already been born as a result of this method.

The growing availability of IVF has raised many questions. Is it the most promising new technology, helping people who cannot conceive to fulfill their dreams? Or does it offer false hope to people who are willing to try anything to have a baby?

There is no doubt that it is controversial. The image of scientists creating human embryos in a laboratory is frightening to many people. They see IVF as leading to dangerous manipulations of life, including selective use of embryos according to their sex and other genetic traits. But for those couples who seek out IVF, the controversies are mostly irrelevant. They have spent years trying to have a biological child, and they often believe that IVF is their last hope. Even though it may reopen a Pandora's box of anxieties and grief once thought resolved, and despite the fact that it is difficult, expensive, stressful, and unlikely to succeed, each couple sustains the hope that for them, at least, it will produce a miracle.

Carol and Tim have been searching for this miracle for almost ten years. For years their lives have been dominated by temperature charts and sex on schedule. Carol has been through multiple tests with several doctors. She has had surgery twice and has taken fertility drugs. For Carol and Tim, IVF is not a radical new experiment. It is simply the last of a long series of intrusive and difficult procedures. It is the end of the line for them.

During these years, Tim has worked hard to build up his own mail-order business and Carol has been enjoying a successful career in family counseling. Yet their minds were never far from their preoccupation with becoming parents. Carol said:

> I had all the usual tests done—everything from A to Z. After years of tests and two operations, the end result was absolutely nothing—unexplained infertility. I went to another infertility specialist to get a second opinion and was told, "Relax, keep trying." They couldn't find anything. I always thought they were implying that the problem was in my mind, and, although I didn't think so, I would wonder. It's the 1980s; they should be able to come up with something tangible. It's like I'm out on a limb; I'm in limbo somewhere.
>
> I kept thinking I had to do something, find more information, see other doctors, or else nothing would happen. It was so frustrating to keep calling and writing people, because it takes so much emotional energy to do that. But I did it anyway because I wanted a baby so badly. Finally, one doctor suggested I try *in vitro*. He referred me to a medical center about an hour from our home that had recently started a program.

For some lucky couples, perhaps 15 percent of those who start the process, IVF succeeds with the birth of a baby. For all those who fail to become pregnant, or who have miscarriages or ectopic pregnancies, it brings renewed stress and grief. For many, it is the final procedure that closes their struggle for a biological child.

The great majority of people in our study who had tried IVF felt it was worth the effort. They may be angry at a specific program, they recall the process as being emotionally and physically difficult, and they might have been unhappy if it did not work. But, despite all the stress, almost no one was sorry at least to have tried. Other studies have also found that the experience of IVF can be extremely stressful, and its failure can result for some people in acute grief reactions, including anxiety, depression, and thoughts of suicide. Women report such responses more often than men, and women without children appear to react most intensely when IVF does not work. These reactions generally diminish over time.[1]

When IVF was first developed, it was intended primarily as a way of bypassing damaged or blocked fallopian tubes. As infertility specialists became more experienced with the techniques of IVF, many clinics began to extend it to couples with other problems such as endometriosis (when pieces of the uterine lining attach to the tubes or ovaries and prevent conception), male infertility, poor sperm-mucus interaction, and unexplained infertility such as Carol and Tim experienced.[2]

The major purpose of IVF has been to join the egg of a woman to the sperm of her husband so that they can produce a biological child together. Eggs are removed from a woman's ovary, either by a surgical procedure called a laparoscopy or now most often with the use of ultrasound-guided needle aspiration. A thin needle is inserted into the ovary either through the vagina or through the bladder. Using ultrasound to visualize the eggs, the physician can remove them through the needle without general anesthetic, and they are fertilized with the husband's sperm in a small shallow container called a petri dish. After waiting two days to see if the cells have divided, the physician inserts the fertilized eggs through the woman's vagina into her uterus.

As IVF has been perfected and gained greater public acceptance, physicians have begun to offer a large number of variations. Fertility centers are increasingly using methods called gamete intrafallopian transfer (GIFT) and zygote intrafallopian transfer (ZIFT). These techniques were developed with the idea that fertilized eggs would implant more readily in the womb if they could start a normal journey through the fallopian tubes first. With GIFT, as soon as the eggs are retrieved, they are immediately placed in a catheter with the man's semen and returned to the fallopian tube. ZIFT differs in that the eggs are placed in the tube only after fertilization.

Physicians appear to have achieved a higher success rate with GIFT than with IVF, but ZIFT is so far no more successful than IVF, and subsequent studies indicate that *where* a fertilized egg is placed is not a key determinant of the results. It may be that GIFT has better success rates in part because candidates for the procedure have less severe fertility problems to begin with. For example, this method is possible only for a woman who has at least one healthy tube. And since it is a somewhat less complicated procedure than IVF, it may be attracting couples earlier in the treatment process who might have eventually conceived without assistance. In fact, one of the best-selling fertility books recommends that people having trouble conceiving skip all other tests and treatments and go right to GIFT.[3]

Some procedures involve other people in the conception or pregnancy. For example, a woman with impaired fertility whose husband also has a low or absent sperm count can have her eggs fertilized in the petri dish by a donor's sperm. If a woman's ovaries are missing or inaccessible, or if she has stopped ovulating, she may receive eggs donated or sold by another woman, which are then fertilized by the patient's husband. Or if she can produce an egg but for some reason cannot carry a baby, the couple's embryo may be transferred to another woman who is hired as a surrogate mother.[4]

The use of donor eggs is becoming increasingly common, and it is proving to be more likely to result in a healthy baby than any other form of IVF. As a result, a number of fertility clinics have organized programs for recruiting egg donors.

Some clinics offer a method called micromanipulation for male infertility. The woman is superovulated, her eggs retrieved, and then a hole is drilled in them to allow the sperm to enter, either on their own or by "subzonal insemination." The success rate is low, but it does work for some couples in which the man's sperm cannot achieve fertilization otherwise.

Success Rates

One of the first questions most couples ask as they are investigating IVF is the likelihood of success. In some clinics they are told it is 50 percent or more, or that if they try enough times they are sure to succeed eventually. The author of a popular book on infertility, which urges its readers to skip all other fertility treatments and go right to GIFT, claims that it succeeds 45 percent of the time. These numbers are highly exaggerated. Even those specialists who cite more modest rates of 15 to 20 percent often do not take into account the chances of success for the couple's specific conditions or age group. For example, women over forty are as a group less than half as likely as women under forty to have a baby after IVF or GIFT. The answers one receives also often reflect a national rate or the experience of the most successful clinics, ignoring the fact that the particular center where a couple is seeking help may have had very few births or none at all.[5]

One center sent us a letter reporting one birth and three current pregnancies out of almost one hundred patients. At best this would be a

4 percent success rate so far. Yet this clinic, in the same letter, claimed a 20 percent pregnancy rate with 50 percent ending in miscarriages. Another program, which had had no pregnancies after several attempts, was featured in a local newspaper report with the claim that success could be achieved as often as 50 percent of the time.

Widespread dissatisfaction about the difficulty in obtaining accurate information led to congressional hearings in 1988 and 1989 and the publication of a government survey of IVF clinic results. In addition, the American Fertility Society and the Society for Assisted Reproductive Technology established a registry in 1987, and its annual reports provide information about average pregnancy and delivery rates for all reporting clinics combined.

These surveys indicate that there is tremendous variation in success rates from one clinic to another, with only a handful accounting for a substantial proportion of deliveries. In 1990, for example, 5 clinics out of 180 accounted for over one-fifth of all IVF deliveries, and 5 out of 135 that performed GIFT reported 45 percent of all GIFT pregnancies. Larger programs apparently do no better on average than smaller ones, so size alone is not an indication of how good a program is. The reports also document slowly improving results from year to year, although this may be a result of people with less severe fertility impairments trying IVF as well as of improvements in techniques.[6]

It is very difficult to state an actual rate of success. Some IVF programs define success as a positive pregnancy test. Close monitoring of the woman may produce an early diagnosis of what is called a "chemical pregnancy," one that aborts so early that in unmonitored women it would not even be recognized. Increasingly clinics are emphasizing "clinical pregnancy," in which a gestational sac is present on ultrasound in addition to the positive pregnancy test. These numbers do not include, therefore, women who become pregnant and then have an ectopic pregnancy. More than one out of four pregnancies, according to registry reports, result in ectopic pregnancy, miscarriage, therapeutic abortion, or stillbirth. It is also hard to give an exact rate because at any given time there are people who are in the middle of the process, waiting to start another attempt, or currently pregnant. Many drop out after one or two tries. Therefore, clinics usually present their rates as the number of pregnancies compared to the total number of cycles in which ovarian stimulation was initiated or to the number of embryo transfers.[7]

The most crucial question, the best measure of success, is how many couples who enter a program actually end up with babies. The answer to that question is still difficult to obtain. Our survey of American IVF programs in 1985–86 showed that the percentage of couples who started IVF and actually had a successful birth ranged from none to 30 percent, with most programs having birth rates below 10 percent. A government study in 1986 calcluated that 6 percent of women have babies for each attempt at IVF. The 1992 IVF-ET Registry report concluded that 20.7 percent of the 19,095 women who began at least one cycle of IVF, GIFT, or ZIFT in 1990 had a baby. Since many women began one of these methods more than once in 1990, it is important to calculate the chances of success for each cycle begun; for clinics that reported results for 1990, there was a successful birth rate of 15.3 percent for each cycle. In comparing the different methods, we discover that births resulted from 19.0 percent of GIFT cycles, 12.3 percent of IVF, and 13.2% of ZIFT procedures initiated. The best success rates were with donated eggs, the lowest with frozen embryos. These figures should be treated with caution; not all clinics report to the registry, and the results are not obtained independently. As we have seen earlier, clinics have in the past misrepresented success rates to make themselves look better.[8]

Those who can afford IVF do not appear to be discouraged by the low success rates. They hope to defy the odds, to prove that this high-stakes gamble will pay off for them. They may be deceiving themselves. In order to begin a program such as IVF, it may be necessary to ignore accurate information about the very low rates of success. Even when the poor chances of having a baby from IVF are carefully presented in advance, couples often do not believe what they hear. A nurse coordinator in an IVF program described this mental screening process:

> The majority of patients are very well read. They know that one place may have a 20 percent success rate, and we have a rate of 10 percent. But for them it's never 10 percent or 20 percent, they all believe that their own chance of having a baby is 50 percent or 70 percent or 80 percent. Maybe they have to believe that to come here.

Physicians and patients alike engage in magical thinking about the possibility of having a baby. Staff members of new programs are convinced that they will achieve high success rates, and they communicate this to couples. A woman who had already been through IVF three times describes how she convinced herself that her chances were good despite the evidence:

> The doctor told me that I was the twelfth woman in the program. He didn't want to tell me if they had had any successes yet, but I kept asking. I wanted to know what my odds were. He had already told me that the chance of implantation was one in seven. When he finally said that they had had no successes yet, I felt really good; it increased my high. I figured if there had

already been one in the first group of seven, then the next one would be number fourteen instead of number twelve. This way it felt like my chances were better.

Many people decide not to take the risk of trying IVF; for them the low success rates are too discouraging. For example, of the women who wrote in our questionnaire that they had considered IVF, more than one-third said they had rejected the idea because of the poor success rates.

Advocates of IVF point out that the natural conception rate is also low. Even fertile people who have intercourse during ovulation have only a one in four chance of conceiving. Some physicians claim that IVF can match and may ultimately exceed the natural pregnancy rate. This remains to be seen.

Carol described her experience of learning about the possibility of success with IVF and how she reinterpreted the clinic's lack of experience to be a positive factor:

> During out first interview, we spoke to a doctor and the nurse coordinator. They were extremely nice and supportive and gave us detailed information about the procedure and what to expect. They told us that the success rate for this procedure was about 17 percent. At that time I didn't realize that they hadn't had any successes at all, and that they had been doing it for only six months.
>
> I would have done it even if I had known that. At least it was a chance and if I didn't do it I would never know whether I had that chance or not. Also I liked the fact that it was a fairly new program because I thought that we would get more attention. It made it seem like we were doing something important, something that probably not too many people in this area go through.

An Experience of IVF

The IVF procedure is based on precise timing and continuous monitoring of the woman's responses. For several weeks the woman's life is dominated by injections of fertility drugs, ultrasounds, blood tests, followed by egg retrieval and more blood tests. Carol described the procedure and the physical and emotional difficulties it entailed:

> After our initial interview, we waited three months before the start of the procedure. It was really very hard once we started. I think because you want this so badly and try to

protect yourself from the hope, especially after so many disappointments, you begin to feel you can't do it. But somehow we kept going.

Tim started giving me the Pergonal injections on the third day of my cycle in order to help produce more than one egg. The shots were a little scary, but the main thing is that I felt I couldn't escape what we were doing. I couldn't try to distract myself or pretend this wasn't happening. I was dragged right into it because I was so physically involved for the entire month.

On the sixth day I started going to the hospital for ultrasounds. Each morning I would sit in the waiting room with other couples, drinking water to fill up my bladder, so that they could see if follicles [the sacs in which eggs develop] were growing on my ovaries. They would say you have three follicles, sized 1.2, 1.4, and 1.7. I kept thinking, am I going to make it? My blood, my numbers, are they going to find follicles? Will they be big enough? Will I make it to the laparoscopy?

At every stage I was terrified that I would fail and not make it to the next step. I was scared and upset, but I was afraid to show my feelings or go to the counselor there. I thought they might ask me to leave the program because I wasn't handling it well. There was also the feeling that I didn't want to say anything because I would be jinxed.

Then they told me the time looked good to release the eggs from the follicles. To do this they stopped the fertility drugs and gave me an injection of HCG [human chorionic gonadotropin, a substance that triggers the release of the eggs from the follicles]. It really drew me in when I saw those eggs on the surface of my ovary in the ultrasound.

A day and a half later, I went into surgery for the removal of the eggs. When I woke up, the doctor told me they had gotten three eggs and they looked pretty good. I felt a tremendous sense of relief at that point. The worst part physically was over—the ultrasounds, the driving back and forth, and then the surgery.

The anesthesia made me sick for a while. While I was vomiting in the recovery room, Tim wanted to know where I thought he should go and masturbate to give his sperm. I couldn't believe it. I just told him to take his *Penthouse* magazine and go find a bathroom. They told me that they took Tim's semen to the lab, washed it, separated the sperm from the fluid, and placed it in an incubator for several hours. Then a lab technician placed a few drops of the most active sperm onto each egg to fertilize it.

Not everyone who starts IVF gets as far as Carol did, since there are several points in the procedure at which something may not work. In an average cycle, approximately 15 percent of women who take drugs to stimulate their ovaries discover that the egg follicles have not developed sufficiently or cannot be retrieved. When eggs are removed, about 15 percent of the time they fail to fertilize. This means that one out of every four women who begin a treatment cycle will not proceed to the stage of having a fertilized egg placed in her body.[9] As one woman who never had eggs retrieved said:

> I'd been there for a week and things were not looking very good. The eggs were not developing the way they wanted them to. That was hard to take. Here the nurse is telling everybody after the ultrasounds to come back tomorrow. Then she sits down quietly in the corner with me and says, "Well, we're sorry to have to scrap this cycle." It was like someone had died.

Carol felt fortunate to be among those who made it through all of the initial stages. She said:

> I burst into tears when the nurse called and told me eggs had divided. I realized I had finally created new life.
>
> Two days after surgery, I went back for the embryos to be transferred into my uterus. When they put them in with the fluid, I was scared to move. I had to stay on my hands and knees with my rear end elevated for the transfer—all of this with eight people looking at me. What a humiliating position. But I guess I'm beyond embarrassment at this point.
>
> It was also *very* exciting. It tasted like hope—real hope. My body was all puffed up from the Pergonal shots and I felt pregnant. I knew a live embryo was in my uterus. This was the closest I had ever been to being pregnant. Then the two-week wait to see if an embryo would implant, and I would be officially pregnant. After one week my hopes were the highest, but I could barely endure the strain of waiting, thinking every twinge from my waist down was either menstrual cramps or early signs of pregnancy.
>
> Then during the second week, I felt I was getting my period. That awful roller coaster we had been living on was coming crashing down again.
>
> The nurse called with the results of the first blood test I took to check for pregnancy. She said it looked good but inconclusive. When I went for the next blood test, the staff were all excited. Maybe I'd be their first success. My hopes were soaring again.

Then they called and told me the latest blood test was negative. Even though I half expected it, I was devastated. I didn't realize how much it would affect me. I thought I was handling it real well, but I couldn't even talk to them.

All those feelings I thought had been resolved came right back again. We had never been so close to a pregnancy—never felt quite this hopeful before. That made it painful. For weeks I lay awake at night trying to visualize those embryos inside of me, trying to figure out why it didn't work.

Tim shared in the terrible disappointment:

The day we heard the news I couldn't believe it. I didn't want to believe it. All my rational sense of the poor probabilities didn't prevent us from feeling that we had just lost a baby. I started to focus on work intensely. I couldn't stand to see Carol's pain—I didn't want to see her cry.

The news of failure after weeks of intense effort and hope is crushing. It is compounded for many by a sense of abandonment, a break in the close and constant contact that binds couples to clinic staff and to others going through the program. One IVF counselor described this rupture:

You call a patient and tell her that you have a negative pregnancy test, the phone call is over, but you know somebody at the end of the line is falling apart. There needs to be some real handholding at that time because of the emotional feeling that somehow the patient has failed, and the medical team feels that way, too. That's one of the reasons we have a hard time dealing with it, because we, too, have failed.

The intense daily relationship between staff and patient is over, often ending without even a goodbye. This breaking off of communication, a frequent occurrence, is particularly hard on couples because they are grieving. They grieve for those living growing embryos that should have become babies and instead died in the woman's body.

"Some women become attached to those embryos in a way that's very similar to how attached women get to a pregnancy," explains a psychologist who counsels infertile couples. "They are really experiencing a failed cycle of *in vitro* as a miscarriage." This is not surprising. Her body prepared with drugs, her mind "psyched" for success, and in many cases having seen live embryos under a microscope and even being placed in her uterus on ultrasound, she has indeed felt pregnant. Just as with a miscarriage, couples may go through intense feelings of depression and anger. They may feel guilty; once again they may blame themselves for having done something wrong or simply for being inadequate. They may be jealous of others who have achieved pregnancies by IVF or who have never had to struggle with infertility.

Despite the trauma they had just experienced, Carol and Tim reminded each other that they had originally agreed to try the procedure at least three times. They figured they would devote one year to *in vitro*. At that point Carol would be thirty-five, and they would then decide what to do next. Carol explained:

> In my head I knew it made sense to try it again. I thought, I've endured one loss and I know what that's like. It's very painful, but it didn't kill me. My choice is to try one or two more times with the months of grief attached to it, and maybe have a success, or not to try hard at all. As hard as it was, knowing that we got so far gave me hope to try again. Maybe the next time would be lucky for us. I'm glad I did it. I don't think I could have rested, knowing that the technology existed, until I had tried it. It was painful, but so were the other years of my life that I was trying to get pregnant. Those were my choices. I could quit or I could try.

Tim was also ready to try again:

> Two months later we were back. It was easier the second time because we knew everybody there and knew what was involved. The part that made the first one hard was not knowing your way around the medical center and feeling bounced from one lab or office to another. You also don't know whether you're going to drop out at any point. They come up with all sorts of little traps along the way and give you only little pieces of information as you go along. I would think we've made it and then find out that no, that was just one piece and there's still another step to be done. We got through all the steps the first time; so I was very positive about our chances of being successful if we tried again.
>
> I was so excited when they told me that this time they retrieved eleven eggs from Carol. They were very encouraging. I felt like we got 100 on a test and this was the time it was going to happen for us.

The development of follicles, eggs, and embryos becomes very important psychological steps for couples going through IVF. As Carol observed:

> You go for these tests and you bring the results back to the nurse there, the picture of the follicles, which wasn't always very

encouraging. She'd say, "Is that all there is? Come on Carol, you gotta get them bigger." What did she think? Of course, I would like to make them as big as possible!

Carol and Tim felt sure that since there were so many eggs retrieved this time, they were going to make it. When the results of the final blood test were negative, they were devastated again. Carol said:

> I was afraid I was going crazy, especially after I got my period. I couldn't go to work and I couldn't stop crying. Again I felt like I had lost a baby, but it would sound strange to tell that to my friends and family. So I couldn't share the feelings very well. There were several months of mourning when nothing else in life seemed worthwhile. I felt physically depleted, not to mention seeing all this money thrown out the window for nothing. We had very little left. I really wanted to run away from it all.
>
> But at the same time, I realized that it hadn't been all negative. At least, after all these years of trying to get pregnant, we knew we could make an embryo. That was one step farther along. And the doctors were still encouraging—they hadn't given up.

A positive aspect of the IVF experience for Carol and Tim was Tim's involvement in the procedure. Tim commented:

> I felt more actively involved with the *in vitro* than with any other part of the infertility procedures. Maybe because I became so involved, I was very hopeful. I thought I was going to faint when I had to give Carol the first shot. I always had a phobia about needles. But it really made me appreciate what Carol was going through physically. Then watching the ultrasounds, watching Carol go into surgery one more time, was really hard. I admired Carol's courage. I don't think I could go through the same thing.

Many couples feel that IVF gives them an opportunity for greater control over the procedure, while others are glad to be told what to do and not worry about control. The programs vary a great deal in how much they involve couples, such as the man giving Pergonal shots to the woman, or the couple taking samples to the lab. But ultimately the outcome is out of their hands. As one infertility counselor noted:

> They make the decision to do it. But are they going to be accepted in the program? That's out of their control. It's all of these hurdles they have to leap over. I think the only control they really have is deciding which program, how many times they will try, how they're going to cope as a couple, and how they're going to utilize their network of family and friends.

Carol and Tim had agreed to try three times, and although they were feeling very discouraged, they decided to stick to that original plan. By this time they knew the ropes and they were feeling close to some of the staff. Tim recalled:

> As much as it had been difficult, and they weren't always equipped to meet our needs, we still felt that they were like family. You can get to know people pretty well in those circumstances. One of the doctors was really super, and we also came to rely on the nurse coordinator a lot. When things got really tough for us after the second cycle, we went to see the social worker at the clinic, and she was a big help.

For some couples, trouble arises because one member of the couple is more interested in pursuing IVF than the other. Often the husband feels that he is just going along to keep his wife happy, but that it is really her project. Some men are very reluctant to see their wives subjected to yet another series of tests and treatment. When the two are not in agreement, a failed IVF attempt may produce a great deal of anger and mutual blaming.

Some IVF programs have a full-time social worker who offers counseling and organizes support groups. Others use a therapist only at the beginning in order to help couples talk about their feelings about infertility and any ambivalence they have about IVF. However, since these interviews are part of the initial screening, many people are reluctant to speak openly for fear of being dropped from the program. In reality, it is very rare for the therapist to recommend that a couple be excluded.[10]

Most programs offer no counseling at all. As one director said:

> We take pride—we do a good job of talking to people. I don't think we do as good a job for someone who really has a more pronounced need, but it's like a lot of other things with an IVF program—someone's got to pay for it, and I think the expense is prohibitive.

For many couples, the contacts they have with clinic staff are all they need, but many more with whom we talked expressed a desire for more counseling as part of the program. Some felt that they were treated very impersonally; although they were not sorry to have tried IVF, they were angry at the staff. As one man said:

> You know, we've been infertile a long time and we finally get to this fancy medical center and pretty soon we realized that these guys were only spending ten minutes with us if we were lucky. We just weren't getting our questions answered, and of

course it wasn't working either. It was just so frustrating. The whole process is so much black magic. You get the impression you're part of an experiment, a little cog in their big machine, just another one of fifty people being herded like sheep through exactly the same thing with no personal interest in you as an individual.

Part of this anger is an inevitable component of the grief from failure. The clinics that make efforts to offer personalized care and support may be better able than the others to help couples through this difficult process. They are certainly more appreciated. But this kind of support is unusual.

One very important source of support is the other couples who are going through IVF at the same time. Tim described the bond he felt to these other couples:

> They were mostly people like us, in their thirties, educated, and from middle- or upper-middle-class areas. They had all been through infertility problems for many years. All these women had their battle scars from surgeries, and their bodies had been probed and prodded. All the guys had jerked off a million times in the bathroom. With all of these things we had in common, there was a lot of mutual support.

There may be a certain amount of competition among people in the same cycle (e.g., who has the biggest eggs?), but ordinarily this is greatly outweighed by the help. These couples sometimes stay in touch with each other long after their connection with the center has ended.

Even before Carol and Tim received that last phone call informing them once again of a negative pregnancy test after their third attempt, they had the feeling that it was all over for them with IVF. They knew they would have to accept that they were unlikely to have a biological child. Carol was glad that at least it was over:

> When the third time failed, I felt exhausted. I was angry and upset, but part of me felt like it was over and that was a relief. I knew I had done it all and now I could stop; I was tired. By the time we finished *in vitro*, I had come to the point where the need to have a biological child had been beaten out of me. I had wanted desperately to be pregnant with our own child. Inch by inch I started to give up that need, and I felt I was ready to consider adoption.

For many couples who do not succeed, IVF can lead to closure. They feel that they have tried everything and now can begin to accept the fact that they are not going to be able to have a child together. Carol and Tim went through the procedure three times before they could come to this point. Couples sometimes reach this resolution after one time, while others are unwilling to give up even after six or more trials.

Many couples have to drop out of the program because it is simply too expensive to go on. The cost of each cycle is usually $5,000 or more, and many insurance companies do not cover IVF.[11] There are additional expenses of transportation, lodging, and food if one uses a center away from home. Because of these high costs, many people cannot even try one time, and others make great sacrifices for this chance. Some people feel it really isn't a choice—"We do what we have to do," they say. Another woman agreed:

> You pay your money and take your chances. What good is money if you don't have the thing you want most—to have children?

Other people express a great deal of anger and resentment about having to spend so much, especially when the procedure fails. One man voiced his opinion:

> The price tag is outrageous! These programs are entirely too expensive. Why should people have to go to the poorhouse simply to exercise their inalienable right of having a child?

For many people the "price tag" makes the decision for them. They may buy lottery tickets in the hope of some day winning a large sum, but in the meantime they simply cannot afford to go on. In our 1985 survey, we found that people with little insurance coverage who made less than about $40,000 per year could not afford to try IVF at all. Money is also the major reason given by the many people who stop IVF after one cycle.

In studies of patients who withdrew from an *in vitro* program, two main reasons were given for leaving. Financial burdens was one. The other major problem was the stress of the procedure. People mentioned the tremendous anxiety, depression, disruption of work or career, and strain on their marriages.[12]

Despite the cost and stress, many couples find it hard to stop. They are encouraged by the programs and by the nature of the procedure to try again and again, in the hope that eventually it will work. Sitting in the waiting room in the one of the leading IVF clinics, it is hard to re-sist the temptation. Beautiful picture albums on the coffee table show all of the babies conceived in this place, together with their beaming fami-lies. There is hope in the air. And a sign on the bulletin board offers the powerful message: "You Never Fail Until You Stop Trying." Stopping—

or worse, not even trying—are presented as personal failures, lack of adequate motivation to have a child.[13]

A social worker at another IVF center criticized this kind of pressure:

> It is a rare bird, the infertility specialist who will say to couples, "Why don't you stop? Why don't you just put it in park?" Even to take a break. It's very hard for couples to give themselves permission to say, "I have done enough." We need to really help people, when they need to say enough is enough, to be able to do that.

Stopping is particularly difficult for those couples who have achieved a pregnancy that ended in miscarriage or ectopic pregnancy. They have tasted success; for them IVF worked, at least for a while. After years of trying to get pregnant, they have finally done it, and they celebrate their accomplishment. The clinic celebrates with them, counting them as a success. As one program director said:

> It took us more than fifteen transfers to get our first pregnancy. If you've done fifteen with nothing, a pregnancy is a real shot in the arm, whether it results in a live birth or not. It's a shot in the arm for the medical team and for the other patients, too, because they always want to know if you're having successes. And for some infertile people, even a failed pregnancy can be better than none at all.

——— • ———

Although a successful birth is still the exception, it does occur. One fortunate couple, whose daughter, Carla, is an IVF baby, are Sharon and Jerry.

Sharon had become pregnant quite unintentionally shortly after her marriage to Jerry, when she was in her twenties. They both knew they did not want another child right away after Alison was born, so they used birth control conscientiously, sure that they were super-fertile. When they decided later to have another child, it never occurred to them that it might not work. Like many couples with secondary infertility, they were astonished to find out that what had been so easy six years earlier was now impossible. It was five long painful years until they finally had another daughter, Carla, conceived in a petri dish at a university fertility clinic during their second attempt at IVF.

Sharon and Jerry described to us their experience with IVF. Sharon, still ecstatic, began:

It's been a miracle. Carla was dropped from heaven and I feel so blessed. It's as if I've woken up from a nightmare. I am a new person—I am not infertile anymore. I got pregnant and probably can again, if I want to. In fact, this turned my life around.

Our problem, as it turned out, was damage to my tubes. I must have the most horrible tubes in fifty states. Even when I first became pregnant with *in vitro*, I had an ectopic pregnancy. But that was hardly my first. During those five years we were trying to get pregnant, I actually conceived three times, but I had a miscarriage the first time, then two ectopic pregnancies, and several operations to repair my tubes. The first ectopic was especially traumatic. I came pretty close to dying that time. I came within two hours of hemorrhaging to death. So much at once—my first major surgery, nearly dying, losing a pregnancy, and discovering how serious my infertility problem was all at once. I was pretty badly depressed after that.

Part of the difficulty in deciding on *in vitro*, even though our doctor said it was our only chance, was the fear of facing one more loss, one more failure. I had terrible feelings of guilt that my body was this damaged vessel that was not capable of letting life continue. It was difficult for me to think that I would be carrying around fertilized eggs that would die one more time. I didn't think I could stand any more dead babies.

The turning point for me came when a good friend said, "You know all those eggs in your ovaries are going to die when you do, and they are dying each month. Now you can take a risk that they'll live to ten or thirty cells, with the chance of becoming a human being, or not live at all." So I decided, okay, together my eggs and I will just take that risk of living to twenty cells or however far they get, with the outside chance that one of them might actually continue—otherwise they'd die anyway.

Jerry continued the account:

We were actually very good candidates for the procedure, knowing that the tubes were our problem. I was more eager than Sharon to try it, thinking of it as a real challenge, almost an adventure into new scientific territory. Besides I just wasn't ready to consider adoption; I really wanted another child that was ours. We couldn't let the opportunity go by. One good thing about the *in vitro* was that it took the pressure off our marriage. I didn't have to perform according to the calendar, and lovemaking became more natural at that point.

Sharon interjected:

> I think everybody goes into it believing it might work. Even though they tell you that the success rate is low, there's something very compelling about it. You get very much tied up into their system—you get to know the physicians and they get invested in you, and you see it work with other patients; so even if it doesn't work, you try again. When you know that there's a chance out there, it's hard not to grab for it.
>
> The whole system has such built-in hope, as you move from one stage to the next, that there's a lot of false optimism that gets built in. You know, all of a sudden, you've got follicles and you get a little excited about that. You go to the laparoscopy and they are able to view the eggs; you get real excited about that. As you move along the process, you get more and more hopeful, so that by the end there's only a very small part of you that's really ready for bad news.

Jerry remembered his feelings at the time of the final stage of the procedure:

> I really believed that Sharon was pregnant after the embryos were transferred. I had even looked in the microscope to see the embryos, and when I said I wasn't sure what I was looking at, Sharon's response was, "What's the matter—don't you even recognize your own kid?" I was so sure that it would work since everything had gone perfectly up to that point. When we found out she was pregnant, we were elated and began to make plans for the birth. We were astonished at the grief and depression we felt when we realized she was having another ectopic.

Jerry and Sharon were both very involved in the *in vitro* procedure. They felt that in many ways it brought them together as a couple, since they were both so oriented to achieving pregnancy, and the procedure was something they could work on together. They were fortunate to have been referred to a clinic that had already been operating for several years, had had a number of successful births, and was less than two hours away from their home. They were able to get the Pergonal locally, and Jerry gave Sharon the shots at home. By the eighth day, however, she needed to be at the clinic early each morning for a week of ultrasounds and blood tests. She moved into a motel near the medical center. Sharon recalled that time:

> Being down there alone did not bother me. I looked upon it as kind of a nice vacation, and I knew that Jerry and our daugh-

ter Alison would be there for the weekend. There were several of us at the same motel, and we tended to spend a lot of time together. Most of the time it was very helpful, but occasionally the anxiety became contagious and that was the downside of it.

Jerry commented:

I think the hardest part for me was the waiting, waiting at home for Sharon to call while she was away to let me know if it was going okay. And of course it was awful waiting for the results of the blood tests to see if she was pregnant.

Sharon continued their story:

After the embryos were transferred in one part of the hospital, they had to take me on a gurney to the hospital itself, because at that time you had to stay twenty-four hours. Well, it was the bumpiest ride I've ever been through and I thought, This isn't good, I'm supposed to be perfectly still and I'm sure things are falling out. And then we had to wait for the elevator, and I was on an incline and I could feel things starting to drip out and I thought, It's all over. I was very pessimistic at that point.

We were ecstatic when the test came back positive. But then I kept bleeding and having pain on one side and I called the doctor and told him this feels like an ectopic pregnancy again. They discovered I was right, and they removed the tube. I was so scared by this experience that I asked them to please cauterize the other tube way down at the base. These tubes were no friends of mine.

At that point I was hopeful because before I hadn't been able to part with my tubes, they were my only chance. Now that I got pregnant once, I figured I could do it again. They could take my tubes—I didn't need them anymore. I think that knowing I could get pregnant, that it worked, made it easier for me to accept the loss. Instead of feeling helpless, I could go on. Also, I'm a somewhat religious person, and I just felt that if God wanted this for me it would be. If not, then that was His will and I could accept what would happen. That was very helpful and kind of got me through it.

The hardest part was probably the emotional aspect of it. I was very psyched for this the second time. I felt very positive about it, knowing that if I could just get pregnant and have it in the right place, I would be on my way. I had decided I would do this as often as necessary to get pregnant, no matter how long it took. And yet I kept trying to tell myself that it might not work, the success rate wasn't good, because I was so afraid of another disappointment. And then the embryo that was to be Carla was transferred to me on Mother's Day—what a good omen!

I knew it wasn't over when that pregnancy was confirmed. I just didn't believe it was going to last, that I could be so lucky. All through the pregnancy I kept waiting for something to happen, for it to be taken away from me. But I also figured that if one embryo survived out of the six that were transferred, this must be a strong and healthy one.

I think I had the same concerns for her that I would have had if I had conceived her naturally. It was a relief when she was born to see that she was a very healthy baby. Now when I look at her, I don't even think about all we went through to get her. She's just Carla, a very special child.

The Risks of IVF

Certainly one concern for couples is the risks of the procedure, both for the woman and for the potential baby. IVF pregnancies are more likely to end in ectopic pregnancy, miscarriage, or premature birth. It has been difficult, however, to assess the significance of the high rates of loss, because the women involved may be at a higher risk of experiencing these losses than other women by virtue of their age and infertility history, and the fact that they are closely monitored to detect pregnancy.[14]

There is growing concern about the risks involved in taking fertility drugs, although physicians generally claim that they have been proven safe over many years of use. In fact, their use has increased considerably in conjunction with artificial insemination and other therapies. Yet there is increasing awareness of the hazards of what is called ovarian hyperstimulation syndrome (OHS), which has occasionally proven fatal for women undergoing treatment for infertility. More commonly, hyperstimulation may result in burst ovaries, ovarian cysts, septicemia, adhesions, migraines, depression, weight gain, and other symptoms. For some women the result of hormone therapy is the destruction of their fertility. Of every 1,000 women who underwent IVF in the United States in 1990, 7 are known to have been hospitalized for treatment of OHS. Severe OHS has been estimated to affect 1 to 2 percent of all women who take ovulation-induction drugs, and some researchers have raised concerns about their possible link to cancer and birth defects. Serious questions have also been raised about the long-term effects of repeated ultrasounds, although the evidence is inconclusive.[15]

Doctors usually minimize the risks, and patients usually do not ask. Many say they will do whatever is necessary and do not consider the possible side effects. As one nurse at an IVF clinic said:

> Patients are not frightened about what is going to happen to their bodies. It's amazing, if you told them we'll have to tie your arms and legs down or whatever it is, they are willing to go through it.

An additional risk of the IVF procedure has been the use of laparoscopy for egg retrieval in IVF and replacement of egg and sperm in GIFT, since any use of general anesthesia carries the risk of complications and (rarely) of death. Many women reported that the nausea after the anesthesia was the most unpleasant part of the whole procedure. The increased use of ultrasound-guided aspiration is making it possible to avoid laparoscopy in most IVF procedures, but it is still used in the great majority of GIFT attempts.[16]

There has not yet been any compelling evidence that babies conceived by IVF are at greater risk of birth defects than babies conceived naturally. Yet most scientists agree that there is the theoretical potential for abnormalities as a result of the procedure. In addition, the higher rate of premature birth and low birth weight increase the possibility of long-term disabling conditions. As more years pass and more babies can be followed up through their childhood, it will be possible to assess any long-range effects.[17]

One risk that is widely acknowledged is that of multiple births. Twins, triplets, and quadruplets are all much more common with IVF, GIFT, and ZIFT; they occur in as many as one-third of all deliveries. This occurrence has presented a serious dilemma: On the one hand, the more embryos transferred, the better the chances for a pregnancy. Yet multiple births increase the dangers for the mother and babies and may present overwhelming problems of parenting.[18]

One woman who underwent IVF dismissed the problem: "For a woman who's infertile, multiple births are multiple blessings." However, another couple who had tried for a long time to have a baby realized they were unable to cope with the prospect of having four and decided to have an abortion instead when they learned that the wife was carrying quadruplets. This was a disaster for all concerned.

Increasingly, women who have conceived several babies at once are being offered the possibility of aborting one or more of the fetuses in order to increase the chances of a successful birth for the others. This puts expectant parents in the agonizing situation of having to decide whether to eliminate some babies after so many years of trying to conceive, or take the chance of having all of the babies be sick or die.[19]

This kind of situation has led some physicians to prefer freezing some of the embryos until a later cycle rather than inserting all of them at once. Freezing also has the advantage of reducing the need for renewed drug therapy on each attempt. But freezing embryos is objectionable to many people and is still not perfected.[20] To overcome the fears of many that frozen embryos will be experimented on or discarded, scientists are working on techniques for freezing eggs before fertilization instead. When this can be done easily and the eggs can be thawed and fertilized in later cycles without damage, it is likely to be used widely.

————— • —————

IVF may seem controversial to outsiders. The U.S. government, source of so much research support, refused for many years to fund IVF research, and many groups object to its use for a wide variety of reasons (see chapter 12).[21] IVF is making possible widespread study of and experimention with embryos and with reproduction, and this makes many people worry about the consequences in the future. But to those who are involved with infertility, it is becoming an increasingly routine procedure. New techniques that avoid repeated drug treatment and surgery are likely to make the experience less traumatic and somewhat less expensive. And the requirement in some states that insurance companies cover at least part of the cost is making it more accessible to middle-class couples.

Scientists and fertility specialists applaud the opportunity they are giving couples to try to get pregnant. However, our initial questions remain. Is IVF a wonderful technology giving people another chance, or is it a false promise? Are couples really freely choosing to proceed, giving them another possibility, or does the sheer existence of IVF make it imperative that they try it? Is this a benign program designed to try to help people, or is it really part of scientists' effort to control women's lives and to master the process of creation? Will IVF make society a better place, or will it reinforce existing inequities and narrow what are considered acceptable choices?

We have seen many people excluded from trying IVF by the cost and by the rules of eligibility. We have seen the torment couples go through, the misrepresentation of success rates, the stress and grief, the reopening of old wounds thought healed. There is the possibility of more loss, the worry about risks and side effects, and a lack of support and follow-up.

Even so, couples told us, it was worth a try. Even if they did not have a baby, at least they had had a chance. And when sometimes, blessedly, it works, the happiness is unimaginable. For these families it seems to be a miracle; for others it is a curse. The effects of these new technologies on society as a whole are still being vigorously debated.

CHAPTER 5

Surrogacy

Although all forms of the new technologies for conception have sparked widespread criticism as well as strong support, the one that appears to have sparked the most heated public controversy is the practice of hiring a woman to bear a child, what has come to be called surrogacy.

The majority of the American public was initially appalled by the idea that a woman could voluntarily agree to become pregnant (with the sperm of a man who is not her husband) and then give the baby to that man and his wife in exchange for money. "How could you possibly give up your own baby for $10,000? What normal woman would ever do that?" These are the questions posed to surrogate mothers by others. There is hostility and bewilderment in the questioning.

A surrogate mother named Jan wrote a letter to the child she was carrying to explain her feelings about what she was doing.

> I'm sure you're wondering why I would do this. I have two children of my own who are very precious to me, and it's hard for me to envision going through life wanting children and not being able to have them. I felt that I could help your mom and dad out by doing this. . . . Being pregnant with you has been very exciting, and something very special for myself. I felt very good . . . but the best thing was the excitement I knew your mom and dad were experiencing. I've never thought of you as my child, but you hold a very special place in my heart.[1]

Despite the public's concern over the motives of women who would willingly become pregnant in order to give up a baby, most people were even more fervent in condemning Mary Beth Whitehead in the widely publicized Baby M case for *not* relinquishing her child after giving birth. Afer all, she had signed a surrogacy contract, she had promised to do it. Witnesses at the trial accused her of being immature and overly emotional, of not knowing how to play with her baby in the "right" way. Her

70

refusal to give up her child was used as "evidence" of her unfitness to be a mother.

The often bitter controversy over surrogacy greatly accelerated as a result of Whitehead's decision and the trial and appeal that resulted, and it has continued to be debated in legislatures and courtrooms as well as in a wide variety of publications. "Pro-family" and religious forces on the right oppose the idea because of its potential for undermining the traditional family, one that is ruled by men whose wives' key roles are caretaker and baby maker. For example, they fear the possibility that women could hire surrogate mothers for convenience, to maintain their own careers. Many feminists are just as critical. They decry the exploitation of poor women and the commercialization of women's bodies to produce children for men. Lawyers and ethicists debate whether this is baby selling, and physician organizations have expressed serious reservations about the ethics and risks of surrogate motherhood.[2]

Opinion surveys on alternatives for having babies show surrogate mothering to be at the very bottom of everyone's list.[3] Some people simply do not understand what it is all about and assume that a man must have intercourse with the surrogate for her to get pregnant. The idea of receiving money for a baby is discomforting, perhaps even more so because it is a woman taking payment for something she's supposed to do for free, as part of her role in life. Over time the public has become more used to the idea, while the organized groups opposing surrogacy have gained ground in limiting its availability.

The term "surrogate mother" is used here because it is the most recognized name for women who have babies for others. It is misleading, however, perhaps intentionally so, since the word *surrogate* usually refers to a substitute for the real thing. At the time of the birth, the surrogate mother is actually the real mother, a mother who has agreed to give up her child to its father. The terminology itself is a subject of debate. While proponents of surrogacy speak approvingly of women who merely "rent their wombs" or act as "human incubators," opponents describe them as the natural or birth mothers and sometimes more disparagingly as "breeders" and "reproductive prostitutes."[4]

An Experience with Surrogacy

All this controversy did not deter Sarah, a thirty-one-year-old legal secretary who had a baby for Alex and Lisa. She feels good about what she has done, sure that it is right:

> I knew how I would feel if I didn't have my children. I mean my children are my whole life. I just can't imagine not having them.

My best friend couldn't get pregnant, and yet it was so easy
for me. I know the kind of anguish she went through. I couldn't
help her, but I felt a need inside me to help someone else. Thank
God I'm healthy enough to do it.

I loved being pregnant. I liked the attention, but my family
is complete. My husband and I don't want any more children
for ourselves—he had a vasectomy a few years ago. At first
the money made it attractive, too, but after I got pregnant and
started to feel so close to Lisa, it didn't seem very important
anymore. I was not even sure I'd be able to accept the money.

I like the idea of doing something unique. But basically I'm
just a normal person, not someone who is out for money. But
I'm not some kind of angel either. I'm just a normal working-
class woman who does it because I like being pregnant and I like
giving other people the happiness that my kids have given me.

A Michigan-based attorney named Noel Keane started the first surrogacy program in 1978. Since then, other lawyers, social workers, and
former surrogate mothers have started their own surrogacy businesses,
and as many as four thousand babies have been born under contract in the
United States alone.[5] In very few of these cases has the surrogate mother
changed her mind and expressed the intention to keep the baby, but those
occurrences have been widely publicized and have formed the basis for
new laws and court decisions affecting the practice of surrogacy.

Who uses surrogacy programs? Mostly affluent couples with a fertile
husband and an infertile wife, for whom other treatments have failed and
adoption is unavailable or unacceptable. The woman may have a genetic
disease that she does not want to transmit or a medical condition that
precludes pregnancy.

How do women who want to be surrogates and couples who want
a baby find each other? Sometimes a couple recruits a woman through
personal networks or advertisements. Occasionally a family member—a
sister or a cousin—offers to carry a baby for her infertile relative. Most
often, however, they are brought together by "matchmakers"—attorneys,
physicians, psychologists, former surrogate mothers, and others—who
have started surrogacy programs.

Alex and Lisa were at first very skeptical about trying a surrogacy program. They had been through a miscarriage, an ectopic pregnancy, tubal
surgery, and three failed attempts of IVF (*in vitro* fertilization). They were
on an adoption list but discouraged by the years they would still have to
wait. Lisa described how hard it was to decide:

I knew how important it was for Alex to have his own baby
and I felt guilty that I couldn't provide that for him. I wanted

one, too, but I had finally begun to accept the reality that I would never give birth to my own baby. I saw a TV program about surrogates but couldn't handle the idea at the time. I got depressed just thinking about it. The idea of giving up on my own body and looking at someone else's and visualizing that person being the biological parent of my child was too painful for me.

A year later we still didn't have a baby, and the thought of a surrogate began to seem more like a possibility. I showed Alex an article about it and was surprised at how enthusiastic he was. I was willing to talk to the attorney at least and find out more about it.

Alex saw the advantages of a surrogacy program right away:

> I figured we'd have more control with a surrogate than with adoption, where somebody arbitrarily thinks this baby will fit well with this couple. I liked the idea that both of us would be there at the start of creating a baby. The child would know that he or she was created not by accident but out of love and a commitment to nurture that child for the rest of our lives. And of course at least we knew that the baby would have half of our genes.

Screening Couples and Surrogate Mothers

Having finally decided to contact a surrogate program, Lisa and Alex were worried about being accepted. As it turned out, there was no screening process whatsoever. The lawyer told them that he accepts all couples who can pay. He explained his reasoning in an interview with us:

> It is his child and he has a constitutional right to do this. We have no basis for screening the couple. They've been through enough torture already. If they were able to conceive on their own, no one would ask them "How many windows do you have facing the lawn?" or "How much money did you earn?" the way people who want to adopt are questioned.

Different programs vary greatly in their philosophies regarding the selection of couples, although financial means is a criterion for all programs. Three programs described here—referred to as the East Coast, Midwest, and California programs—represent some of the variation that can be found in selection of couples and other practices. For example, some programs, such as the East Coast one, require that couples be married and childless and have a documented fertility problem. Otherwise they have no screening of applicants. The Midwest program, on the other hand, accepts everyone who applies. The couples may see a psychiatrist, but only if they request one.

In contrast, the California program has very different policies. The psychologist interviews all the couples who come to the program. Acceptance is far from automatic, as explained by the psychologist:

> What I screen them for is appropriateness for a surrogate mother program, not appropriateness for parenthood. I'm not like an adoption agency. I want to know if they can handle our philosophy and how we work. I say to them, "Let me help you decide if this is the way that's best for you."
>
> They're very anxious for a child and willing to be flexible. But occasionally we have a couple who is not ready for a surrogate. They have to come to terms with the third party in a very physical way—the woman may be in the delivery room or at Lamaze classes, and she'll be talking to the surrogate periodically. If a woman's infertility is not resolved to the point where she can handle being with the woman who's carrying her husband's child, it's going to be painful.

The three programs also have conflicting ideas about how to select the women to be surrogate mothers. All have some kind of screening by a psychologist or psychiatrist, but with very different intentions. The psychiatrist who sees applicants to the Midwest program, for example, feels strongly that all applicants should be screened. But he also believes that if he finds a woman who wants to be a surrogate competent to make an informed decision and wanting to be a surrogate, she has a right to be one. He said:

> I function by helping surrogates to screen themselves. I explain all the possible risks, and then the responsibility to decide is up to them. Professionals have no way to predict who will be okay. Even if we did know, our job should be to help them decide, not to be paternalistic and decide for them. What I advise is, "If you're not sure, don't do it. It's forever; this is one of the most important decisions of your life."

He had interviewed well over 500 applicants and had yet to turn one down, but a large proportion decided to drop out on their own.

Women were accepted in the Midwest program whether they were single, married, gay, or had children. The first surrogate in this program was an unmarried virgin, the infertile couple's friend who volunteered to have their baby. The program directors prefer, however, that the women already have children. They used to think it was better if surrogates were single or divorced, anticipating possible complications from a husband.

Now they believe that having a husband may be valuable for support. It also may be easier for the woman to give up a baby because it is not her husband's.

The psychologist in the California program also screens the women who apply to become surrogate mothers. In contrast to the open-door policy of the Midwest program, she turns away at least two-thirds of the applicants. First, she requires that they already have children at home, explaining that a woman who has never had a pregnancy and delivery cannot really know what she is agreeing to. She also eliminates anyone who, in her judgment, would suffer from being a surrogate mother.

> I feel that it is my job to make sure that no one gets into this who would get hurt. Even though it's very difficult sometimes, I do tell women I think it's simply not in their best interest to be a surrogate, that they are so needy and that this isn't going to fulfill their need. We see ourselves as very protective.

In California, the psychologist also sees husbands of potential surrogates to be sure that the women will have a supportive home environment. Once accepted, the woman is required, and the husband invited, to attend a monthly support group meeting. She is also in frequent contact with the psychologist.

The East Coast program has a different approach. Unlike the California program, which looks at the benefit or harm to the surrogate mothers, the East Coast program is concerned primarily with their emotional ability to give away a child. According to the psychologist who screens all applicants, he looks for women who are strong-willed and reliable, and he accepts fewer than half of those who apply.

The Relationship Between Surrogate Mother and Couple

Lisa and Alex were not aware of all these differences when they picked a surrogacy program. They had, similarly to many other couples, simply gone to one that was located near their home. They were pleased, however, that the lawyer said they could meet Sarah before deciding if they wanted her to have a baby for them. Alex described what they were looking for:

> We wanted a nice normal human being that has above-average intelligence. We wanted her to be emotionally stable, kind of a solid person. We thought it was important for her to be healthy and loving so that we would be able to communicate that to the child.

In a number of programs, the couple picks a woman from pictures in a book that includes details of the surrogates' history and motivations. Some come to the office to meet several women. Sometimes, if they request it, the director suggests a particular woman for a couple and then has them make the decision. All three people involved have to agree with the choice.

At the East Coast program, the attorney makes the match strictly according to the couple's place on the waiting list. When a woman becomes available, he sends her description and a photograph of her and her children to the first couple on the list. If possible, two such profiles are sent, and the couple makes the decision.

In contrast to programs where the couples select among a number of women, the psychologist in California decides on every match. She sends to the couple and to the potential surrogate information about each other; if they are pleased with what they see, they must meet together with the program staff. Each party has a chance to veto the match, but as the psychologist says, "If I've done my job, it shouldn't happen, and it rarely does."

The most important difference among program staff is their attitude toward the relationship between surrogate mother and couple. Some programs leave that decision up to the parties involved. Other programs take definite but opposite stands on this issue. In California a meeting is required and a relationship encouraged, while in the East Coast program complete anonymity is the rule.

The psychologist for the California program explained why she and her colleagues feel so strongly about openness:

> If the couple really doesn't want to meet the surrogate or they want to make sure she doesn't know where they are or what their last name is, it's not going to work. The surrogate is going to feel she's not being appreciated or that they don't trust her, or that they're still ashamed of this. And separation from the baby will be much harder. It works for us because she cannot imagine hurting this couple whom she knows and likes so much.

The East Coast program takes the opposite view. The program's directors feel strongly that if a relationship were allowed to develop the surrogate would have a harder time detaching herself from the couple and the child. And they worry that she might refuse to be inseminated by an unattractive man, or that she would say, "This guy looks like Burt Reynolds, how can I give up Burt Reynolds's baby?" Therefore, couples and surrogates never meet and never learn each others' names or addresses. All communication is through the attorney's office.

So many differences; yet the key people in each program are confident that their way works best. They all base their policies on a notion of what they believe to be psychologically healthy and most efficient. Until impartial follow-up studies are carried out, however, we cannot know which, if any, will prove to be the best for surrogate mothers, for couples, and especially for the children.

Generally, the couples seem to be more interested in anonymity than are the women they hire. They feel uncertain about what part a known surrogate mother should continue to play in their lives. They worry about a meeting leading to problems. One woman explained:

> Suppose she didn't like my husband's glasses, or his freckles. Considering the enormity of what she's doing, something trivial like that could set her off. We just didn't want to take the risk. We had all the information we needed about her and the pregnancy from the lawyer.

Some women fear that if they get to know the couple, it will be hard to separate from them as well as from the baby. They prefer a more "businesslike" arrangement, with no contact or information.

A more common situation is that of the woman who agrees to have a baby for an anonymous couple and then regrets the lack of contact. We heard stories, for example, of women who requested the baby's picture and received no response. One surrogate recalled:

> Once I was pregnant, I starting having a lot of thoughts about the couple, wondering what kind of people I was going to be giving this baby to. I knew I could never meet them, and that began to bother me. I just hope that when the baby's older they'll tell her about me and let her come see me if she wants to.

Occasionally both parties are obsessed with secrecy. Birth mothers tell everyone that the baby died, and infertile wives pretend to be pregnant for nine months. We do not know what the consequences of these behaviors are, but we strongly suspect that such deception will be harmful to the people involved.

Lisa, Alex, and Sarah discovered that it was very valuable for them to know each other. Eventually they forged strong bonds of commitment and friendship. Their relationship was stronger than most between surrogates and couples because they all wanted it that way. Although their story is unusual because of the closeness they developed, their experiences and feelings are shared by many others who become involved in surrogate programs.

The relationship began with a difficult introduction in the dark-leather conference room of a law firm. Sarah remembered that day vividly:

The meeting was very awkward at first because you're going in feeling, I really want to do this and I really want to please them. They're going in and they want to show that they really would be good parents and want a surrogate to have a baby for them. After about five or six minutes of awkwardness, we started to chat and then we even got into talking about things like my period and her uterus and ovaries. It was odd talking about intimate subjects to people you just met. It was important to me that they have a very religious sense, that they believe in God, and not be cold people. They were wonderful, and I knew by the end of that meeting that I wanted to be the mother of their baby. When they said they were sure they wanted me to be their surrogate, I was so thrilled—I felt an immediate bond with them.

As friendly as this threesome felt, they were very uncomfortable about starting the inseminations. Sarah had started charting her temperature every day, and when she thought she was about to ovulate, she called the program's physician. He arranged for her and Alex to come in the next afternoon. Sarah described what happened then:

It was all very odd. Lisa came with him and she and I are sitting there chatting in the waiting room while Alex goes into the bathroom. He comes out with the stuff and then I go in the other room to have it inseminated. Then we all leave on the elevator together just like this is an everyday occurrence.

When I got home it hit me all of a sudden that I had another man's sperm inside me and I might get pregnant by him. It felt really creepy for a few minutes, but then it passed. When I got my period that month, I was really disappointed that it hadn't worked and eager to try again.

The second month Alex wasn't able to get here at the right time, and Lisa decided to bring the sample by plane, since they live four hours away by car. I always laugh when I picture her running through the airport with her little lunch bag. She didn't want it to go through the x-rays, and the security people asked, "What's this?" She tried to be casual: "Oh, it's sperm," and they let her through.

When it took that time I was ecstatic. I called the lawyer's office right away to tell him. I had a bouquet of balloons sent to Lisa and Alex to let them know I was so happy being pregnant. I proudly told everybody around me that I was pregnant. I told my two sons, who were three and a half and seven at the time, that I was having a baby for Alex and Lisa. I explained to them that Lisa's tummy didn't work and I would be carrying this baby for them. When I referred to the baby, I would always say Lisa and Alex's baby. They didn't have any problems with it. My son even told his class at school, "Guess what—my mommy's pregnant and we are not keeping the baby."

My sister and parents accepted it very easily. The only family member that gave me a hard time was my husband's aunt—she is a very staunch Catholic. She said, "God will punish you for this." "Aunt Rita," I said, "I find it hard to believe that God would punish me for giving so much love and happiness to someone else. I am happy with myself and feel good about what I am doing."

My pregnancy was easy—I wasn't tired or sick. But suddenly this all changed. During my tenth week I saw some blood. It hit me in the face like a thunderbolt that I could lose this baby. A few days later, blood started pouring out and I had excruciating labor pains—I thought I was really dying. However, I only worried about what I was going to tell Lisa and Alex. What a failure I was! Would they give up on me?

Sarah seemed to have had a strong need for Lisa and Alex's approval. She was more concerned about them than about the trauma her own body was going through. This is not unusual; some women become surrogates because of the positive attention they receive from the couple as well as from the professionals who run the program.

Fearful of rejection, Sarah wrote a letter to Lisa and Alex explaining how badly she felt. She said she felt she was their last hope and had let them down. She hoped they would want to try again with her.

Lisa and Alex were very discouraged by the miscarriage. They began to wonder if they just were not meant to have a baby. But Sarah's determination infused them with new hope. They called Sarah and told her they felt very lucky to have her and that they wanted to continue as soon as she was ready.

After the miscarriage, Lisa and Alex visited Sarah's home and met her family for the first time. Each meeting was bringing them closer together, and now Sarah's husband Mike became more involved as well. He commented:

After they left, I talked to Sarah that night and told her, "That couple deserves to have a baby." Just because the woman he chose to marry cannot have children, that does not negate his right to have a child. And because I was lucky enough to marry someone who can have children, does that give me more of a right to have them? I just can't believe that. I think what Sarah's doing is fantastic—I'm really proud of her.

By the time they started trying again, Lisa felt that they could do without the physician. After all, insemination is a simple procedure, one that can be accomplished with a store-bought syringe, and she wanted her baby conceived in a more personal environment. Lisa replied:

> We invited her to our house for a few days and I helped her do it several times. She and I would lie on my bed and put up our feet together and just talk for an hour. It's so special that our baby was actually conceived in our own bed.

Lisa and Alex almost held their breaths until the second pregnancy had progressed beyond the first trimester. Even then they were still very tense. We talked to Lisa halfway through the pregnancy:

> I'm excited, but nervous, too. There's just been so much suppressed feeling for so long and we're trying to suppress it for another four or five months—it's hard. I think the uneasiness is irrational, it's nothing specific. But just to have a baby live, you know—I just sort of hold it in and try to stay very busy.
>
> I'm really very glad though that the baby's in her uterus and not mine. It would be dead if it were in my body, and so there's really a feeling of relief and trusting her body over mine.
>
> We've already been there for a couple of prenatal visits. Hearing the heartbeat, seeing the baby on ultrasound—I can't tell you how thrilling this has been. We even framed the ultrasound picture and hung it by our bed so we could see it whenever we wanted to. Sarah is incredible—she sent us Mother's Day and Father's Day cards and a tape of the baby's heartbeat. We played it so many times the tape wore out. I talk to her at least once a week to find out how she's doing. It keeps me feeling very connected to the pregnancy.

Alex did not have the frequent contact with Sarah. He dealt with the anxiety by trying to be more detached. It didn't help that he was still uncomfortable with the whole idea. Alex described his feelings:

> I still would rather it be Lisa carrying my baby, and sometimes I get angry at Sarah for not being Lisa, for being able to do what my own wife cannot. I know that's not fair, but I can't help how I feel. In some ways it would have been easier if we didn't meet her and know what a wonderful human being she is. It's more difficult than just renting a womb, so to speak. And she needs a lot of attention from us—if Lisa doesn't call one week, Sarah starts to wonder what's going on.

Sarah did want the attention and the reassurance she gained from those visits and calls. She relied on Lisa to help her through the difficult times when she was feeling ambivalent or uncertain. Sarah recalled:

> Whenever I had any maternal feelings toward the baby, like when it first started to move, I would call up Lisa and talk it through with her. That way I just transferred those feelings to Lisa. I never felt this was my baby. I tacked a picture of Lisa and Alex on my refrigerator so that all of us could keep in mind that I was doing this for them. If I ever thought about keeping the baby, all I'd have to do is look at that picture and think what they've been through.
>
> Not everyone was as lucky as me, having Lisa to talk to. I've talked to other women who are having a very hard time. I think support groups should be required for us, to help handle the criticism for one thing. Also, being able to deal with the fact that some day you're going to have a child in your arms and you are going to hand that child over to somebody else. You can gear yourself up for the nine months, but when it comes you're still going to have a difficult time.

Lisa moved into Sarah and Mike's house two weeks before the due date, wanting to make sure she was there for the baby's arrival. She felt very close to Sarah's family during that time.

Everyone worried about how the hospital staff would react to their situation. Would they allow Lisa into the delivery room? Would she be able to hold the baby? As it turned out, with some help from the program's physician, the labor nurses reluctantly agreed to go along. Sarah remembers the delivery vividly:

> When I started pushing, Lisa was pushing with me. There were tears in her eyes when she saw the baby's head. I was so happy to see Lisa's pure joy. They handed the baby to me first and I looked at her for a minute and handed her to Lisa. Mike was by my side, and they let Alex come in to see his daughter. She was a beautiful seven-pound, two-ounce healthy little girl. They named her Emily.
>
> The nurse told me she had been on the labor floor twenty-five years and never in those twenty-five years had she ever witnessed such love in the delivery of a baby.

Alex had arrived at the hospital only a few minutes before Emily was born. He describes the incredible feelings of that moment:

It's a little hard to convey how wonderful that experience was. I was standing in the delivery room thinking, What do I do now? and there's this little pink prune squawking its head off and grabbing my finger. There's a bonding that takes place—there's no lightning flash, but it's there. It's a moment that will be there forever for me. At that moment I had a daughter.

Sarah stayed in the hospital for three days. Lisa and Alex were staying at her house, but they spent every waking moment at the hospital, sharing in the care of the baby. This was not an easy time for Sarah, as she recalls:

In the hospital the second night, the baby was in the room with me, and I looked down at her sweet face and thought she looked just like me. I immediately called Lisa to talk to her about how well her baby was doing and my feeling about the baby. As I was talking the baby fell asleep and I felt better.

Lisa and Alex stayed at our house one more night after I came home from the hospital. That night I had a difficult experience. The baby was in Lisa and Alex's room and I could hear her screaming. They were trying to calm her, but just like any new parent, they weren't sure what to do. I felt torn between wanting to help the baby and feeling that it was important to let them handle her themselves.

The hardest part was saying goodbye to them the next day. I had a much harder time saying goodbye to Lisa than to the baby because I had such an intensely close relationship with her. Even though I knew our relationship would continue, it would be different. That goodbye really caught me off guard because I hadn't expected it.

After they left, it was like that feeling I have the day after Christmas. The parties are over, the presents have been opened, and all the anticipation, all the fun is over. All that is left are empty boxes and torn wrapping paper. Mike put his arm around me and told me how wonderful he thought I was, and how much he loved me. It really helped having his support. One of the things that was hard for both of us was the fact that the baby was a girl and we have two sons. If it had been a boy I think it would have been much easier.

Lisa was simply overwhelmed by all that had happened. She remembers:

I was just so grateful to Sarah, and ecstatic to finally have our baby. I told Sarah she had made it possible for us to have the family we never thought we could have, and to experience a pregnancy as much as we ever could. There were no words to tell her how happy she had made us, but I'm sure she understood. I worried about her though; I hoped she would be okay.

During the first few weeks after Emily's birth, Sarah and Lisa talked on the phone often. They needed to reassure each other that everything was all right. Sarah said:

> I probably have my highest euphoria when I am talking to Lisa. When I hear her talking to Emily or she's drinking her bottle while Lisa's talking to me, I think, she just sounds like a really different person than what she did when I met her. She sounds very content now, like she is complete. That is the biggest gift that she could have given me, just letting me hear her be happy like that.

One month later, Sarah was in court, declaring before a judge her intention to relinquish all rights to the baby. She knew that up until that time she could change her mind. But whenever she was tempted to do so, she thought about how ecstatic Alex and Lisa were and realized she could never break their hearts. She had taken on a very important job, had done it well, and had gained very valuable friends. She knew that she would be part of their lives in some way, that she could always know how the child was doing.

All of that made it hard to her to think about accepting the money that would arrive after the day in court. The payment is often a troubling subject for surrogate mothers, and they are sensitive to accusations that they are selling their babies. They remind people, however, that they are giving the baby to his or her own father, not to strangers who have no connection. Some are very reluctant to take the money, while for others the idea of a contractual obligation keeps them committed to relinquishing the baby. Sarah said:

> It was never my major motivation. If you think about it, $10,000 isn't a lot of money for all of the inconvenience and discomfort of the inseminations and pregnancy and birth. At least I didn't have to abstain from sex with my husband during the inseminations like most of the other women. We were grateful for that vasectomy. Even so, it was a year out of my life.
>
> Mike and I had decided that we couldn't take any money from Alex and Lisa. Yet they insisted, telling me I deserved it, that there is no way that any amount of money they could give me would ever be enough to reward me for what I had done for them. Lisa made me feel comfortable about taking the money, just as I had made her feel comfortable about taking the child when she was worrying so much about taking her from

me. There was something else, much more important than the money. The day we signed the papers, Lisa gave me a string of pearls. I had no idea it was coming, and I wear them all the time.

Sarah used the money to go back to school and start a new career in counseling. She felt that she had given a precious gift to Alex and Lisa and had received in turn a new direction for her own life, a new sense of confidence and specialness.

Obviously not many couples can afford the $30,000 and more that an average surrogacy program costs, including legal, medical, and counseling fees as well as expenses and the fee for the birth mother. Those who can, however, are happy to pay it. A private adoption, or five or six IVF attempts, would cost as much. As Alex said:

> I think the surrogate deserves a larger fee for everything she's done. There's so much else involved for them. For us, it wasn't easy to come up with such a big amount. Let me put it this way—I could have bought one helluva Porsche. But then, on the other hand, if I had bought a Porsche, that's all I'd have, and there's no comparison to having Emily.

Problems with Surrogacy

The experience we have described is in many ways unusual. Most surrogates and couples do not develop such a close relationship. Some women who sign up with surrogacy agencies want this kind of relationship with the couple, or at least more contact than they have, but they do not know how to make it happen. The program may not allow it, or the couple may not want it. Other surrogates prefer to think about what they are doing as more like a job and manage to maintain a certain detachment from the whole process. Program psychologists are surprised by the number of women who do not seek any support or any information about the couple and the baby.

Are the birth mothers fooling themselves by treating surrogacy as if it were, in the words of some, a "temporary job"? Are they rationalizing away bothersome emotions? Or are they simply unique women for whom being a surrogate mother brings sufficient rewards (emotional or financial) to outweigh any discomfort or pain? Some women even decide to have a baby a second time, for the same couple or for a different one. Critics wonder if what this really means is that the need for attention or for fulfillment or for absolving of past losses simply wasn't met the first time and never can be. What are we to make, for instance, of the following quote from a woman who is waiting to be matched to a second couple? She has a son at home and receives photographs of the daughter she relinquished to the first contracting couple: "She looks just like me. She looks more like me than my own son. When I saw the last picture I started cry-ing. It's so nice to know I have a baby out there who looks like me."[6] Are those really tears of joy?

There is no doubt that for most women being a surrogate mother is very difficult. It requires tremendous commitment and has the potential to create serious problems. Uncertainty about the relationship to the couple, negative comments from others, and especially grief for the baby who is gone are all common. There are physical risks as well from the pregnancy and delivery, and additional risks for those women who are superovulated before being inseminated. One young woman who had agreed to be a surrogate mother tragically died of heart disease, apparently as a result of the pregnancy.

Even the best-prepared surrogate mothers may have a difficult time adjusting, and they often find it hard to admit to needing help. One woman told us:

> I think with surrogates there is this image you feel you must keep, that you are a "super surrogate" and you're not going to feel any feelings after the baby is born other than happiness for the couple because they finally got their child. But that's not true, because for nine months you carried this child. Every night you lie down in bed and you're lying on your side because the baby's there. And you get home and that baby is not there. It was not so much that I wanted to change my mind. It was just the feeling of emptiness because there wasn't a baby there when there should have been by all laws of nature.

A few programs provide support groups or individual counseling for the surrogate mothers while they are pregnant. Most women we inter-viewed felt there should be more, and that the feelings of loss should be addressed.

One woman who has become a resource for others in the program she was involved with explained some of the problems:

> Sometimes other surrogates call me because they are afraid to talk to the couple. Maybe they haven't met the couple and want to but aren't sure how to go about it. Or the couple does not want them to hold the baby at all in the hospital and they want to. I tell them, "Until you sign the papers giving up custody of that child, that child is yours. If you want to hold that baby, no one can stop you."
>
> Sometimes they want to find out more about the baby after it's born but can't. I think there is a need for more of a mediator

between these people, and a way for them to talk to surrogates who've done it already.

Patricia Foster is a woman who changed her mind about giving up the baby but was unsuccessful in gaining custody despite a prolonged and expensive legal battle. She describes her feelings about the pregancy:

> I thought (wrongly) that the baby wasn't conceived out of love, that since I was to be artificially inseminated, I would feel differently about this baby. But by three months he was moving and by four and a half months I saw the baby on an ultrasound screen in the hospital and watched his little fist swinging and saw his little legs kicking. I couldn't take my eyes off the screen. He was mine and I loved him no matter how hard I tried to convince myself otherwise. . . .
>
> The surrogate company keeps telling you that this is the couple's child. But your body takes over. Your mind and heart don't agree anymore. This little person takes over. He moves. He kicks. He reminds you twenty-four hours a day that he is there. You start to see this little person grow and grow. . . .
>
> The guilt you start to feel because your heart is taking over! Putting your hands on this tummy that grows and this little person who responds to your touch. Praying every night that he's a healthy baby. Crying yourself to sleep at night because you are scared of your feelings. . . . Praying not to go into labor so you and the baby can't be separated. . . . You leave the hospital with empty arms and feel cheated. Now the suffering, the pain, the feeling of emptiness, the great sense of loss at being separated from your child. How can this be, how can this be allowed to happen?[7]

Mary Beth Whitehead has also written about the feelings of loss she experienced, feelings she had not anticipated when she signed the surrogacy contract:

> I genuinely believed that this was a way for me to help better the world. Looking back, I now believe that this was a form of brainwashing. . . . I was completely devastated about having the baby taken from me. I felt like I was used for one purpose and was no longer needed or wanted. I was distraught for my child, for my own flesh and blood. I remember the inseminating doctor telling me that I was giving away an egg. I didn't give away an egg. They took a baby away from me, not an egg. That was my daughter. That was Sara they took from me.[8]

Occasionally it is the couples who have to confront grief. An early case that received publicity was that of a surrogate mother who decided to keep her child even before the birth. The coupled filed suit seeking custody. Before the trial it came out that the wife could not have children because she had had a sex change operation. Fearful that this information would work against them in court, the couple dropped the case a day before the trial and gave up any rights to the child.[9]

Another couple, who never had contact with the woman who was to bear a child for them, flew six hundred miles to pick up their baby on the day his birth was scheduled to be induced. When they arrived, they were shocked to find out that the mother had never even checked into the hospital. The wife wrote to us about her traumatic experience:

> We called the person running the program to find out what happened. She seemed very upset on the phone and said the surrogate had gone to another hospital where no one would know about this baby's origin. And then she told us she would be right over to our hotel with the baby. As she handed the baby to us, she said we would not be able to keep him because the mother had changed her mind. She stood outside in the hall for twenty minutes while we stood inside the room too stunned to talk or look at each other. We just watched our little baby boy, who we would probably never see again. Then she knocked on the door, and like robots we handed her back the baby. There we were in that strange room far from home, surrounded by all the baby clothes and diapers we brought with us.
>
> We signed a legal document that said we weren't sure who the biological father was and gave up all our rights and responsibilities and got our money back. We didn't sue because we were sure we wouldn't have a chance of getting him. Who would take a nursing baby from his mother?

This couple was in a program in the Midwest where the surrogate and couple are not allowed to meet. Although they exchanged letters through the program office, the wife feels the main reason the surrogate mother kept the baby was because of this policy. The wife said:

> We were anonymous to her, we weren't real people. She needed emotional support and wasn't getting it from the program. We should have been there to give it to her. Instead, we were strangers that she was supposed to give her baby to. *We* knew we would be good parents, but she had no way to know that.

This woman was sure that no court would award her the child. Yet, in a complicated and dramatic New Jersey case that brought a great deal of attention to surrogacy, one genetic father did challenge in court the surrogate mother's decision to keep her child. The mother, Mary Beth Whitehead, had given the baby to the father, William Stern, and his wife, but a few days later she asked to have the child back for a week. When the week elapsed and Whitehead did not return, police officers came to her home to arrest her. Whitehead fled the state with the baby and was discovered several months later in Florida by private detectives.

The judge who ruled in her case upheld the surrogacy contract as binding, claiming that she lost all parental rights at the moment of conception; the only exception he conceded to her was the right to abort, since this was protected by *Roe* v. *Wade*. (Many surrogacy contracts require the woman to have an abortion if prenatal tests reveal any medical condition unwanted by the contracting couple.) Condemning Whitehead as an unfit parent who could not give the child the same educational benefits as the Sterns, he awarded them custody and immediately completed adoption proceedings. An appeal to the New Jersey Supreme Court resulted in a reversal on the contract decision, with the court ruling that it is illegal to pay a woman to have a baby. However, the custody decision stood, with Whitehead given expanded visitation rights.[10]

Although there have been a few surrogate mothers who have won custody, they have been the exception. The Baby M case, however, has had a major influence on the future of surrogate programs. Until this case, the legal status of surrogacy had been largely untested and therefore unclear. Most states have long had laws against paying a birth mother for a baby. Since the Baby M case, a number of legislatures have passed bills to limit or prohibit surrogate mothering.[11]

The whole subject of women having babies in order to give them to the genetic fathers and their wives (who are increasingly also the genetic mothers) continues to be fraught with intense controversy. What may have seemed for some people at the beginning to be a relatively simple solution to their desire for a child has come to symbolize and embody a much larger struggle over the meaning of motherhood, the rights of women, the definition of parent, and the best interests of the child.[12]

Opponents of surrogacy arrangements question the social implications of rewarding women for *not* bonding with the babies growing inside of them. They point to the enormous potential for emotional damage—to the mothers who give away their babies, to their other children who see that Mom could give up a child she has borne, and to the babies who are separated from their birth mothers. Proponents respond that such effects are not inevitable, and that in any case it is paternalistic, indeed anti-woman, to ask the government and the courts to protect women against making their own informed decisions about how to use their bodies.

Opponents further contend that surrogacy contracts are unenforceable since they violate constitutional protections such as due process and the ban on slavery and state laws such as those forbidding the sale of babies. Proponents respond that surrogacy is neither baby selling nor slavery but compensation for a woman's time and effort and willingness to relinquish her parental rights. If this is true, counter the critics, why does the same amount of time and effort merit $10,000 if the baby is alive, but only $1,000 if the baby dies at birth? Surely it is the product, not the process, that is being purchased. And if the $10,000 were indeed compensation for a woman's time and effort, then she is being grossly underpaid, in violation of the fair labor laws.

How can this transaction be considered baby selling? respond the supporters of surrogacy. After all, the baby is going to his or her genetic father. How could he be buying his own child? The child is half the father's, the argument goes, and in case of dispute he has at least equal claim to the baby, indeed more than half because he has a contract and he can provide better financially than can the birth mother in almost every case. If his wife's fertilized egg was transferred to the woman they hired, then of course it's completely their child.

"Outrageous!" is the answer. How could parenthood be defined only by genes? How could the bond between a woman and the baby growing inside her, indeed growing with and because of her, be so totally discounted? If sperm donors in the case of donor insemination have no legal rights over the babies they father, why should the sperm donor in the case of surrogacy have the *only* rights? If women who donate ova to infertile women undergoing IVF have no rights to the babies that result, why should the woman whose ova are fertilized and transferred to a hired birth mother be considered to be the only "real" mother?

These situations are exactly comparable in terms of what occurs genetically and biologically, and yet they have been treated in exactly opposite ways by the courts. The difference between sperm and ovum donation on the one hand and surrogacy on the other is one of intent, often embodied in some form of contract. Yet in a number of cases the courts have ignored the laws and precedents relating to donor insemination and have ruled in favor of genes as the dominant factor in determining who has custody, in defining who the parents are. It is certainly not irrelevant that there are usually significant class differences between hired birth mothers and the couples who employ them.

Indeed a key element in the critics' concern about surrogacy is that only well-off couples can afford to hire a birth mother, and the women who agree to bear children for these couples tend to be financially (and/ or psychologically) needy and therefore vulnerable to intimidation by the couples as well as the brokers. The inequality in this relationship means that the deck is stacked against the birth mother, and her rights and feelings and preferences will ultimately be ignored.

The introduction of "gestational surrogacy," in which the couple's embryo is carried by a hired woman, has greatly accelerated the problem. With no genetic contribution, the mother's legal rights are greatly diminished. In some cases, she is legally declared *not to be the mother* even while she is still carrying the baby inside her. The full-time contribution of blood and belly and careful nutrition and nausea and varicose veins and risks to her health, and the subtle but constant physical and psychological interaction of mother and growing fetus over the course of nine months are considered irrelevant in comparison to the ejaculation of semen and the extraction of eggs, to the microscopic gametes and their precious chromosomes.

The rights of birth mothers are even further diminished when they are women of color, the black and Latina women who are beginning to appear in news stories of troubled surrogacy arrangements. They are among the least powerful people in our society under any circumstances, and when they are hired to carry an embryo, they have no more rights than if they were hired to clean the house.

The story of Anna Johnson reveals what is clearly a growing trend. Johnson, a working-class African-American woman who had been on welfare, was hired by a white man and his Filipina wife to have their embryo implanted in her uterus. As the baby grew, Johnson decided that she could not give away this baby, and she sued for custody, asking at least to have joint custody or visitation rights. The judge ruled that two mothers might confuse a child, and he terminated all of Johnson's rights to the baby. One author suggests that the contracting couple picked a black woman on purpose to increase the likelihood of this outcome in case of a dispute— after all, they are supposed to have reasoned, what judge would give a white baby to a black mother? Gena Corea's prediction in 1985 that a breeding class of poor women would be developed to meet the needs of white and wealthy men seems closer to reality.[13]

Racism, class oppression, patriarchal rule over women. By accepting surrogacy, say the critics, we permit these evils, which already exist in our society, to flourish. We legitimize the victimization of individual women. We resurrect the era of slavery, when black women made babies for their white masters.

Not at all, say the supporters. We are promoting altruism, people helping each other. We are permitting women, not legislators, to control their own procreative choices. We are giving unhappy, even desperate, couples a chance to exercise their right to be parents.

No, respond the critics, you are mostly helping men to be genetic fathers, as if the male genetic tie were the supreme value. And you are helping lawyers and physicians and other brokers to make large profits by taking advantage of needy and vulnerable women. This is only peripherally about women wanting babies; it is really about men gaining greater and greater control over reproduction.

The adherents of each position continue to argue with each other, in print, in court, and through a variety of organizations created to promote or halt surrogacy through legislative action. There are women who have been surrogate mothers in the past who are active in both camps. Ironically and sadly, feminists who agree with each other on many issues are often deeply divided by this one. Some strongly defend a woman's right to choose how she uses her procreative abilities, even if it may ultimately be to her detriment. Others are equally vehement in opposing the exploitation of women and would abolish all commercial surrogacy.[14]

Many state legislatures have debated, and some have passed, laws that would ban, limit, or in some way regulate the practice of surrogacy. In July of 1992, New York State, the location of a large proportion of the surrocacy business, passed a law that made it illegal to pay either a broker or a birth mother for having a baby. Yet in many states it is still possible to become a surrogacy broker with little or no limitation.[15]

Despite the wide diversity of laws and court precedents, each program has so far managed to find legal ways to accomplish its goals. According to one program director, "We do not confront laws anymore; we find out procedurally what's the easiest position to take. We find out where the least resistance is in order to complete this." Noel Keane, the first, the busiest, and best-known broker, closed down his Michigan office when that state passed a law against surrogacy, and centered his operations in New York. When that state banned commercial surrogacy arrangements, he made plans to move to other states. He is also arranging matches overseas, including the recruitment of American women of Asian descent to carry babies for Japanese couples.[16]

Sarah maintains that her experience, at least, has been a positive one for her, although she does long for the baby and sometimes wonders what life would be like if Emily were with her:

> When I think back about the whole experience, I really feel good about myself and what I did for them. I wear my pearls almost all the time and I talk to Lisa pretty often. However, as time goes by, Lisa calls less often, and I feel disappointed. They

invited all of us to come visit them on Emily's first birthday. I was glad to see her mom and dad so happy and they are really good parents to Emily. But it was a shock to see Emily. She looks so much like me. Seeing her reminded me how much I had wanted my own baby girl.

Lisa and Alex asked me if I would think about having a brother or sister for Emily. I told them I didn't think I could do it again.

Being with them, it felt just like an extended family. It was hard to leave though. I knew it would probably be a long time until I saw Emily again.

Altruism or exploitation? An independent woman's choice, or co-ercion and manipulation of poor women with low self-esteem? Another expression of racism and sexism, or a welcome opportunity to solve a difficult problem? Profit making at women's expense, or a sympathetic response to the sadness of infertility? Surrogacy is all of these, not one or the other. It is a complex phenomenon, one whose risks and costs are becoming increasingly apparent, just as it is becoming more commonly practiced and more publicly accepted.

CHAPTER 6

The Rise and Fall of Ovum Transfer: A Cautionary Tale

In January 1984, the first baby to have been carried by two mothers was born. This young boy was the product of an unusual partnership of medical researchers, financiers, and a livestock breeder. He was conceived inside one woman who had been inseminated with the sperm of the other woman's husband. Five days after conception, the tiny embryo was removed without surgery and transplanted into the uterus of the second woman. This woman, who was infertile, then carried the baby to term and gave birth to him. His birth, and that of a girl born several months later, represented the first—and almost the only—successes in the United States of a method called ovum transfer (OT).[1]

OT was highlighted in major media outlets, including *The New York Times Magazine*, the Phil Donahue show, and *People* magazine, as another breakthrough for infertile people. It was heavily marketed to the public and to investors, and it continues to be the basis for articles appearing in the medical literature about its past success and future promise. Yet OT was a monstrous failure, both medically and financially. Its story is important because it illustrates some of the ways in which women have been used as guinea pigs in questionable scientific experiments and misled by profit-driven entrepreneurs who see infertility treatment as just one more commodity from which to make money.

Ovum transfer was presented at the outset as having the potential to create major changes in the process of reproduction that could affect fertile as well as infertile women. First, the procedure presumably offered infertile women a nonsurgical alternative to IVF. Second, the commercialization of the OT program departed from the usual medical approach at

93

the time. In addition to being financed by investors buying shares through the stock exchange, the program also operated out of profit-making clinics, and sought to patent the entire procedure as well as the instruments. Third, OT was envisaged from the beginning and continues to be viewed by some of its advocates as the basis for diagnosing the genetic makeup and potential health problems of embryos very early in their development.[2]

OT was not a new concept; it had been widely used in the cattle industry for many years in order to increase the number of offspring of genetically superior cows. These high-quality cows are inseminated with the sperm of prize bulls. Their embryos are then removed, to be carried by more common cattle, so that the superior cow can be inseminated again very quickly. Beginning in the late 1970s, superovulation was introduced to maximize the number of high-quality embryos and ensure the profitability of this method of breeding.[3]

Richard Seed, a consultant to the livestock industry, had a vision of saving Western civilization by increasing the number and quality of American babies. Together with his physician brother Randolph, Richard began a corporation in 1978 named Fertility and Genetics Research (FGR). Its purpose was to apply ovum transfer to humans. Their grant to Drs. John Buster, John Marshall, and colleagues at Harbor UCLA Medical Center made it possible to carry out the first experimental phase in 1983 and 1984.

The developers of this new method for humans called it "ovum transfer," even though it is a five-day-old embryo that they tried to transfer. The avoidance of the term "embryo transfer" in the OT program appears to have been designed to allay public worries about scientists playing with embryos. Dr. John Buster, the professor of OB/GYN who directed the original OT research, talked about the careful selection of a name for the program:

> We chose the word "ovum" because, in 1980 when we prepared the protocol, we were concerned that there would be people parading with signs outside that we were transplanting things with arms and legs and eyes that we called an embryo.

Ovum Transfer as an Infertility Treatment

The developers of OT presented it as an ideal solution for women who cannot produce their own eggs, either because they have had their ovaries removed or experienced premature menopause. In addition, they considered it the best method for women who are not infertile but who do not want to take the chance of passing a genetic disease to their children; these women might welcome the chance to be pregnant by carrying another woman's egg fertilized by their own husband's sperm.

FGR, in its promotional literature, listed these as the types of problems that would bring couples to OT, but the research had either not included, or not been successful with, women in most of these categories. Only one OT baby, born in Milan in 1986, had a mother without ovaries. The mothers of the two OT babies born in California did not fit any of these groups. They both had normal ovaries but scarred fallopian tubes, the type of condition for which IVF was first developed. In fact, the owners of FGR expected a major portion of their customers to come from the growing ranks of women who may have tried other methods such as IVF and failed. As FGR president Twerdahl told us:

> If a couple can afford it and they have their own sperm and eggs, we presume they would prefer IVF. But perhaps they can no longer afford IVF or they failed at IVF a couple of times. Perhaps the patient can't tolerate surgery and anesthesia anymore, whether she can't physically or psychologically. Then ovum transfer becomes a method for them.

The OT program recruited its first donors by putting a small ad in the newspaper: "Help an infertile woman have a baby. Fertile women age 20–35 willing to donate an egg. Similar to artificial insemination. No surgery required. Reasonable compensation." Of the four hundred women who answered the ad, many lost interest after their initial contact, and others were screened out. Only forty-six were finally accepted. Dr. Buster talked about the donors:

> To answer that ad was a pretty cavalier thing to do and so we got a large number of people that had high psychopathic scores. After screening out a bunch of them that weren't suitable, we were left with a few great ladies.

Those "few great ladies" were selected on the basis of psychological stability, medical suitability, proven fertility, and compliance. They and their husbands were questioned at length to make sure they could handle the procedure and any possible side effects. Infertile couples who applied were also carefully screened to be sure they would fully cooperate with the program.[4]

Public relations were, from the very beginning, a key concern. As Dr. Annette Brodsky, the psychologist in charge of screening, explained:

> You need people who are going to be stable enough to handle the fact that OT is a new procedure, that there might be publicity around it, that they won't get completely overwhelmed

or thrown by the fact if something goes wrong. We didn't want them to be so invested in having a baby that, should prenatal testing reveal that the baby is deformed, they'd say they would want it anyway. Then the first baby in the project is deformed and the whole world stops wanting to think about it again.

After being matched with a recipient woman, a donor arrived at the clinic at the time of ovulation, to be inseminated by the sperm of the infertile woman's husband. The sperm had already been carefully examined for genetic information and the possibility of venereal disease. Five days after the insemination, the donor returned. With a specially designed catheter, about two ounces of fluid were flushed into her uterus. In a procedure called "lavage," the fluid was then removed again through the catheter. If an embryo was growing in the woman's uterus, it was unlikely to have attached itself yet to the uterine wall and therefore should have emerged with the fluid. One woman who was a donor described her experience:

> It's a simple procedure and doesn't take very long, about fifteen minutes from start to finish. You get undressed, get up on the table, put your feet in the stirrups. They use a speculum and then the catheter. There's a little bit of cramping; you feel a little tug for a second. It's pretty much like a regular exam.

The fluid that was taken from the donor's uterus was checked for embryos. If one was found, the recipient woman was called, and the embryo was transferred, again by a catheter inserted through the cervix, into her uterus. If everything went as planned, the embryo that started in another woman's body then implanted in the infertile woman's uterus and grew there normally.

While the endless waiting and lack of success were undoubtedly harrowing for the couple, the major physical risks of OT were for the donor. She was exposed to the possibility of infection from the insemination. She also took the risk of remaining pregnant if the "lavage" process did not work. This happened at least three times in OT research, and one of the donor women had to have an abortion. The other two aborted spontaneously. Ectopic pregnancies were also a possibility, since the fluid could wash an embryo back up into the tubes.

In its second phase, in addition to putting ads in local newspapers to recruit donors, the OT program asked infertile couples to help find their own donors. If a couple brought a friend or relative into the pool of donors, they were promised a priority position on the waiting list. Since there were 2,900 names on the list by the time the Long Beach clinic opened, this was an incentive that put a great deal of pressure on couples and their families.

In FGR's plans to establish OT clinics nationwide, there was the possibility that donors and couples would be matched through a central computer. In a few collection centers around the country, "professional" donors would have numerous embryos washed out of them every month. These embryos would be frozen and shipped out to OT centers elsewhere in the country to waiting couples and their physicians. A collection center could even be in the basement of a high-rise office building in the center of a large city. Thousands of women working upstairs could easily descend during their lunch hour for a quick insemination or lavage.

The Commercialization of Ovum Transfer

Once the "research phase" was completed, FGR sought financing to expand its operations. In December 1985 the company's stock was offered over the counter under the symbol BABYU. The company made plans to create OT clinics in joint ventures with hospitals and physician groups in California, Chicago, and other major population areas.

When the OT procedure was first publicized, and FGR made known its intention to seek patents for the catheter and the process, there was a great deal of criticism. Jeremy Rifkin, a leading opponent of genetic engineering, threatened to bring a lawsuit to contest the patent, claiming it "reduces the process of human reproduction to a commercialized product to be bought and sold in the marketplace." The medical community was equally opposed to FGR's approach to research. An attorney for the American Medical Association explains: "It's always been the view of the medical profession that you should have as widespread dissemination as possible of anything that would be beneficial to patients." [5]

"We're a technology company, just like any other. . . . We're no different from Polaroid or any other company that invents a new process and wants a patent to protect it." [6] This comment came from Lawrence Sucsy, an investment banker who did much of the fund-raising for FGR. For him and many others in the financial field, infertility is a growth business, a booming market aimed at highly motivated and affluent consumers.

FGR was hardly the only infertility company to offer shares on the stock market and set up joint ventures for profit. Private infertility clinics offering a wide range of treatments have followed the same path. Franchise operations and IVF chains have appeared throughout the United States and many parts of the world.[7]

What difference does the form of organization make for infertile people? From the point of view of FGR's John Buster and James Twerdahl, it could only make things better. They believed that central control guarantees high quality, a large enough pool of donors, and uniformity of performance from one place to another. According to Dr. Buster:

The financial issues and the patient care issues and the quality issues are usually about the same. The company does well by contracting only with first-class organizations. It will do well only if it serves the people well, if it is perceived as taking good care of the women. If not, it will fail.

Of course there are many corporations that have done extremely well financially by treating their customers, workers, and neighbors very badly. If ovum transfer had had any success, FGR would not *have* to have treated people well, because infertile people would come to it anyway; it failed because it simply did not work.

Buster also claimed that, without private financing, the research for OT would never have been possible. He describes himself as having been driven into the arms of Wall Street types by the unavailability of funding:

> The alternative is to do nothing at all. Wall Street will never help you unless they get their money out. It's kind of analogous to going swimming with sharks. I mean, the sharks are pretty vicious, but their behavior is predictable and if you do exactly what they want and understand that predictable behavior, it is fine. You have to understand that getting money out of it is what makes their system work for them, even though that relationship compromises some of the dear academic principles we've always espoused.

Centralized control might be an advantage, especially when compared to the very uneven performance of different IVF centers that have been started independently. Profit-making health programs, however, are not necessarily any more efficient or cost-effective than nonprofit ones. The incentives for them to cut corners and to concentrate on the most profitable activities are very strong. As Dr. Buster himself admits:

> There is a very delicate balance between keeping the Wall Street crew happy, keeping the physicians happy, and keeping the patients happy.

The Fall of OT

The second phase of OT started in the fall of 1986 in Long Beach, California, at a private medical center. Ultimately, according to James Twerdahl, a former electronics executive who became president of FGR, the intention was to have thirty to fifty such OT centers in North America. Once the first clinics proved successful, FGR planned to develop new ones in almost every metropolitan area in the United States, all under the corporation's control.

Yet within a few short months, all of these plans were abandoned. The Long Beach clinic suspended its operation, and the dozens of people who were on waiting lists to be either recipients or donors for OT were informed that they should look elsewhere.[8]

Why did this project, with such great ambitions and media hype, fail so completely and so rapidly? Investors and potential patients were all sent letters early in 1987 informing them of the development of the GIFT procedure at a nearby medical center. GIFT's apparently greater success rate, compared with IVF, made it unlikely that OT could compete effectively for patients for whom IVF was an undesirable option. Investors were told that this "competing technology . . . could adversely affect the company's operations." Patients were informed about the GIFT procedure and told, "While we strongly believe in Ovum Transfer, we nevertheless want only what is in your best interest."[9]

The reality, however, was that OT had never worked well at all for infertile women, and that it was causing risks for the donors as well. Despite the claims that this method would solve a wide range of infertility problems, the research results were so poor that they could in no way justify marketing the procedure as proven. Dr. Buster spoke expansively of a 60 percent success rate, but his published reports of the first trials are considerably more cautious. It is true that 60 percent of the blastocysts (the most developed fertilized ova) that were transferred resulted in pregnancies. However, only *five* blastocysts were recovered after eighteen months and fifty-three inseminations of ten donor women. Three pregnancies resulted (hence the claim of 60 percent success, or three out of five blastocysts), but one ended in a miscarriage. It is striking that four of the five blastocysts came from only one donor, although all ten donor women had been carefully screened for fertility. Twenty less-developed embryos were also transferred, but only one produced a pregnancy. This was an ectopic pregnancy, and the woman's tube had to be removed.[10]

During the first eighteen months that OT was attempted by Buster and his colleagues, thirteen women received embryos. Thirteen women, two babies. This may sound pretty good for a first trial. But ten donors had been inseminated fifty-three times. Two babies after fifty-three attempts is hardly 60 percent; it should more accurately be represented as less than 4 percent. In addition, recipient women experienced a miscarriage and an ectopic pregnancy, and one of the donors retained two pregnancies after lavages, resulting in a miscarriage and an induced abortion. Most disturbing perhaps is that the only women who had babies became pregnant within the first six months of the program. For another year until the research ended, and in subsequent trials at the Harbor campus, no additional births were reported.[11]

Similar trials were carried out in Milan, Italy, between May 1984 and

February of 1986, but with better results. Of forty-two couples in the research, eight became pregnant; two of these had spontaneous abortions and four had given birth at the time of the researchers' report. One donor out of forty-two retained a pregnancy after lavage.[12]

Further experimentation resulted in more complications for donors. A report of 265 lavages between 1982 and 1987 claims a "rare (3%)" complication rate, but this is figured on the basis of the number of procedures. Since there were only twenty donors, four instances of infection or retained pregnancy means that 20 percent of donors were adversely affected by the experience.[13]

The developers of the OT method pointed out that the initial trials were only the experimental phase. With more donors, more drugs to eliminate retained pregnancies in the donors, and more money, they hoped to limit the losses and improve the rates considerably. Yet subsequent research at the University of Southern California Medical School in 1987 and 1988 attempted, with dismal results, to overcome the failures of OT. The problem of very few embryos retrieved was addressed by superovulating the donors with hormone treatments; the drawback of retained pregnancies was to be averted by giving all donors an endometrial curettage and contragestive drugs after each lavage. Despite these procedures, which presented more risks for the donors, twenty-eight lavages of six donors resulted in only one embryo transfer, but no pregnancies for recipients and two retained pregnancies in donors.[14]

Clearly this is a method that had moderate success in Milan but very poor results in California, with problems for the donors severe enough to lead even OT's strongest proponents to conclude that the risks were too great to proceed. The subsequent development of ovum donation combined with IVF eliminated any indication for using lavage, as it meant that egg donors no longer have to be inseminated.[15]

On the basis of his very limited and mostly unsuccessful experience with thirteen women, Dr. Buster had proclaimed in 1985 that "the research is completed, the success of the procedure is proven," and the plans for a national marketing campaign were launched. Good medical research, however, requires a much larger sample, trials by other researchers, and better evidence of safety and effectiveness before making a procedure available to the general public. The American Fertility Society's ethics committee concluded in 1986 that, because of reservations about the procedure, OT should be carried out only under carefully controlled experimental conditions.[16]

Ovum Transfer for Prenatal Diagnosis

Human ovum transfer was first used with infertile couples. Long before it failed, however, John Buster already had other plans for using the ovum transfer technology, but this time with all pregnant women. He has long since moved on to this new research. His concern now is not with making babies but with improving their "quality." He described the embryo to us as a "little microchip," a package containing an incredible amount of information. Now he is researching that package, decoding the information to discover defects in the chip. In an interview carried out in 1985, Dr. Buster told us:

> In another five years infertility will be a non-issue, when there's an abundance of human ova available. Women are going to be much more concerned about the quality of life than they are about whether or not they can have babies.

More than five years have passed. Today infertility is hardly a non-issue, and OT has failed to live up to any of the promises. Yet John Buster continues to be optimistic. In recent publications he describes uterine lavage as "safe," and in 1991 he was quoted as saying that in ten more years it would be perfected enough to give all women the possibility to diagnose their embryos even before they implant in the uterus. Women who are now advised to have prenatal testing must wait at least until late in the first trimester and then agonize over the possibility of an abortion. With the lavage method (that worked so poorly for OT), they could have a newly fertilized egg washed out of their wombs after five days, checked out in a laboratory, and reinserted only if it is healthy.[17]

Thus a new field has developed, called preimplantation genetics. Eggs that are fertilized and grow in a laboratory as part of IVF are already being biopsied to detect sex and genetic disease; Buster's proposal is that uterine lavage should be used to remove embryos from women who conceive naturally, before they implant in the uterus, so that they can be diagnosed for genetic "quality."

Scientists claim that very soon they will be able to detect not only genetic diseases in new embryos but also even tendencies to diabetes, heart disease, and other disorders. Will all of the embryos with these problems be discarded? Will future children with the wrong color hair or shape of nose be tossed out, with the woman trying again the next month for a more perfect "package"? According to the scientists, no embryos will be discarded; instead, they will be frozen until methods are developed to repair the defects. We wonder, though, how many people would go to the expense and trouble of genetic repair—when it becomes feasible—of an embryo if it is relatively easy to produce new ones.

All of the reproductive technologies have this potential for applying eugenics to human procreation. They all will eventually allow parents to pick their children's characteristics. OT may be unique in that one of its founders, Richard Seed, became involved with it in the first place because he considered it a means of improving the number and quality of American babies. According to journalist Martin Stuart-Harle, Seed believed that "there has always been a shortage of humans in Western civilization" and that OT could be a key to "the success of Western civilization."[18]

OT is not likely to contribute very much toward achieving this racist vision. It is more likely to be used by fertile women who are worried that they might have handicapped children and who are able to monitor the possibility of a pregnancy from the very beginning. These would tend to be more affluent and educated women with access to the most advanced medical resources. They are the people who, if they have handicapped children now, push hard for better services. When only poor and uneducated women have children with serious problems, how much influence will they have over the allocation of resources to help such children?

The history of OT is a disturbing one. It demonstrates the worst of science and business combined, with women the experimental subjects paying for their own subjection to unproven and risky procedures, and no outside body empowered to provide any oversight or regulation. The media also played an important role in promoting the program, just as they have consistently highlighted the very few successes of other reproductive technologies and ignored the many negative dimensions for those involved. If GIFT, whose success is also overplayed, and oocyte donation had not been developed around the time when FGR was beginning its operations, it is likely that the program would have continued on hype and hope for several more years before its failure brought it down. But lack of success both scientifically and commercially has hardly discouraged the promoters. This is evident from the current attention in both the press and scientific journals to the use of uterine lavage with "preimplantation genetics." It would not be surprising to find FGR, which is still in the infertility business, setting up franchised embryo check-ins around the world in a few years.

Significant Others

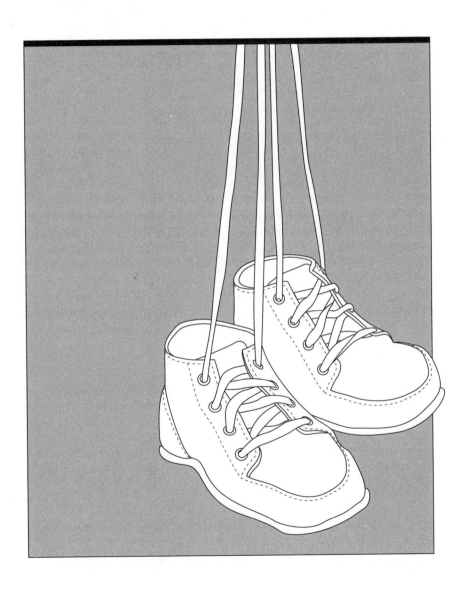

CHAPTER 7

Donors and Surrogate Mothers

Bob had not yet finished unpacking his bags when, glancing at the clock, he realized his first class was about to begin. As he sprinted across the quad, he felt the tension rising inside him. It was the start of his second year of medical school, and everyone agreed that this year was the worst. Besides, the tuition had just gone up again. He felt that he was being slowly sucked into a quicksand of debts. It was hard to imagine how he could make it through the next year.

As he passed the mailboxes, he noticed an official-looking letter inside and prayed that it would not be another bill. Instead, it was a letter from one of his professors in OB/GYN, telling him and the other men in his class about the need for sperm donors. The professor described the growing problem of male infertility, and, like a military recruiter, he ended with "I'm looking for a few good men."

Bob stopped in his tracks, realizing that this might be a solution. He recalled later:

> The line that caught my eye was the one that said, "I will pay you $35 for every specimen." I thought, this could make a dent in my bills if I do it regularly! I looked at it as a lot easier than selling blood, which I was chicken to do anyway. Here was a way I could help people and do myself a favor at the same time. And frankly, I think I've got pretty good genes—I figured I'd be a great candidate.
>
> The letter said that if you're interested, fill out this form describing yourself—stuff like hair and eye color, height, race, special interests. Then there was a medical history form—what did your grandmother die from, things like that. I had never been tested for genetic diseases like Tay-Sachs, but I couldn't think

of anyone in my family who's had a problem so I just said no to the question about genetic problems. Later I took a genetics course and realized that I had had no idea which diseases could be inherited or how.

It turned out to be so easy. As far I was concerned, the most difficult part was getting to the office early in the morning and getting out of there before the women arrived. I have to admit that I wondered about these women and their husbands. Occasionally I'd imagine this beautiful girl carrying my handsome baby. Most of the time, though, I just wanted to do my job, get my money, and be out of there to get to class on time.

I was glad when it ended after a year. I was starting to feel uncomfortable about possibly having so many children that I don't know. The closer I came to starting my own family, the more real the idea of fathering became for me.

Who Becomes a Donor or Surrogate Mother?

Who are the men and women we call donors? Who are these people who sell or donate sperm or eggs, or who become pregnant for nine months in order to create a child for someone else? Why do they do it, and how do they feel about having children they may never know? The answers to these questions are different for male and female donors, and from one method to another.

Unfortunately, little is known about the donors. This is understandable in the case of egg donors because there have been few of them so far. There have been hundreds of surrogate mothers, however, over the past decade, and several studies of them exist.[1] There is a great deal of curiosity about who these women are and why they would become surrogates.

In contrast, there has been a lack of interest in the United States in studying sperm donors and their reasons for doing it, despite the fact that AID has been practiced for over one hundred years. Tens—if not hundreds—of thousands of men have sold their sperm in the United States alone during that time. Yet hardly a single American study of these men exists.[2]

The lack of research on male donors says a great deal about the obsession with secrecy that surrounds AID. Most of what we do know about the feelings and motivations of sperm donors comes from anecdotal information, from interviews and informal contacts, and from studies carried out in other countries.[3]

We do know that, until recently, the vast majority of sperm donors in the United States were medical students or residents providing fresh sperm. In a 1979 survey of American physicians who performed AID, 85 percent reported using fresh sperm. Of these, more than three-fifths relied solely on medical students or residents, 10 percent on other students, and 18 percent on a combination of both.[4]

This picture has changed, however, as the demand for AID increased and sperm banks made frozen semen more available and easier for physicians to use. With frozen sperm, doctors no longer have to worry about screening the donors themselves or about the logistics of arranging for donors to be in the right place at the right time. Most important, men can be screened for HIV infection both at the time they sell their semen and again six months later, so that the possibility of HIV transmission is practically eliminated before the semen is ever used. With these developments has come some change in the pool of donors. They are still selected for academic achievement, but not only in the medical field. They are also more likely to consider selling their semen as a long-term job.

Even with these changes, the motives of sperm donors appear to have changed very little. Some are curious about their fertility, wondering if their sperm is any good. Others are motivated by sympathy for people who want children. For many men, however, the major reason to be a donor is the financial incentive.[5]

Surveys in other countries such as Australia and New Zealand found many donors stating their willingness to continue even without payment. Yet where payments are low or nonexistent, as in France, it has been difficult to recruit men. One Australian physician who doubled the fee experienced an immediate increase in applicants. In contrast, a feminist sperm bank in Oakland, California, looks for men with altruistic motives and may pay them with a service, such as a cholesterol check, rather than with cash.[6]

The desire for money was the major factor for a law student named Ken, who saw an ad placed by a sperm bank. He thought this would be an easy way to buy the car he had always wanted. He said:

> I felt a little strange answering the ad. I told a few close friends I was thinking of doing this as a joke. We all laughed. When I went into the clinic they gave me a physical exam and had me masturbate in the bathroom to examine my sperm. I then asked the doctor, "How does it look?" I always wondered how good my sperm really is. After looking at it under his microscope, he said, "So far it looks good, but we won't know until other tests, including a karyotype for genetic information, are done."
>
> A few weeks later they called and asked if I wanted to try being a donor. By then it wasn't a joke anymore. I had decided to go ahead.

Ken has been a donor now for two years, and he figures he is making as much money for five minutes in the bathroom as he does for several hours at his job as a law clerk. He takes his sperm donor job very seriously. He keeps himself in good shape, watching his weight and never smoking. He also makes sure not to have sex for forty-eight hours before each trip to the sperm bank.

Ken was proud of being one of the sperm bank's star donors. He recalled:

> Until I started being a donor, I wasn't absolutely sure if I could get a woman pregnant. It turns out I must have been a super stud, because they asked me to do it a lot of times.
>
> I wonder once in a while how many children I have out there in the world. Of course, I've never asked at the sperm bank—they probably don't even know and if they did, they wouldn't tell me anyway. Sometimes I try to calculate: If one child is produced every time I make a donation—let's see, that would be about 112 children! Of course, that's unlikely.
>
> What I do know for sure is that so far I've made $5,600, $50 every time. Not a bad record. The children don't feel real to me—it's as if they're not really there. But my car is, and every time I make another payment I feel great that the extra money helps me afford it.

If being a sperm donor is so easy and lucrative, why don't more men offer their services? According to one physician who recruits donors in a medical school, fifty letters from him can produce twenty responses one year but only three or four the next. The reluctance on the part of the majority must be more than a concern with inconvenience.

Some men may be put off primarily by their uneasiness about masturbation, especially on demand and in a hospital bathroom. Others fear that a child they never knew existed might come back one day to demand money or disrupt their lives. Many men are reluctant to father anonymous children, feeling some responsibility to care for, or at least acknowledge, their offspring.

Men who decide to become sperm donors may be kidded by their friends, but they do not have to face any serious social stigma. It is also possible to keep this activity secret from others if they want to. In Robyn Rowland's study of Australian sperm donors, 77 percent had told someone about being a donor. Yet 31 percent of those who were living with a partner had not told her and had no intention of telling her.‾

For a man to sell his sperm and "father" unknown numbers of children for profit does not seem to disturb or intrigue the general public. When it comes to surrogate mothers, the situation is very different. The idea that a woman could give birth to a child for $10,000 and then give it away is considered "unnatural" by many people. Of course, giving up a

baby after nine months of pregnancy *is* very different from a quick ejaculation of semen. The motivations of surrogate mothers are therefore very
different from those of sperm donors.

Jenny is in many ways typical of women who decide to have a baby
for someone else. She is married, with children, and had never heard about
this type of program until one day when she noticed an ad in the newspaper saying, "Surrogate mothers wanted to bear children for infertile
couples." She recalls:

> I showed it to my husband just to see his reaction. I was sur-
> prised that he didn't oppose it. All he said was, "As long as you
> don't have to sleep with the guy, if you want to do it, it's okay."
>
> In the beginning I wanted to do it for the finances, because
> we were very much in debt. After carrying the baby, the money
> didn't matter so much. It was just the feeling of giving someone
> the gift of life. Maybe I was destined to see that ad and this is my
> part to give to humanity.

Women who become surrogate mothers emphasize their empathy
for the infertile, and their desire to do something special. Many of them
love being pregnant but do not want any more children to take care of.
For many, it is a chance to do something that fits with a traditional role—
having a baby—but in a unique way. The first "generation" of surrogate
mothers received a great deal of media attention, and for some women
this was a big advantage. According to Dr. Nancy Reame at the University
of Michigan, most surrogates are women who see few possibilities for
satisfaction in their lives. "This is their one chance to shine."[8]

Women who respond to ads from surrogacy brokers are also a more
varied group than sperm donors seem to be. According to Burton Satzberg, attorney for Surrogate Mothering Ltd., in Philadelphia:

> The women, interestingly enough, have very little in com-
> mon with each other. Some of them are highly educated, others
> are not; some fairly well off, and others are not. Different reli-
> gions, different interests. Some are homebodies and some are
> out there in careers. The only things they have in common are
> that they enjoy being pregnant and they all have had very posi-
> tive birth experiences.

Despite this variety of backgrounds, some patterns do emerge, partly
due to program requirements. The majority are married, have one or two
children, and have completed at least a high school education. They are
strong-minded and willing to do something that might be disapproved
of. They are almost all white and Protestant or Catholic. Psychologist
Hilary Hanafin of Los Angeles described the women she selects as "really

neat people," who are emotionally healthy. This last characteristic is not necessarily true of women involved in other programs.

It is increasingly possible, due to the spread of egg donation programs, for a woman to be a donor without becoming pregnant. Yet the women being recruited as oocyte donors share some of the same motives and characteristics of surrogates. They are empathic, often having a friend or relative who is infertile. Some want to feel special; others are trying to compensate for a past abortion. One unusual woman who is a regular donor in California is the daughter of Holocaust survivors; she sees her activities as "my way of getting back at Hitler. . . . He took the Jews off the world, I'm putting them back in."[9]

The women who offered to be embryo donors for the first experimental round of the ovum transfer program are described by Dr. Annette Brodsky, a psychologist who screened them, as "not the average lady off the street." She found them to be adventurous, but also concluded that many were trying to make up for an unstable past. One OT donor explained to us why she likes what she is doing:

> It's a gift of God to pass on. It also helps me with self-confidence. I've always been shy and let other people walk all over me. When I was in school I had a lot of friends; then I got married and devoted myself to my husband, that was it. It makes me feel good to do something for somebody—every time I leave there I'm on a high. And where would we be today without guinea pigs?

Egg donors are recruited in a variety of ways. Since the removal of eggs requires an invasive procedure, physicians sometimes approach women who are already having surgery and ask them to donate some of their eggs. Women who are having tubal ligations or hysterectomies or who are undergoing laparoscopies as part of IVF or other infertility treatments have been the most likely candidates. According to physicians, such women are highly sympathetic to the problems of infertility and rarely say no. They certainly are in a vulnerable situation, and would be reluctant to refuse their doctors' requests.

With the widespread use of superovulation in conjunction with egg retrieval, however, it has become more difficult to ask women who are about to have an operation for sterilization to first undergo drug treatment and daily monitoring. And with the greater availability of cryopreservation to freeze embryos, women in the process of IVF are more reluctant to give away any of their eggs. Over the past few years, therefore, as oocyte donation in conjunction with IVF has become more common, the most common donors have been those recruited by the recipient woman herself, usually friends or family members, and women who respond to advertisements by fertility clinics. This second group are generally the only ones to be paid, and they usually do not have any contact with the couples who receive the eggs.[10]

As donor programs become more routine, the characteristics of the donors are already changing. Those who are attracted by the potential for media attention and the desire to be pioneers may be less likely to apply. More donors are being recruited by friends who have already been surrogates or donors. Some surrogacy programs are reporting that more highly educated and emotionally stable women are now applying than in the past.

The Ideal Donor, the Ideal Surrogate Mother

We asked program staff and couples to describe what they were looking for in an ideal donor. Although health was always a major factor, the other priorities differed greatly depending on whether they needed a male or a female donor. The differences were closely tied to sex role stereotypes.

Most programs that need sperm donors, for example, look for intelligent men. The profiles of donors at IDANT, a New York sperm bank that is one of the largest in the United States, include grade point averages, and 3.5 to 4.0 is common. An extreme example of this requirement for intelligence is seen in the policies of the Repository for Germinal Choice in Escondido, California (better known as the Nobel Sperm Bank). It dedicates itself to improving the human race by using only donors who have superior intelligence.

Several other sperm banks in California cater primarily to single women, both lesbian and heterosexual. They provide more detailed information on the donor, sometimes including his motives for being a donor as well as eating habits and musical ability.[11]

In contrast, when it comes to surrogate mothers, qualities such as stability, warmth, openness, physical attractiveness, strength of character, and compassion are considered more important than intelligence. So is the ability to cooperate with a program and follow its guidelines. All surrogacy programs and some egg donor programs screen applicants for psychological makeup. We are aware of only one program, in Belgium, that screens potential sperm donors psychologically and turns away those considered to be unstable.[12] The difference is striking. The father should be intelligent, the mother should be nurturant and pretty as well as compliant.

Some of this is logical. Surrogate mothers certainly give a great deal more of themselves to the baby, and often to the couple as well, than do sperm donors, and that does make personality traits, at least, much more important. However, the case of oocyte donors supports the view that powerful stereotypes are at play here as well. Their role is in many ways similar to that of sperm donors. They are often anonymous, and their involvement is much more short term. Yet they may be screened like potential surrogate mothers, with attention to personality and psychological stability. Intelligence does not appear to be an important factor.

The difference in priorities when selecting a male versus a female donor is based on a traditional view of the ideal father and the ideal mother. Perhaps the professionals who do the screening and the prospective parents as well are trying to create a balance they assume a child born of the two of them would have.

Finding One's Own Donor

More people are deciding to do without the professional "matchmakers" who recruit and screen donors and manage the relationship among all the parties. They prefer to select their own egg donor, sperm donor, or surrogate mother, in the last two cases often performing the insemination themselves. Some IVF programs that use donated eggs require that the couple find their own donor, as they do not have sufficient donors available. Increasingly people who want to become parents are approaching friends and relatives or placing ads in the newspaper ("Carrier Mother Wanted" reads the headline on one such advertisement). One survey found that 63 percent of the medical students studied and 78 percent of a sample of infertility support group members agreed that AID recipients should be allowed to select their own donors.[13] This is a surprising statistic in light of the current prevalence of anonymity.

There are some advantages to finding one's own donor. It avoids the control and the biases of professionals and is almost always less expensive. Noel Keane, the lawyer who started the first surrogate mother program, was introduced to the idea by a couple who were having a young unmarried friend carry a baby for them and just needed an attorney to handle the legal aspects.

Another reason some people prefer to choose their own donors is so their children will have the option of knowing who the other person is who contributed genetically and/or biologically to their birth. Some known sperm donors do in fact take a part in the child's life. For many other people, the choice of a relative has the advantage of making the child genetically closer to the infertile parent or to the woman in a lesbian couple who is not the biological mother. Increasingly, couples are turning to brothers, sisters, and cousins to be sperm and egg donors, and occasionally to mothers or other female relatives to serve as surrogate mothers. News reports of women over fifty bearing children for their own children are appearing with greater frequency.

Having a known donor is not always an advantage. A sperm donor may want much more involvement with the child than the mother had intended, and occasionally the mother and the donor end up in court together battling over visitation and custody. Single women, both heterosexual and lesbian, are particularly vulnerable, because courts have ruled in the sperm donor's favor in custody disputes when there was not another man around to be the father. Even as they have sometimes denied visitation rights to a lesbian partner who helped raise a child after she and her lover separated, some courts have given priority to the genetic father, even one who has had no contact with the child.[14]

The problems may become even more complicated when family members are involved. Sisters are not allowed to be oocyte donors in England and parts of Australia, due to fears of psychological harm to the children.[15] One woman we interviewed worried about such effects:

> My sister offered to have a baby for me. She figured it would be ideal, because the baby would have genes like mine and she would still be Aunt Betty just as if I had given birth to the child. But as great an idea as it is in theory, I knew it would be a disaster. She's the kind of person who would want to be telling me how to raise the kid, and never let me forget what she did. I'd rather have someone who isn't so close to me.

Both donors and recipients often realize that their relationship will change with a successful pregnancy, as it may with no pregnancy or if the child suffers any health problems. Both may expect that their relationship will be closer, but it may well be complicated by a strong sense on one part or the other of enormous obligation to the one who made this pregnancy possible.

Sometimes having a relative be a surrogate mother or sperm or egg donor does work well. Family members made such private arrangements long before the current era of procreative alternatives. A close relative, a brother, or sister, is likely to offer empathy as well as genetic similarity. There may be disputes over parenting or conflicts with the donor's spouse, but we have heard of several instances of women having babies for sisters and still maintaining close relationships between the two families.

Lesbian couples who want to find their own donor in order to avoid the scrutiny of professionals sometimes discover that it is more difficult than they expected. One gay woman reported:

> We got turned down, I don't know how many times. They'd say, "Oh, I don't know if I could handle it." "Nobody's asking you to handle anything," we said, "just give us your sperm!" We weren't asking for any financial support; the kid didn't even have to ever know who they were. We had a lawyer ready to sign

every legal document in the whole world. We were all prepared. But they'd say, "But I'd just know that there was this child." We were so angry that they couldn't just give us sperm—two seconds you know.

Since private arrangements with sperm donors and surrogate mothers are largely unrecorded and therefore unstudied, we cannot know how frequently this happens or how well it works. When it doesn't work and ends up in court, we are more likely to hear about it. Such was the case of a young Mexican woman brought to the United States by cousins living in California who told her she would be pregnant for them only for a few weeks, but later informed her that she would be carrying the child to term. Her objections and subsequent decision to keep the baby were met with threats to have her deported as illegal and prosecuted for using the American cousin's name for insurance coverage, as she had been told to do. Despite her lack of English and precarious legal situation, the young woman was able to get legal help and win joint custody of the baby.[16]

The matchmakers who run programs usually prefer, of course, that the selection be left up to them. One surrogacy program director, for example, reasoned that the safeguards involved in his screening procedure are essential. Certainly, a thorough health screening is important, but there is no reason that an individual or couple could not arrange to have a donor screened. It is also true that the screening of donors by physicians is not always as rigorous as it should be.

Risks for Egg Donors and Surrogate Mothers

People who become donors usually talk about the positive side of their experience. They feel very good about helping others, and the extra money that many earn can be a big help. In many cases, the egg donor is contributing her ova to a friend or relative who she knows has suffered a great deal because of infertility, and being able to help gives her great satisfaction.

There are risks as well, however. The risks are particularly great for the women donors, both oocyte donors and surrogates mothers. They face a multitude of physical risks, ranging from minor discomforts of pregnancy to infection during egg retrieval to possibly severe or even fatal compications from an ectopic pregnancy or ovarian hyperstimulation syndrome or childbirth. Surrogate mothers are artificially inseminated with sperm that may not be carefully screened, exposing themselves to the possibility of infections, venereal disease, or even AIDS, which threaten health, future fertility, or life itself.

Psychologist Annette Brodsky explains why donors in the now-defunct ovum transfer program ignored the risks:

Some donors say: "I trust this program, I trust the people, if they think it's okay, and they've researched it, and they've looked at it, then I'll be okay." We tell them all the risks—we can't let them out of here without knowing. But, there's a lot of not wanting to know.

A risk that is of concern to some women who become surrogate mothers is the possibility that the couple may reject a child if he or she is born with a handicap. One highly publicized case made the entire country aware that this might happen. The baby in that instance was born with microcephaly, indicating a likelihood of retardation. The presumed father questioned whether this was his baby and raised the possibility that he would not take the child. The results of blood tests were revealed in a bizarre manner—in front of a national audience on the Phil Donahue show; they showed that the surrogate mother's husband was actually the father, and she agreed to keep the baby.

A much more common problem for surrogate mothers is the emotional trauma of giving up the baby. One woman described her own experience:

Through the whole pregnancy I was motivating myself, trying to put my state of mind into what I wanted it to be for the delivery and after. But it was still very hard, that separation, much harder than I thought it would be. I wonder how she's doing, what kind of life she'll have. I wish I had thought to ask the couple if I could be the guardian of the baby if anything happened to them. But I know I have to try not to think about her. Her birthday is especially hard. I always get depressed then.

I wanted to keep in touch with the baby's parents—after all, we had gotten to know each other pretty well and you'd think they'd want to know how I am. We had agreed from the beginning that after the baby was born we would not contact each other. But I hadn't realized how hard it would be saying goodbye to them. I haven't heard from them since that day we said goodbye.

The birth mothers face grief from loss of the baby and frequently from the loss of their connection with the couple. Psychiatrist Philip Parker, in his follow-up study of thirty surrogate mothers, found several who had severe grief reactions and required treatment. One of the first surrogate mothers, "Elizabeth Kane," was frequently interviewed in the media and insisted that it had been easy to give up her baby. Seven years later she appeared on television to express her remorse. She is now active in opposing surrogacy and feels that she and her other children have been damaged by her experience of giving away a child.[17]

As surrogacy programs are increasingly combined with IVF, the emotional dimension for surrogate mothers may change somewhat. In these cases a woman becomes pregnant with the embryo of a couple, and she may feel more like a "hired womb." A woman who was trying to conceive with frozen embryos explained her feelings about it:

> This has nothing to do with me at all. It's not my egg and it's not my husband's sperm. I'll be an incubator, that's really what it is. You know I'm just going to take care of their baby, like baby-sitting it for nine months. It's kind of long to baby-sit somebody, but that's the way I look at it.

What does it mean for women to carry and give birth to babies that are not "theirs" genetically, yet have been part of their bodies for nine months? Is it really easier, or is that another form of self-deception to suit the needs of others? How is it possible for a woman to believe that "this has nothing to do with me at all"? The effort to detach herself from what is going on in her body, to perceive herself as a machine (an "incubator"), is difficult to sustain. After nine months of the most intimate connection, it is not surprising that some women find it just as hard to give up a baby, regardless of its genes.

The emotional risks for surrogate mothers may be eased by professional counseling and support, but it is rarely available after the baby is relinquished. Some women feel that seeing the happy family together helps them cope with the loss. But what about those women who never see the baby again and do not know where he or she is? They do their best to detach themselves from the experience and go on with their lives. Are they repressing grief, only to see it emerge again months or years later as has occurred with many birth mothers who relinquish babies for adoption?[18] No one knows the answers yet; women who have come forward to fight either for or against state bans on surrogacy give very different accounts of how the experience has affected their lives.

There may be risks for the birth mother's family life as well, something about which we do not have much information. For instance, many women said that their husbands were very supportive. Is it really irrelevant to these husbands that their wives are pregnant from the sperm of other men, especially affluent, well-educated men whom the women have come to believe will make great fathers? Will the marriage suffer if the woman feels her husband pushed her into being a surrogate for the money? Can their other children really understand that "Mommy is baby-sitting Ray and Betsy's baby for nine months because Betsy's tummy doesn't work" and not wonder how Mommy could give away their baby sister or brother? What will be the long-term effects on these children? Several women who now regret their involvement with surrogacy say that their other children have suffered as well as they themselves have.

The women we interviewed felt confident that, so far, their families have not suffered. They give instances instead of how encouraging their husbands and other relatives had been, how easily the other children hadaccepted the situation. Until follow-up studies are done, there will be no way to know how many women, or members of their families, suffer long-term damaging effects.

Many egg donors stay in contact with the couple and child, either because they already knew each other or because they had requested reports and pictures of the child. There have been no instances yet of donor women claiming any rights to the child, but it is certainly possible that this could happen.

Some women donors mention as a benefit the attention that they receive from prestigious people. They are courted and cared for—if only temporarily—by physicians and lawyers, and may even appear on television. This need for attention may ultimately backfire. Program staff remark that some women return regularly for favors and advice, expecting to receive continued support. They do not always get what they are looking for and end up feeling angry and disappointed.

One woman, whose experience as a surrogate mother can only be described as destructive, was ready to do it again because of her continuing need for approval by the program directors:

> The pregnancy made me feel sick as a dog, I've never been so sick in my life. I was going through a great deal of emotional problems and admitted myself to a hospital to get some rest. I had to place my children in foster homes for the rest of the pregnancy.
>
> The pregnancy kept me going through all that, and also my relationship with the program. I would trust those guys with my life. They really care about me; they tell me I'm their star. They're my knights in shining armor; they've helped me through a lot. Even though I'm having a hard time getting pregnant again, I'll keep trying for them.

Hilary Hanafin, who counsels women for a Los Angeles surrogacy-program, believes that some women may actually benefit from being a surrogate mother. She said:

> It's not unusual to hear that a surrogate has decided to go back to school and finish her degree, or put a down payment on a house she's always wanted. I think it's a combination of finances and of also having achieved something unique that really gives them that boost, that transition from being a housewife to attacking another career.

Risks for Sperm Donors

Physicians who work with artificial insemination or who have donated sperm themselves do not believe there are any emotional problems associated with donating sperm. If there is any risk, it is that a child may find the donor father who would prefer to remain anonymous. There have in fact been a number of children who have tried to trace their fathers through medical school records or yearbooks.

The chance of this happening, however, is still small. Most of the children do not know of their AID origins, and if they do, the possibility of finding the biological father is slim. Records are poorly kept or destroyed. Only in Sweden is it required that a record be kept of the donor and that children have the right to this information after they reach the age of eighteen.

A surprising number of donors would like to have contact with the children, or at least would not mind it. Robyn Rowland, in her study of Australian sperm donors, discovered that 60 percent of her sample would not mind meeting the children they had fathered. Forty-two percent claimed that they would still donate even if their names were given to the couple. Daniels's study of donors in New Zealand had similar results; four out of five think about the children they may have, and two-thirds would not mind being contacted by them.[19]

Often it is the donor's wife who is more concerned. She may worry that some of her husband's dozens of offspring may come looking for him, perhaps threatening her own children's well-being as well as their inheritance.

In an unusual case in which a supposedly anonymous donor came to know a child, it was the boy's mother who contacted him. As she had worked in the fertility clinic, she had a pretty good idea who was the genetic father of her child. Divorced from her husband, she wanted the child to know his biological father. Fortunately, in this case, the sperm donor and his wife, who were not able to have children of their own, were delighted to meet the boy, and he has become an important and joyous part of their lives.

Donors and Recipients

The great majority of donors and recipients have no contact and very little knowledge about each other because secrecy has been the rule for donor insemination. Surrogacy and egg donation programs vary widely in their policies, from those that forbid any contact to others that require it. Of course in the most common type of IVF, where there is no donor involved, there is no problem about secrecy. When sperm donors are brought into IVF, they are almost always anonymous; in contrast, egg donors in IVF are often known to or met by the recipient couple.[20]

Professionals who advocate secrecy sometimes justify it by claiming that a relationship between donor and recipients would intensify fantasies about each other, which could lead to trouble. According to psychologist Howard Adelman of Surrogate Mothering Limited:

> If the surrogate meets the couple, there's the possibility of fantasies starting. She starts really liking this guy who is the father, and maybe thinking she'd like to have this child of his and keep it and even—in very unrealistic situations—possibly he'll leave his wife for her. So when they ask what he looks like, I make a joke out of it—I say, "He's very short, fat with a big belly, and bald," and they laugh.

Anonymity, however, offers no guarantee of eliminating troublesome fantasies. Perhaps it is harder to act on them, but they may actually be exaggerated by lack of reality. Donors and recipient couples who never meet often have fears and fantasies about each other. Many times these revolve around racial or religious prejudices. Fantasies about other characteristics are often present as well. "I hope he doesn't look like John Belushi," a woman commented after being inseminated.

Some people who advocate secrecy in a surrogate program fear that the birth mother will "blackmail" the couple later in order to receive more money. In addition, anonymity has the advantage of diminishing the couple's sense of obligation to do more for someone who has given them such an important gift.

The major argument against secrecy is the same one used in discussions of adoption—harm to the children who may want or need to know their parentage. In addition, many surrogate mothers want to know the families to whom they are giving their babies. Like many other birth mothers who give up babies for adoption, they need to know where the babies are and how they are doing.

One woman who developed a close relationship with the adoptive couple described the reasons for her feelings about contact with the child:

> I was adopted and knew my birth mother, and I realized that I couldn't handle anonymity. So we decided before I even got pregnant that it was very important that the child know who I am and feel comfortable enough to call me if he felt the need to talk to me, that he would have that right to do it.

This woman has already visited the child twice and speaks to the parents regularly by phone. Their situation, however, is not very common.

One element present in most relationships is the payment. Whether it be $50 for a sperm donor, anywhere from $1,000 to 4,000 for an egg donor, or the typical $10,000 that surrogate mothers have received for over a decade, very few people become involved with one of these methods for free. As George Annas, professor at Boston University Law School, suggests, they are not donors, but vendors.[21]

There are pluses and minuses with payment, just as with secrecy. Both appear to increase the likelihood that a sufficient number of donors will be available. Both present difficult conflicts for many of the people involved.

In his classic study of blood donation, "The Gift Relationship," Richard Titmuss found that those countries in which blood donors are paid have major problems with donors concealing information that would have disqualified them.[22] The same may be true for some sperm donors, who have been known to split one sample of semen into more than one donation, and also to misrepresent their medical histories.

Some people who do not really want to be donors may feel compelled to do so because they need the money. Payment is also troubling because of the implications of "baby selling." In an ideal world, people would give of themselves for altruistic reasons, to help others in need. Unfortunately, we have seen from the experience of some other countries that altruism is rarely enough of an incentive to begin to meet the demand for donors.

A great stir resulted from the announcement at the end of 1993 about animal experiments being conducted in Great Britain using aborted fetuses as a source of ova for IVF. The questions raised in this chapter about donors' motives, psychological characteristics, and relationships with recipients would be irrelevant if this practice were followed with humans. But it raises many other difficult ethical issues for society and may pose particularly hard social and psychological challenges for the recipient family and the child who is born from a fetal mother's egg.

Often donors enter into a program as a lark, or from financial need. And often they discover that they are giving a very precious gift, one that may make others incredibly happy. Many couples told us about their feelings of gratitude, feelings they rarely get a chance to express to the donors:

> I love my son with all my heart. But I can't forget that a stranger played an essential role in my child's conception. Without him, my son would not exist. I know we'll never meet the donor, but sometimes I wish he could visit us and see for himself what a precious human being he has helped to create.

CHAPTER 8

The Professionals

It had been a particularly rough day for Dr. B., the director of a fertility center. He shut the door of his office, sat back in his big leather chair, and sighed. He was clearly exhausted. He was willing to be interviewed about his work, but he was distracted by thoughts of the phone call he had just made. He explained:

A couple came in last year who had two children; she then had a tubal ligation. Later one of the children died and she wanted to have another. Tubal surgery didn't work, so IVF was their only chance. She told me they were people of meager means. They had sold their second car and raised $10,000. They figured that, with insurance, they had enough for three chances. "Here we are, Doc," they said, looking at me with hope in their eyes. Today I got the third negative pregnancy test. I just feel the lowest of low.

It's really, really tough. If I think too much about every patient's pain and sacrifices, I wouldn't be able to focus on developing new procedures that may help them. If I spend more time consoling and talking to them, there will be no time for the next person. I know they're angry and desperate, but I just can't always deal with it.

The hardest part of my work is trying to treat such a large number of patients. It requires such extraordinary patient-physician interaction, so much emotional energy involved in it, and after a while, it is wearing. My God, they are all lined up out there—one side of my brain says I'm obliged to treat every person that I can and the other side says, if you treat any more, you won't even know their names.

People who try the new methods have entrusted their futures to powerful individuals. They bring to these physicians and lawyers their

121

hopes and anxieties, their vulnerable overtested bodies, and often their life savings. They seek understanding and compassion, information and support, and most of all, of course, they seek a baby. What they find is that the professionals they depend on often fail to understand their emotional needs. These professionals frequently focus only on the technical or legal details and do not realize how crucial their support is.

Professionals and Their Motives

Who are these people who are offering the reproductive alternatives? Two entirely different images emerge from what has been written about them. In one image, commonly found in the media, these are extremely hardworking, imaginative, and dedicated people. They are creative scientists, empathic attorneys, and caring physicians and nurses, devoting enormous energy to helping unfortunate couples achieve their most precious goal. They are pioneers, miracle workers, even saints.

There is also another image, painted by those who are critical of the new methods. They write of the "pharmacrats," the egomaniacal madmen whose search for fame and fortune is exploiting women today and may ruin society in the future. In this view, the infertility professionals are single-minded devotees of "science" who pursue "progress" without regard for the human and social consequences. Hiding behind the mask of benevolence, they are the manipulators and controllers of women.

Both pictures have some truth to them. In our interviews with professionals, we observed the complex merging of these two images. We met individuals who are motivated by the challenge of working at the frontiers of science and by the prestige of being at the top of their field. They are ambitious go-getters who feel there is no reason to be concerned about the present risks to women and possible future dangers. At the same time, they work very hard to help infertile couples. They share in the joys and disappointments of their clients and cannot understand why they would be considered exploiters of women.

When we asked directors of infertility and surrogate programs why they became involved in this kind of work, their answers usually centered on scientific and career concerns. The lure of scientific discovery, the chance to be a pioneer, is a principal motivation for many professionals. As one director of a fertility program put it:

> My thing in life is not to be just in the front running: I want to be right out there in the very front. The grant money in my area dried up; so I became interested in infertility. Personally, it is important to me that the work I do helps women. But by far the

most exciting part professionally is the research and the new data we get.

Another physician remarked:

Delivering babies became too routine for me—it just wasn't very creative. But IVF is really an exciting intellectual problem. It has unlimited potential.

Dr. Alan DeCherney, director of Reproductive Endocrinology at Yale University School of Medicine, represents this viewpoint most vividly. He wrote:

We can only be overjoyed . . . to be working during a period of time when such paramount advances have been made. How thrilling it must have been to be Chaucer writing when Gutenberg invented the printing press, or to be a physicist working on the Manhattan Project! . . . An individual who is interested in fertility, who is not involved in IVF, is very similar to the West Point graduate who is educated in military science but never goes to war.[1]

There is something very troubling about the imagery here. The physician is compared to a warrior; the researchers on women's bodies are similar to the creators of the atomic bomb. The prestige and satisfaction of discovery, and the possibility of developing and using new skills, appear to be more important than helping women become pregnant.

Dr. DeCherney himself is also worried about the physicians who go into infertility treatment with little or no training and whose motivation is essentially financial. In 1989 he appeared before a congressional subcommittee investigating IVF and criticized the OB/GYN doctors who decide that malpractice issues make obstetrics unattractive, take a two-day course, and then advertise themselves as able to perform IVF. "Any doctor that is licensed in this country is licensed to do anything. I can do neurosurgery in my kitchen if I have a mind to," DeCherney pointed out in warning of the possibility of exploitation in medicine. DeCherney and ten other leading specialists around the country issued a similar warning in the journal *Fertility and Sterility*, charging that exploitation of infertile couples exists due to lack of regulation of practice and false advertising.[2]

The other side of this picture is that many of the academically inclined or profit-driven professionals derive a tremendous satisfaction from the personal side of their work. For some, the desire to help people who are infertile has led them into this specialty in the first place. One infertility specialist explained:

When I was a resident, my wife and I became friendly with the couple next door in our apartment building. She had a fertility problem and needed somebody to give her a Pergonal shot. That was how I learned about the terrible pain of infertility, and it was the dawn of my new career.

Another physician recalled:

I was working with infertile couples, and it was so frustrating to always be saying, "There's nothing else to be done." I joined an IVF program so that I could offer more.

Does it make a difference why these professionals went into the field of infertility? After all, without driven scientists and entrepreneurial lawyers, there would be fewer options for the infertile. And from the point of view of people trying to have children, the motivations of providers may not appear to be important, providing they can achieve success.

However, these physicians and lawyers are powerful people who hold the fate of many families in their hands and in their laboratories. If their priorities are science or prestige or financial gain, they should not be entrusted with decision making about the future of these procedures. And in the short run, it may be difficult for them to provide the needed emotional support for their clients.

The Power of Professionals

The professionals' power extends to many aspects of the methods. They decide who will be allowed into a program and what their experience will be like. They determine what procedures will be used and how much information the clients will have. They select the surrogate mothers or the donors and decide what new directions the research will take. The only control they do not have is over the outcome.

Control over access to services is an important source of power. There is no open-door policy with the new methods; every program sets criteria for screening clients. Marital status, age, fertility history, and emotional stability are usually considered before someone is allowed to try an alternative.[3] The ability to pay is the only standard shared by every program.

Many infertile people never get inside the well-guarded gates of fertility programs. The professional gatekeepers in many programs have declared them to be too old, too poor, too single, too far down on the waiting list, too neurotic, or medically unqualified. Some of the restrictions were instituted because the programs were new and the directors were worried about public relations. They believed that by accepting only married couples who were psychologically stable they would avoid bad publicity.

In some countries the requirement of marriage is written into national policy. In one case in England, a woman found out that she had been removed from an IVF waiting list (without ever having been informed) because she had worked years earlier as a prostitute. Her appeal to a court was turned down.[4]

The psychological testing is the one aspect of the screening that bothers applicants the most. One woman recalled her session angrily:

> We had a horrible experience. The coordinator refused to tell me over the phone what the assessment was about and insisted that we just come in for the appointment. Additionally, we had to pay in advance and our check had to arrive before we went through the program. In retrospect, I should have been suspicious then. The actual assessment included intrusive, lengthy questionnaires about our sexual practices (questions beyond imagination!). A final interview with a psychologist revealed that this was a research study to determine if couples applying for IVF had sexual problems as well. She assured us that she didn't think that this was the case, and that as a group she found us "disgustingly normal." There seems to be an attitude among professionals that we are experimental guinea pigs even though we are paying (and the price is high) for the opportunity to try something with no guarantees or assurances.

Psychological screening may help patients to consider whether they can cope with the stress of the procedures. It may also, however, reinforce the emotional distress of the infertile couple who, already feeling inadequate, must prove their qualifications for parenthood. This is a challenge never presented to those who can conceive on their own; infertile people may wonder why they have to meet higher standards than other prospective parents.

According to the studies of couples who have applied to AID and IVF programs, very few have ever been rejected for psychological reasons. Some couples voluntarily change their minds after a full discussion of their motivations and plans; a few are referred for further counseling.[5] But the fact of screening gives a great deal of power to the physicians. Even though they may not turn away many couples, they could.

When there were not many programs available and few of them had a reputation for success, the long waiting lists became the greatest obstacle to acceptance. At one point a staff member of the Norfolk IVF program, for instance, estimated that it would take ten years to accommodate everyone already on the waiting list. In this kind of situation, assertiveness and personal connections often help move a name to the top of the list. Physicians may favor their own and their friends' patients, and lawyers may turn first to the couples they know or like the best. Now that there is a great deal more competition for clients, the waiting lists are shorter and the standards for admission have become somewhat less restrictive.

Some physicians feel that their role in "gatekeeping" should be limited to giving the facts. One fertility specialist who practices AID told us:

> If a woman comes in here and she is unmarried, or a lesbian couple comes in and they decide they are in a stable relationship and want a child, who am I to decide that they shouldn't? My job is to inform them of the dangers and ask if they've thought about all the possibilities. If they have, I'm just playing a technician at that point. They could just as easily go to a bar and have sex with somebody to get pregnant. They might as well do it in a controlled manner.

Even the most liberal professionals, such as this doctor, see control as an essential part of their role.

Most people entering programs in which there is a donor trust the professionals to screen out problems effectively. For example, most women who tried AID told us they were sure that the sperm donors had been medically screened. Yet we have seen that selection is based more on academic accomplishment, and health is often checked very poorly. On the other hand, a woman who had a baby as a surrogate mother told us she was certain the adoptive couple was screened for suitability as parents. Yet the director of the program that recruited her told us that if couples can afford it, they are accepted. He sends only surrogate applicants to the psychologist, never the couples.

Sociologist Marcia Millman describes the ways in which physicians "enact trust" from their patients. By withholding information and discouraging questions, they force patients and their families to fall back on the belief that the physician will do the right thing.[6] While some degree of confidence is important between patient and doctor, blind trust can be harmful. One woman said:

> I've had four laparoscopies in the last four years. I wouldn't think of changing doctors, even though I still haven't gotten pregnant. I think part of that is just the way I trust my doctor—if he wanted to cut me anywhere I'd say, "Fine, go ahead, do what you want."

Denial is a powerful force for self-protection in humans. It protects people from seeing or feeling what they would rather avoid. It is all the more powerful when reinforced by a lifetime of learning that one should trust people in authority, especially doctors. So when a kindly physician or psychologist tells someone that what he or she is about to do—whether it be open heart surgery or ovum donation—has possible risks, most people have learned not to listen. They trust that it will not happen to them.

Another concern about the control of professionals is related to the potential link between these methods and a growing movement called eugenics. People who believe in eugenics want to "improve" the population by limiting the reproduction of "inferior" people. Since it is the doctors and lawyers who choose prospective parents, donors, and surrogate mothers, will they decide to produce only babies with superior intellect or other specific characteristics? This is already happening, particularly in the way sperm donors are now selected for intellectual ability, and in the beginning of genetic screening of embryos before they are transferred to a woman's body.

Perhaps the greatest power of these practitioners is the control they have over the creation of new life. "We are truly playing God," a psychologist with an IVF program told us. The potential for—and existence of—abuse of such power is what worries many observers of the new technologies.

Meeting the Needs of Clients

The professionals who work in fertility programs are crucial in the lives of the people who go to them for help. It is not surprising, then, that they evoke such strong emotions, both positive and negative. These conflicting comments from two women who had been through IVF are typical:

> They were incredible human beings, always there for me. I think of them as family. They really helped me get through the hard times.

> I didn't feel that they were very understanding about the pain I was in. We were dealt with as objects, as guinea pigs. Not that they wanted to; they just didn't have the staff. They didn't have the training. We were just numbers to them—it was much too impersonal.

Many professionals—attorneys, physicians, and staff—are very caring to their clients; just as often they are viewed as distant and lacking in understanding. Often they simply do not know how to deal with the emotions of people struggling with infertility. Unfortunately, their comments and attitudes have a tremendous impact. An unsympathetic staff person can intensify the stresses of an already difficult process. One woman was very upset about her doctor, who had said, "Why do you deserve to have a baby?" She explained that he had six children and thought that the better the person, the more children God would give you. A woman who was having artificial insemination was also very upset with her physician. She said:

> It's hard for anyone to meet your emotional needs, but the one person who did the least of any one I know was my doctor. First of all, he had pregnant women in the waiting room at the same time I was there. And then he would hardly talk to me. When I complained one time, he said that he had thirty other women out there in his office just as anxious as I was and he had to see all of them in one hour. I really didn't have a choice because he was the only one in our area doing inseminations.
>
> It would infuriate me when he would unexpectedly go out of town and not have anyone cover for him. Here I was planning my whole life around this schedule, I would be ovulating and he would be out of town. He said he couldn't ask another doctor to cover for him because then the donor would be known to some-one else. I felt that if he was offering a service, he really owed it to the people to be there. However, he was more concerned about the donor than about his patients.

Lack of understanding, lack of time, lack of personalized attention. There are the themes that recur in the comments of people who have tried the alternative methods. We asked people what, if anything, they would change about the program they were in. By far the most frequent response was that it should provide more emotional support and counseling. There are so many pressures, expectations, frustrations, and feelings of isolation and anger, it is no wonder that a person would benefit from a professional counselor and from more contact with other couples. Though some receive the help they need from program staff, or from informal support groups, most people feel that more is required.

Formal support groups are rare for most programs because funds are scarce or because staff members believe there is no need for them. For example, Dr. Howard Jones of the Jones Institute of Reproductive Medicine in Norfolk claimed in a speech that IVF patients have no special emotional needs compared with other infertility patients and therefore programs to provide support are unnecessary.[7] In other programs, support groups have been announced, but they met at inconvenient times or were not presented as an essential part of the program. Under such circumstances, it is not surprising that they failed. At one university hospital, a more formal group has been set up where couples are encouraged to attend as part of the program. In addition, every couple is introduced to one or two other couples as a buddy system for support.

People going through these programs need support and contact from the staff at all stages of the process. They also need to be prepared for the possibility of failure. Feelings of isolation and depression are especially acute during waiting periods and after conception fails.

While the relationship between staff and patients may often be very good and helpful as long as the patients are physically at the program, this support often vanishes once they go home. One woman recalled her feelings:

> After the eight embryos were implanted and I went home, I felt the staff were very far away. I would call up and they would seem very, very distant—it seemed like they were billions of miles away. They were very curt and would say, "Send in your blood and we'll find out the results."

Many people told us they felt they were not getting from the professional staff honest information about the procedure and their realistic chances of success. They needed accurate information to make their decisions and were angry if they felt they had been misled. One man who wrote to us was furious when he learned, after his wife had gone through IVF, that her chances of success had been only 1 percent:

> After the fact we were told we were admitted because the clinic personnel thought that it was psychologically beneficial to experience failure, to which I say, "Hogwash!"

When their needs are met, even if the treatment is not successful, the gratitude is boundless. An example is a woman who gave birth after three attempts at IVF in the Norfolk clinic. She spoke about the founders, Drs. Georgeanna and Howard Jones:

> I'll never forget the fact that the Joneses were there. You know, she held my hand and patted my back during the transfer, and he did the transfer. I think of them as our child's grandparents.

One couple who were trying AIH told how appreciative they were of their doctor's dedication. The husband said:

> After three months of trying, we told him the procedure was too expensive for us to continue. We were surprised when he quickly said he would cut the fee in half. He's just doing everything he can to get us a baby—not everything he can to get a large bank account.

The physician who made extra visits in the hospital to a woman whose family was far away, the hospital staff who made a couple feel welcome in the delivery room while a surrogate mother gave birth to a child for them, the doctor who opened his office on Christmas to do an insemination, the receptionist who kept a woman company for the three hours she had to lie still after an embryo transfer, the nurse whose humor and friendliness made it possible to get through another day of tests and uncertainty—these people are remembered forever.

Stresses on Professionals

Infertility programs are certainly stressful for staff members as well as for the people who are infertile. The emotional difficulties for the professionals, however, are even less well recognized.[8]

Because the professionals have so much of their training and energy invested in these programs and so many people counting on them, they are often faced with difficult emotional stresses as well as technical challenges. They know that people are using up their retirement funds or the money they had saved for buying a house. They know they are frequently targets for the anger and frustration of the people they are trying to help. The pressure for success is intense.

For some, the frustrations arise mainly from the technical challenges. For example, several IVF physicians told us that the single most difficult aspect of their work was the situation where they were not able to retrieve any eggs. It means that something went wrong in the process of monitoring hormone response. They feel more responsible at that point. It also seems more final than when a woman at least has some eggs that can be fertilized, even if she does not get pregnant on a given cycle.

Often the nurse coordinator of an IVF program is the one who is most intensely involved with couples. Joan is one such nurse; she has been part of a busy IVF center for two years. She described her role in the program:

> I get involved with every couple. It's hard not to, because the nurse is the person they see every single day. I'm the constant in the whole process. I'm the "good news, bad news" person. Everything goes through me. I see them every morning following their ultrasound and talk with them on the phone every evening with the results and instructions. I'm available at home if they need to call me for any reason.
>
> Yes, you do get wrapped up in it. It's very hard for me to call a patient with a negative pregnancy test. Emotionally it's the most difficult part of the job. But then there's the elation of calling those women who have a positive pregnancy test. I think I

experience the same kind of emotional roller coaster they are experiencing because I want so much for it to be successful for every couple.

One of the toughest situations for people working in these programs is when their efforts are frustrated by a change of heart, such as the surrogate mother who decided to keep the baby, the woman who was so nauseated during her pregnancy following AID that she decided to have an abortion, or the IVF patient who went through hormone treatments only to refuse to undergo the laparoscopy because she had already experienced so much failure in her life and was afraid to fail again.

Professionals who work in surrogacy or AID programs are less troubled than IVF staff people by the difficulty of achieving a pregnancy. They are matching up two people who have no known fertility problems, and therefore they ordinarily see high rates of pregnancy. Their frustrations are more with the logistics of making the match—recruiting sperm donors and coordinating their schedules with the recipient women's cycles, or finding women who would be good surrogate mothers.

Programs that carefully screen surrogate mothers are caught in the difficult situation of needing women and yet sending many applicants away. The staff members feel stressed by the responsibility of making sure no one is hurt. Being in a situation for which there is little precedent also creates stress, as noted by Dorie McArthur, a psychologist who works with a surrogacy program:

> The hardest part is that every week we consider an ethical, legal, philosophical, social issue for which there is no answer in any book. We're just ordinary human beings in this world, trying to figure out how to do it in a way that won't backfire. If it does backfire, what will the repercussions be? When do we take the risk and when do we not?

How do staff members deal with the stress? IVF programs, in particular, have informal supports for the team members. They take breaks between cycles, rely on the social worker or psychologist on the team to provide help, or they find contacts with other programs. One nurse coordinator found relief from the stress and pressures of her job by phoning a woman who had the same job at a different IVF clinic. She said:

> For a year, we were best friends on the phone. It was so great because we could really support each other. Her pregnancies really helped me when we had none. And when she was down, when she went through a real grief, a real dry spell, then my pregnancies helped her.

For some, the ability to keep going comes from the patients and their own inner strength. Another nurse said:

> When I have to give bad news, they feel almost as bad for me as I do for them, so it's more of an "Oh, my God, what are we going to do?" feeling. They know I'm feeling bad. I also do a lot of blocking—that's my defense mechanism, and a lot of joking. Laughter is my way out instead of crying.

Do these professionals feel they are special, that they are involved in creating life? For some, there is a thrill in making new life possible. They feel a special tie to the children, maintaining a long-term relationship like that of an aunt or uncle. A lawyer who runs a surrogate agency described the satisfaction he derives from his work:

> There's such a fulfillment when you hand that baby over from the surrogate to the couple. It does feel like I'm part of creating life. You just look back and think these people had absolutely nothing till they came to us, and look what we've given them. It's something you just don't get in the practice of law. In practicing law you might get someone a bigger settlement, but in a few weeks it's going to be spent or put in the bank. That's nothing to compare with making a family.

Other professionals say they think about their work as being just like any other form of medicine. The director of an IVF program claimed that the procedure has received too much attention:

> It is a normal treatment of infertility, and if you do it every day, it becomes a part of your daily work. We're not creating life, we're just making it possible for two germ cells to meet where otherwise they might not meet. It's just a normal extension of nature.

When we asked people who work with alternative methods what they like best about their work, the two dimensions—driven scientist and caring professional—appeared often. For some, it was the prestige of finding a new technique or the challenge of overcoming a difficult technical problem. For others, it was the excitement of a woman becoming pregnant. In the words of one doctor:

> What's the most satisfying part? Oh, my God, that's easy. Easy— the joy of those people.

Effects on the Family

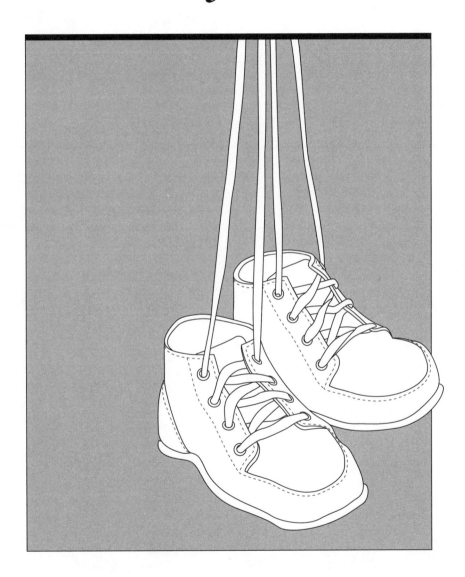

CHAPTER 9

The Couple

Infertility tested our relationship to the limit and strengthened it immeasurably. Of course we have had our fights. We grieved together and separately, but I feel we are stronger for it.

This man's comment is typical of the many we heard from infertile people. In different words, with different details, they all told us of the tremendous strain their relationships had endured. The negative feelings seemed most overwhelming for those who were still in the midst of the struggle to get pregnant. Those who had completed their ordeal—who had adopted, were expecting or already had a child, or had decided to stop trying—expressed the most positive views. They had a strong sense of having overcome the difficulties.

The experience of infertility profoundly challenges a couple's relationship. The very survival of a marriage may depend on a husband and wife's ability to meet this challenge together.

Helen and Dave tried IVF twice and are now waiting with excitement for a surrogate mother to deliver a baby for them. Dave described how much their lives had changed since the simple and carefree time when they were first married:

> We were just going along and having a good time. We had a lot of friends and we were both excited about our work. When we realized that we might not be able to have a child, everything fell apart. For years after, it seemed like every thought, every word, was focused on what we had to do to get Helen pregnant.
>
> It's very difficult for me to imagine that anything else could happen that would require more of us than what we've been through over these last five years. We found out just how much we need each other. We are a team. Our marriage is strong. We did it!

135

Helen explains why it was so difficult:

> Sometimes I wondered if we were going to get through this as a couple, and sometimes I wondered if I was going to survive at all. The years seemed endless. Sex became a burden, and there were so many procedures that were painful, tiring, and expensive. At times I felt I was going crazy with depression. Dave tried to be supportive, but from the beginning, the emotional intensity was much less for him that it was for me.
>
> I finally came to understand that he just didn't experience it the way I did, so now I accept that difference. And he tried to understand my feelings—the disappointment, and the guilt I felt for being jealous when friends got pregnant. By the time we made the decision to try *in vitro*, we had worked out a lot and turned into a pretty good team. I think we will be better parents for it.

Stresses on the Couple

It is the rare couple who experiences infertility without some strain on their relationship. There are many reasons for this stress—the emotional ups and downs from month to month, the financial drain, the distortion of lovemaking into scheduled baby making, and the tremendous physical risks taken by the women.

The financial demands alone can take their toll, as people give up so many other things they want or need in order to spend their money on physicians and lawyers. Some women quit their jobs to be available for treatments, reducing the family income at a time when expenses are greater. Some people resent the high costs of treatment because getting pregnant seems to be "free" for everyone else. They are also angry at the insurance companies that will not cover their treatment, claiming that it is not medically necessary.

Resentment, anger, and feelings of deprivation can undermine a relationship. The same is true for low self-esteem. Individuals who do not feel good about themselves find it hard to be loving and to be loved in turn. A woman who has undergone AIH unsuccessfully for a year wrote:

> Probably the worst effect infertility has had on our marriage is that it made me an incredibly serious and depressed person. My husband is having a hard time living with this new me—we used to have so much fun together.

For many couples, the dramatic swing from despair to hope and back to despair again is hardest to deal with. Many people described this as a roller coaster, from which they cannot get off until they are successful.

Once a couple decides to attempt an alternative, they must go through procedures that are often rigorous and demanding. The testing, the timing, the visits to the doctor, the waiting for results all put tremendous stress on a couple attempting to be supportive of each other. One social worker at an IVF program said that some couples find that the procedure puts too much strain on their relationship, and they quit after one attempt. Other couples may need time away from the program to work out their differences or seek marriage counseling before trying again.

Infertility is often discovered early in a marriage, before couples have ever needed to work out how to cope with a crisis. Sometimes couples have difficulty knowing how to give each other support. The woman may find her husband preoccupied and unsupportive, and he may be angry and frustrated about not being able to make her feel better or to find a solution to their problem.

Even when anger is not an issue, even when a couple has had a close relationship, they are still two individuals whose responses to infertility are bound to be different from each other. It is impossible for two people to feel the same way at the same time. Grief is a lonely process, and even the most loving partner cannot know all the other's feelings or make the guilt and depression go away. One woman who had been trying to conceive for five years wrote:

> I cried, and my husband couldn't understand why I was so upset, so I cried more! A vicious cycle!

Another woman who has been infertile for ten years told us:

> I try to be understanding, and I do think I understand much more now than I did when we first went into this process. But I also feel that I don't have a lot of energy left over to be real supportive of him. I gotta hold myself together, too. He's worked very hard to keep his feelings down and I'm afraid he's just never going to work through it. But I can't do much more; I can't do it for him. He has to handle it his own way.

Infertility is not an event that occurs and then slowly recedes into the past, like most losses. It is an ongoing, recurring loss, one that forces couples to make many decisions at a time when their relationship is already strained. They must choose at various times whether to stop or continue. Should they get another opinion? Can they afford another round of IVF? Is it worth going for one more test, one more month of Pergonal? Can they live with having another woman bear their child? Which adoption agency might give them the quickest results? When they disagree about the best direction to take, they must work hard to resolve the conflict.

So often these stresses are faced in isolation. Family and friends often cannot understand or do not know how to be supportive. Partners are forced to turn to each other for most, if not all, of their support. It is a heavy burden for them to help each other while feeling so vulnerable. One man wrote us reflecting on how much better he felt after finally talking with others who are infertile:

> It has been a painful growing experience. We handled the first two years alone, confiding in few people. Only recently have we realized how well we had managed an issue that many find almost intolerable. Despite many hurting moments, we are closer than ever.

Men and Women: Different Responses

There appear to be sharp distinctions between the way most men and most women react to the crisis of infertility. Many individuals see the conflicts in their relationship as arising from their own or their partner's personal failings. Yet there is a common pattern of male-female differences that often puts further stress on a couple. Researchers have concluded that women generally appear to be more distressed and preoccupied by infertility than are men.[1]

The way in which men and women cope with their feelings, for instance, tends to be different. Very often the men withdraw while the women prefer to talk. One woman, for example, talked about how busy her husband would become at the difficult times during their struggles with infertility:

> The day we heard that the IVF didn't work, my husband threw himself into a community project. He really needed to do that so badly because he is very threatened by my feelings of loss. He can be supportive for a while, but then he always backs away and gets angry when I cry.

One man described his way of dealing with the tension. Instead of withdrawing emotionally, he would try to joke about the situation. He said:

> The most difficult part, I think, was supporting her. She was the one who was feeling the most physical and emotional stress. I tried to make it better by being as silly as possible because it was an absolutely absurd situation going through all this stuff. Somehow I knew that silliness was not what she wanted, but it was the only way I could deal with the IVF procedure.

Women are more likely to talk to others about what they are going through. They are more likely to organize and attend support groups.

When we placed notices in local and national RESOLVE newsletters asking for people who would share their experiences with us, every one of the eighty-five letters we received was written by a woman.

A woman is also more likely than a man to want to discuss marital conflicts with her spouse. For example, one woman said:

> He really doesn't want to talk to me about what we are going through. When we start to talk to each other we end up yelling. We resolved that by talking only very briefly. When I suggested we see a therapist he would say, "I'm a boy, boys don't need this." I think that's his way of backing out. I know he feels terribly guilty because it is his infertility problem. I felt I would go crazy if I didn't talk to someone.

The difference between men and women in feelings about secrecy can be another particularly difficult source of trouble. This difference is especially hard on a woman who needs to talk but feels she must comply with her husband's wishes to keep their infertility problems a secret. In our research, most couples said they agree with each other about whether to tell others of their experiences. Some couples, however, particularly those who used AID, found this to be a problem. Generally, the men were more likely to want to keep everything secret.[2] A woman whose baby was conceived with AID explained:

> My husband insisted we tell no one about the AID procedure, and that was very hard for me. I felt that, in trying AID, I would be carrying another man's sperm, and if the process worked, I would be living with a "lie" the rest of my life. I finally broke down and told a close friend. It felt like I was releasing an enormous pressure from my mind.

Another couple found secrecy an issue between them when using a surrogate mother. The wife said, "I didn't feel as much a need of confidentiality with the surrogate as my husband felt. He was really worried about any contact with her."

We found only one instance in our research where a woman said she wanted to keep her infertility a secret and her husband disagreed. The husband explained, "My wife felt a need to be more secretive about the treatments. As she was diagnosed as having the infertility, she was more sensitive than I."

In most cases where there is a difference in opinion about infertility issues between husbands and wives, it is the husbands' wishes that prevail. Judith Lorber, a sociologist who specializes in the study of health care and gender issues, writes that in our society men's wishes tend to win out in all areas of decision making around fertility. For instance, she cites a study of childless couples in which it was found that if the husband wanted a child and the wife did not, they usually divorced. But if the wife wanted a child and the husband did not, they tended to stay together and not have children.[3]

Not only do men's opinions usually prevail, but as one social worker remarks, many women said they would cover up for their husbands' infertility, saying that the problem was their own. If they had previously told friends that the infertility was their husband's problem, and then they used AID, they would change the scenario to protect their husbands. A woman who wrote to RESOLVE expressed her bitterness about having to cover up her husband's infertility by letting others think that she was the one with a problem:

> I was trying to get away from responding to infertility like a case of "cooties," something you feel compelled to pin on "the other guy." So even though I knew my sexual identity was intact, it felt like a hollow reassurance. I seemed to be the only one who knew this. . . . If everyone else sees you as infertile, it is hard not to react as though you are.[4]

Another woman wrote to RESOLVE about the difficulties she was experiencing because her husband wanted no one to know that he had had a vasectomy during a previous marriage. The cover-up even affected the woman's relationship to her own mother, who felt guilty about her daughter's supposed infertility.[5]

Why are women more likely to cover up for men? According to psychologist Dr. Ellen Herrenkohl, "It's more acceptable for a woman to admit to having a problem. When couples come to me for marital counseling and circumstances require that one spouse be identified as the patient, it is almost always the woman who volunteers."

This is particularly true when the problem is infertility since, in males, fertility is often confused with virility. One husband who has a Ph.D. in biochemistry offered an explanation:

> Society has sterility and impotence all mixed up. Who should understand the difference between sterility and impotence better than I, but my first reaction to learning I was sterile was that I must be impotent. I should know better, but that was my first thought.

Male infertility may also disrupt the unspoken assumption of the man's dominance in a relationship, giving the woman more power than either of them feels comfortable with. Some wives even say they feel guilty about being "whole" when their husbands are not. There are accounts of women actually ceasing to ovulate when AID treatment begins. Do they feel, whether consciously or unconsciously, that they are supposed to be the ones who are infertile, especially since that is what everyone else assumes? Does her assuming the responsibility for infertility restore the previous state of power between them?

Inequalities

A couple's infertility is further complicated by unavoidable inequalities that add to the male-female differences. Every element of the process—the diagnosis, the treatment, the commitment to keep trying, and in many cases the genetic connection to the child—affects the two people in different ways. Inevitably this imbalance also affects their relationship.

Diagnosis

Most often only one partner in the couple is diagnosed as having the infertility problem. Couples can agree that infertility is not anyone's "fault," but it is difficult to avoid bad feelings on both sides. For many people, parenthood is part of their expectation from marriage. It is hard for the fertile person not to resent a partner who has in some sense not lived up to his or her part of this implied pact. The affected spouse, on the other hand, often feels guilty and inadequate, convinced of having deprived his or her spouse and having failed the marriage.

The fertile partner is usually relieved at first not to be responsible. He or she may try to be reassuring. As one man said:

> I kept telling her I still loved her just as much, that I married
> her for herself and not for the kids she would have.

The inequality of diagnosis often means that partners have to be very cautious in how they discuss their situation. They feel they must be gentle with each other, not pushing the partner with the fertility problem to do something he or she is not prepared for. This caution makes decision making more complicated, sometimes leading the fertile partner to resort to subtle pressures. In one study of couples seeking AID, the authors made this interesting observation:

> Most often it is the husband who makes the first sugges-
> tion [to try AID], possibly because in the majority of cases the
> problem is felt to be particularly his. As far as the woman is
> concerned, she is afraid of hurting him or provoking some un-
> expected reaction by broaching the subject of AID. . . . [But] we
> often had the impression that the wife had done everything in
> her power to persuade the husband to suggest AID.[6]

Commitment

Usually women appear to be the most committed to finding a solution for infertility. It has traditionally been considered a woman's problem, and the woman is defined as the patient. Most women are the activists in pursuing alternatives. They do the work, they make the connections, they undergo the tests and treatments. They are identified as needing children the most. It does not matter that the man's condition may be the reason for infertility—the woman is the one who must get pregnant.

Yet in the background we can often detect the subtle but real pressure by the men. It is the men who most often resist the idea of adoption, who want most to have a genetically related child. It is for the men that many women are pursuing a pregnancy, to have "his" child.[7]

Men and women both usually confirmed the view that women are most involved in seeking treatment. One man who has a child from a surrogate said:

> My wife was the one; she was the driving force. Put "force" in capital letters.

Most professionals whom we interviewed agreed that the wife usually appears to be more involved. For example, a psychologist who screens couples for IVF believes that it is often the woman who is pushing to try the method, that the man is just going along. She explained:

> These women have a real sense of rage. They feel entitled to motherhood. This by all rights should be theirs, and it kind of excludes the men from the whole process. It's their body; it's their business. IVF is really a rigorous procedure, so the men are on the outside. There's a lot of empathy, but they just can't feel what it's like to go through all that.

The apparently greater commitment of most women fits with the popular idea that women want children most and benefit from them the most. There is another side to this picture, however. Many clues point to a more complex explanation for women's greater involvement.

An important clue is to be found in feminist analyses, which have challenged the idea that children are necessary to a woman's fulfillment. Feminist authors have emphasized how much motherhood has been an institution controlled by men for their benefit. Childbearing has had the purpose of providing heirs for men. For women, having children has meant distress and often death. It has also been used to justify women's low pay and lack of opportunities in the work force. Only by glorifying motherhood, by making a myth of how important it is to women, has it been possible to keep women producing children, even when it is the men who want them and benefit from them the most.[8]

As mothers and as feminists, we cannot agree with the view that children are only a trap for women, for we know the extraordinary pleasure they can bring. And more recent feminist writings have also recognized the value of mothering for many women.[9] But this does not negate the importance of the idea that women's desire for children and their active pursuit of fertility is at least partly instilled by the values of a male-dominated society.

Some of the women say they are driven only in part by their own desire for a child. Their commitment to finding a solution comes from guilt, from their sense of having failed as women because they cannot provide children *for their husbands*. This is expressed by a woman who had turned to a surrogate mother to have a child:

> My main emotion was guilt; I felt really guilty that I couldn't provide him with a biological child. If he had married someone else, he probably could have had biological children. Having a surrogate took care of my guilt because I paid for it from the money I had earned, and now he has his own child.

Some of the apparent differences in enthusiasm are a matter of differences in personal style between most men and women. She is emotional and involved, even obsessed, with the efforts. He is the quiet one, apparently detached. Yet he becomes terribly depressed when she gets her period, and he becomes intensely excited by a success.

A psychologist who works with infertile couples observed:

> The women tend to be more open in general. Some of the men are so controlled, reserved, cautious. Once there is a pregnancy, they just let themselves go, and even their wives are surprised. They just weren't willing to get their hopes up until it was a reality.

Some men told us they feel reluctant to encourage further treatments because they cannot stand to see their wives going through any more tests or suffering any more disappointment. It is not that they want a child any less, but they recognize that it is their wives who must endure the physical and emotional strain of treatment. Usually, then, they do not want to push too hard, agreeing to go along if she really wants to proceed.

When one partner is more committed to seeking a solution than the other—whether it be the man or the woman—this imbalance can cause serious problems. One woman whose husband was ambivalent about having a child described the result:

I desperately wanted a child, and my husband went along with doing AIH, but he really had a lot of conflicts about it. Asking him to produce a sperm specimen twice a month in the doctor's office became an unbearable chore. He just hated the whole process. We had so many fights, now I can't even tell him when I get my period. I have to hide the little wrappers from the tampons because he gets so depressed.

Treatment

No matter how united a couple is, the man is inevitably a bystander when his wife is trying to get pregnant. At best, he can be supportive. He can take the woman's urine or blood to the lab, sit with her through ultrasounds, wait for her to wake up from laparoscopies, or hold her hand during inseminations.

There is usually one task that only he can do. In the diagnosis stage and for all of the methods except AID, he must produce sperm. He must go into a bathroom in the hospital or doctor's office and masturbate into a cup.

This simple act is not so easy for many men. Women have their most private parts examined and invaded by a host of strangers, over long periods of time, yet the man's solo encounter with himself in the lavatory is fraught with discomfort. Whether because of embarrassment, religious reservations, or a strong overlay of performance anxiety, our interviews were filled with awkward joking about this one aspect of the treatment. A man whose sperm was used to inseminate a surrogate recalled the friendly teasing of his friends:

> There was a point where we thought it might be twins and some of our friends started calling me "mega-sperm." They would joke around and ask how it feels and I would say, "Oh, it's all in the wrist."

For women, resentment may arise from this imbalance in involvement. One woman recalled:

> It was his problem, but they did very little to him. They turned to me and did a whole bunch of tests just to double check if everything was okay. It doesn't seem fair.

Another woman had been through one cycle of IVF and was being encouraged by her husband to try it again. Her response:

> It's easy for a man to say, "Let's do it again"—they don't have to go through it!

Women who go through IVF for male infertility may have the most cause for resentment. After all, they are presumably healthy. Yet they become the patients, undergoing powerful and potentially harmful drug treatments, daily ultrasounds, and sometimes surgery under general anesthesia in an effort to have "his child."

Many women did not express these feelings. They accepted the difficulties and stresses as necessary to achieve their goal. It had to be done, they felt, and would all be worthwhile if they could only have a baby.

Parenting

When deciding to try a technique that requires using a donor, there are many more issues of inequality for a couple to consider. A social worker at a fertility program explained:

> The most complex component is that one person is the biological parent and the other is not; so they start off on an unequal footing even before the birth of the child. They have to resolve with each other what the meaning of being parents is and the difference between biological and social parenting and how they feel about this inequality in biological parenting.

When couples talked with us about this imbalance, they expressed strong feelings and widely differing opinions. One woman said:

> I would rather do AID and have a donor than adopt—at least it's half of ours.

Other people expressed the opposite point of view. They felt they could not deal with the imbalance. It would create too many problems either for themselves or for the child. One man explained his decision:

> I want it to be our child biologically or not our child biologically, not half. I don't want to feel involved in something where my wife wouldn't be. I'd rather wait for a new technology that might come along while we are still in our childbearing years that would allow us both to be biologically connected.

In many cases, infertility occurs in second marriages. If one partner already has children, and the other one would like to have a child with the new spouse, the imbalance between the two can be very painful. A letter in the *RESOLVE Newsletter* describes the strain this can create:

> I resent my stepchildren and the relationship my husband has with "his" children, and I no longer feel like a couple dealing with grieving the dream child. I feel as if my husband is the

person I've always avoided when I felt weak . . . the person who
has children. . . . He can pick up the phone anytime and talk with
"his" children. I feel very alone.[10]

Several women whose husbands had children from previous marriages wrote to us expressing similar feelings of insecurity, isolation, and
resentment. One woman said she just could not believe that her husband
was as interested in trying to have a child as she was: "No matter what
happens, he still has kids. I don't."

Effects of Stress

The stresses of infertility and of the treatments may affect every aspect of a couple's relationship. They may have a profound impact, for
example, on a couple's sex life. The physical and emotional strain of treatment, as well as the depression that accompanies failure, often reduces
interest in sex. Sex is no longer a spontaneous expression of love and
desire—it becomes a planned, charted, and highly charged activity with
the goal of conception. Dr. Wulf Utian, director of an IVF program, writes
that "the fantasied presence of the gynecologist in the bedroom directing
the sexual activity of the couple" can destroy any desire for intimacy.[11]

Utian also observed, as have other researchers, that a couple's problems may lead the husband or wife to have an affair. He concludes that
some people may be trying to test their fertility with other partners.

Infertility can affect a sexual relationship in another way. For instance, psychiatrist David Berger studied sixteen men diagnosed as having
a very low or absent sperm count and discovered that eleven of them
became impotent for several months following the diagnosis.[12]

So many stresses, so many problems. Do they lead to divorce? Occasionally, when the struggle is just too difficult. The husband and wife
are simply too far apart in their motivation, their commitment and their
feelings, and they cannot find a way to bridge the gap.

Some couples need a therapist to help them resolve their differences.
They may need someone to help them communicate the feelings that they
have been afraid to share—the fears of abandonment, the ambivalence
about trying again and again.

For others, going to RESOLVE meetings is a helpful step. One man
said:

> I was surprised to see other people in the same situation
> as us and many having even more problems. I realized other
> women could be very emotional, just like my wife, and saw how
> people can help each other.

Success is a strong antidote to stress. Couples who told us that their relationship was in trouble were likely to be still trying to have a child. Those who had succeeded in having a child, whether through adoption or one of the alternative methods, generally felt much better about themselves and about their marriages. People who had reconciled themselves to not having a child also experienced happier relationships.

One woman who adopted a child after a long bout with infertility and pregnancy loss wrote:

> The adoption has reunited us and made us a real family, not two frustrated housemates. I truly believe that the old saw, "Children can't save a marriage," is bullshit. Without our daughter, our marriage was headed for the garbage heap. We couldn't have lived together much longer without a child to love.

Children do not always save a marriage. In fact, some therapists have observed that couples who finally do have or adopt a child then break up. The stress has been too much, and the child cannot "solve" the problems that have festered for so long. Sometimes the couple has gotten used to a childless lifestyle and after so many years cannot adjust to the major changes a child brings. Or the child they have dreamed about and worked so hard for may fall short of the perfect baby of their fantasies.[13]

Most couples do survive, however, with or without children. They claim that their relationship is stronger than ever, that their partners' love made it possible to survive so much trauma. Many comments from people we interviewed reflected this process of change and growth. As one woman said:

> It may be a cliché to say adversity has strengthened our marriage, but I think it probably has. We went through everything together. We have bonds and trusts that other people don't have. We know how to deal with each other's disappointments and have learned that, despite all our problems, we are very fortunate. We know our children are miracles, and we're so grateful.

CHAPTER 10

High-Tech Children

*These are very much wanted children. These kids, you know,
are dropped from heaven. I wonder how that's going to
affect them.*

—Mother of a child conceived through IVF

Will being so special—the "miracle babies" who came after years
of infertility—create problems for these children? Perhaps they will not
have any special difficulties. It is possible, though, that their parents will
overprotect them or worry excessively about their health. Such children
may find it hard to live up to everyone's expectations. Perhaps they will
be teased by their friends about coming out of a test tube.

When a donor is involved, the repercussions for the children are
likely to be even more complicated. How much should they be told? How
will they feel about having a "third parent"? Should they have any contact
with the donor?

It is not surprising that the parents of "high-tech children" are uncertain about the answers to these questions. No one really knows the
long-term effects of the alternative methods. We will not know what they
are for many years, since almost all of the thousands of children born from
IVF and surrogate mothers are still very young and almost no research at
all exists on these questions. We know very little even about the tens and
probably hundreds of thousands of children born through AID who have
already reached adulthood, because of the lack of follow-up studies. We
know nothing about the future of children born from IVF with donated
eggs or sperm, or those who were carried and given life by grandmothers
or aunts, since these are still relatively uncommon. With no information
on the potential dangers (or benefits), these children must be considered
part of a massive social experiment for which they have not volunteered
and which is not even being evaluated.

When prospective parents think about the risks of the new alterna-

148

tives, their immediate concern is with the physical risks—the health of the child—rather than with long-term psychological effects. They have realistic fears that egg or sperm donors may harbor unknown diseases, such as AIDS. The idea of conception in a test tube arouses fears of mix-ups in the laboratory or some scientific mishap. Some prospective parents are concerned that a surrogate may not be taking good care of herself during the pregnancy.

The data that exist so far show that children born of AID and IVF are generally healthy, although some experts worry about both the short and long-term effects of these methods. What might be the effect of drilling ova for insemination, or of freezing and then thawing embryos? High rates of prematurity and multiple birth with IVF, and the risks of damage from use of superovulatory hormones and repetitive ultrasonography are reason for concern about the health of these children.[1] There are no studies yet on the health of children born to surrogate mothers, but neither is there any reason to expect that they will differ from other children.

Special Problems for the Children

Once a child is born and appears to be healthy, the parents begin to think more about the psychological issues. With hardly any information to guide them, how are they to know what is best for their child? What insights we have are gleaned primarily from the literature on the adoption experience, which, although not the same as the methods discussed here, is concerned with many similar issues for the children. Adoption is obviously most like the methods that involve donors. However, even children who are born from AIH or IVF and who are related genetically to both parents may face some of the same problems as adoptees. In most of these situations, the children are part of their families because of their parents' infertility. Their future is very much affected by the parents' ability to resolve this part of their lives comfortably.

A number of researchers have claimed that adoptees exhibit more emotional problems and are more likely to seek therapy than non-adoptees. This appears to be particularly true once they are of school age; studies of young adopted children and their families show either no differences or even better adjustment than in families of nonadopted children.[2]

Evidence of problems has been attributed by some to the fact of adoption. Others disagree on the reason, suggesting that adoptive families may simply be more comfortable asking for professional help. Some psychologists also point out that if adopted children do have more problems, it is probably not because of the adoption itself but because of the stigmatizing reaction of others or because of poor communication in the family. Both parents and children may use adoption as an extra "weapon" in the normal parent-child struggles.[3] Arthur Sorosky, Annette Baran, and Reuben Pannor, authors of *The Adoption Triangle*, agree that the impression of adoptees as having major problems is exaggerated, but they point out that pitfalls do exist:

> Although we would agree . . . that it is wrong to blame all the adoptees' problems on the adoption experience, there is evidence to suggest that adopted children have unique areas of vulnerability. Adoptive parents must be acutely aware of their children's special needs. . . .[4]

What are these "unique areas of vulnerability," these "special needs"? One important concern for many adopted children is the feeling that they are not the parents' first choice. Psychologist Dr. Ellen Herrenkohl, for instance, says that adoptees with whom she has worked often exhibit an excessive need to please their parents and fears of being rejected by them. When there is not a genetic tie to the parent, she explains, the child may feel that it would be possible to "give him or her back," that the connection to the parents is not eternal and unconditional.

Adopted children are often told that they are extra special because they were "chosen." Yet, according to Betty Jean Lifton, author of *Lost and Found: The Adoption Experience*, "chosen baby" stories are more upsetting than reassuring. She writes:

> Many adoptees have told me that the stories made them feel twice rejected: by the natural parents who didn't keep them, and by the adoptive parents who couldn't have a baby of their own. Being *chosen* meant being second best.[5]

The reality is that most parents *would* have greatly preferred to have a child the "normal" way. Adoption or IVF or AID was not their first choice, but something they turned to when their efforts to conceive failed. This is not necessarily a problem for the child unless the parents have not accepted their infertility and see the child as a constant reminder of failure.

Smith and Miroff, authors of *You're Our Child: A Social Psychological Approach to Adoption*, comment about their research on adoptive families: "The ease with which the child fully accepts his adoptedness is directly related to the degree of success the adoptive parents have achieved in accepting their own status of adoptive parents." They add that the parents who talk too much or not at all about adoption, who are unable to handle a friend's pregnancy, or who are "struggling with fantasies of how their own biological children might have looked or behaved" will communicate to the child a feeling that something is wrong. These observations apply not only to adoption but to families who have used the new methods of conception as well.[6]

Some parents, for example, form an excessively protective relationship with the child. Having waited so long and being so aware of the preciousness of this child, they cannot let him or her out of their sight. One woman, in a rather extreme situation, tied red ribbons between herself and her daughter and never left her side.

People who have children after so many years of effort often have unrealistic expectations of themselves as parents. They cannot imagine complaining about the daily hassles, for they are going to be perfect parents. This can cause a great deal of strain for them and the child. After all, "miracle babies" spit up and cry at night and have temper tantrums just like any other kids.

The parents may also have unreasonably high expectations of the child. This child, born of science as well as intense devotion, can hardly turn out to be average. Their expectations of children may be even greater with AID, because the donors are chosen from highly intelligent, successful men. The reality is that the children may (or may not) be more accomplished than the parents, but they are unlikely to achieve the level of the most brilliant biological father.

The child may also have impossibly high expectations of him- or herself. After all, the parents suffered and worked hard to have him or her. They spent a lot of money, devoted all their energies to becoming parents, and dreamed about the wonderful child they would have. The child may feel that he or she has to be perfect to satisfy the parents.

On the other side, if a third party was involved, it becomes easy to explain undesirable behavior as coming from "bad blood." "Surely she couldn't have gotten that from me!" the parent may say. Even normal misbehavior can be construed as a problem, one that was inherited from someone else. When the donor is unknown, such thoughts are more likely to occur.

In most cases of adoption, the child imagines a birth mother who was young and poor and became pregnant carelessly outside of marriage. She could not even take care of her own child. As a result, adoptees often feel ashamed of their origins and, as adolescents, may act out with rebellious and, ironically, promiscuous behavior.[7]

A surrogate mother, in contrast, did not create the child by accident. She is likely to be married and can be presented as a generous person who wanted to help the parents. Yet questions will certainly still exist in the child's mind. How could she have given him or her away just for money? What kind of cold-blooded person could she be? Not the adoptive child's fantasy of an immoral or poverty-stricken mother, but surely a concern about whether the mother cared more about money than about the child.

A child born of AID reflected a similar feeling about the role of money in her conception, as quoted in a study by Davis and Brown:

> I wanted to know how he could have sold what was the essence of my life for $25 to a total stranger, then walk away without a second thought. . . . Why couldn't he connect the semen to the human being it would create?[8]

Children as well as the parents who raise them often wonder what traits they may have inherited from the donor or birth parent. This opens the door for children and parents to fantasize. One adoptee quoted in *How It Feels to Be Adopted* reminds us that there can be very positive sides to the fantasies:

> The best thing about being adopted is that I can have wonderful fantasies about my birth mother. And if you're a dreamer, which I can be, your mother can become anyone you want her to be. I happen to like opera a lot, so for a while my real mother was Maria Callas. She was such a strange and wonderful lady, and I thought it was neat to have such a bizarre and exotic mother.[9]

A child born from one of the new methods is different from an adoptee in at least one important way—he or she is usually genetically related to at least one parent. This may be an advantage over adoption, since the child will feel connected to part of his or her family heritage. It may also present problems for the family, however, if it becomes the source of power struggles between the parents. In almost all two-parent families, there is an imbalance of power. It is also normal for children to favor Mom sometimes and Dad other times. The danger in families that use alternative methods is that common situations will be interpreted as having genetic meaning, creating unnecessary anxieties. One woman who had a child from AID gave an example:

> There are times when I feel my husband is not taking his full share of responsibility for our child. This conflict would probably have arisen no matter what the circumstances of conception, but I wonder sometimes if my husband feels his son is more mine than his.

Many people who are trying to conceive already have one or more children. These children could also have special problems with their parents' infertility. They may feel the anguish of their parents' ordeal, sometimes assuming—as children do—that it is their fault. A woman whose son was six when she started infertility treatments recalled:

> He started having panic attacks, and I was so concerned, I took him to a psychiatrist who helped him verbalize his feelings.

It turns out he thought we were angry at him, that it was his fault. He even asked me if giving life to him had ruined me so I could no longer have any more children!

If a sibling does arrive, will the usual rivalry be worse because of the circumstances? Will this very special new child seem to the older sibling to be more wanted, more loved?

Although the parents may feel very comfortable handling any problems that arise within their family, they may still fear that disapproval by others will hurt their children. The popular view assumes that a child is best off with his or her biological parents. Often-heard phrases such as "Blood is thicker than water," "Is she your own?" or "Is that your 'real' mother?" convey this message.[10]

Approximately one in every one hundred Americans (and 2% of all children under eighteen) were adopted by nonrelatives; in addition, many children live with parents who are not genetically related to them.[11] There is still a "cultural lag," however; most people's values have not caught up with the reality. Our society still holds on to the norm of a "traditional" nuclear family, a norm that no doubt affects the many children who do not fit the ideal model.

The Search

Adopted children often report a need to know their origins, to know they weren't "dropped from heaven" or "hatched in a social agency." One thirteen-year-old year quoted in *What It Feels Like to Be Adopted* said:

> Adopted kids . . . need to know where they came from, instead of thinking that they just appeared on this earth from outer space . . . everyone goes through an identity crisis at one time or another and everyone needs to know where he or she came from. As soon as I searched and found the information I was looking for I felt more worthwhile in the world—as though I belonged better. Beforehand, a part of me had always been missing. . . .[12]

No matter how good adoptive parents (or the parents who have used alternative conceptions involving third parties) are in relating to their children, the children will always have some normal curiosity about their origins. This interest surfaces at major turning points in their lives, such as during adolescence. It may subside after that, but later life crises often reawaken the yearning for their roots. Marriage, pregnancy and parenting, death of an adoptive parent, and the presumed old age and possible death of the birth parents are all reminders of the adoptees' separation from their genetic heritage.

Many times adoptees who seek information about their origins realize that the parents are uncomfortable with their questions, and they learn
it is better not to ask. This lack of openness can only create further problems. One adopted woman quoted in *The Adoption Triangle* talked about
this issue:

> I was very curious about my birth parents, but felt that my
> adoptive parents became angry because I wanted to know more.
> They felt they had failed me because of my curiosity.[13]

Questions about origins can be threatening to the adoptive parents. Yet
studies suggest that reunions between adoptees and birth parents lead to
even better relationships with the adoptive parents.[14]

A major theme in the adoption literature is "the search." Adoptees
often respond to their need for a biological connection and concerns
about identity by looking for the birth mother. This has been extremely
difficult, since the laws and adoption agency policies, and sometimes the
adoptive parents, put obstacles in their way. Yet the desire for reunion
persists on both sides, and the courts and adoption agencies have recently
started to pay attention to this need and consider revising their policies.

It is interesting that female adoptees are more likely to search than
males, and mothers are more accepting of a search than fathers. The
search is almost always for the birth mother. As in so many other areas
of social life, it is the women who are forging the connections that link
them together.[15]

We expect that children born to surrogate mothers will also want to
find the women who gave birth to them, even though one genetic parent
is known. They will engage in a search for the same reasons adoptees do,
to know about their origins and to meet the women who carried them and
gave them away. They may be at an advantage compared to most adoptees, since the adoptive parents ordinarily have much more information
on birth mothers who were surrogates, and no laws require the sealing
of records. How easy it will be depends, however, on the wishes of their
parents and the policy of the particular surrogacy program.

Most surrogacy programs act as a go-between for couples and surrogates whenever they want to have information about each other. This
gives the possibility for updates on medical information and can be a way
to locate each other at a later date. One program in California requires
that changes of address be sent to it by both parties for eighteen years
after the birth. There are no guarantees, of course, that this information
will be sent to the programs or even that the programs will survive.

Some surrogate mothers may search out the child themselves, as
birth mothers of adopted children are doing increasingly. No matter who
initiates the search, there is a strong likelihood that many surrogates and

the children to whom they gave birth will meet each other. Egg donors, in contrast, are much less involved in the child's creation than a surrogate mother. Some want to maintain contact with the children; others consider their donation to be like AID—short term and impersonal.

The likelihood of AID children meeting their genetic fathers is very remote. Even if they do find out about the conception, so few physicians keep records that it is usually impossible to trace the donor. Yet some adults conceived by AID are searching anyway, resorting to medical school yearbooks and attempting to obtain information from the physician. The government of Sweden passed a law requiring that records be kept of sperm donors and recommending that the children be told when they reach eighteen. Some American experts have urged that records of at least the donor's characteristics and medical history be kept and made available to the children, but it is unlikely that this will happen soon.[16]

When Sorosky and colleagues examined the outcome of hundreds of reunions between adult adoptees and their birth parents, they were impressed with the intense emotional quality of the search and the benefits of its success:

> For a human being who has been unnaturally separated from his/her origins, the reunion with a birth parent is an integral event in his/her life. . . . The reunion provides a bridge to the adoptee's beginnings and answers questions about the past and present. Whether the outcome of the reunion fulfills fantasies is not so important as the fact that it gives the adoptee, finally, a feeling of wholeness.[17]

The Child's Relationship to the Donor or Surrogate Mother

Surrogacy raises the additional dilemma of what kind of relationship the family will have, if any, with the woman who gave birth to this child. Should she be like a favorite aunt who visits on holidays, a close friend of the family, or a more distant figure? What will be best for the parents? What will be best for the children?

One possible model is "open adoption," which has been an important response to the difficult search experiences of so many birth mothers and adoptees. In open adoption, the adoptive couple may meet the birth mother, often prior to the birth, and continue a relationship of some kind after the adoption, or they may correspond with each other through the agency.[18]

Some variations on this approach have been followed by many couples who hire a woman to carry a baby for them. In some cases, the adoptive parents and the birth mothers have maintained contact, and the children have already met their biological mothers once or several times. This may also occur with egg or sperm donors who were picked by the parents.

An ongoing relationship between child and birth parent could be very positive, or it could cause problems. The birth mother or surrogate may be in a position of competing with the adoptive mother for the child's attention, or she may disagree about how the child should be raised. This may be particularly true when the donor parent is also a family member. The adoptive mother is vulnerable to feeling insecure in this situation because she has not given birth to the child. One father of a boy born to a surrogate mother told us:

> I suppose eventually he will want to meet her. I don't think you can deny the child that or the biological mother if she wants it. I don't have a problem with that. I just think it could be a little confusing for the kid.

A fifteen-year-old adopted girl quoted by Jill Krementz confirmed that knowing two mothers does have its difficult aspects:

> It's confusing because I don't know how to categorize my relationship with Alison [the birth mother]. I don't want to think of it as purely biological, but I don't know how else to define it. I feel ridiculous introducing her as my friend and yet I certainly don't think of her as my mother. . . . My birth mother's the person who gave me my heredity and my life, and while I don't want to push her away I also don't want to take anything away from my mom.[19]

A growing proportion of surrogate mothers have no genetic connection to the child at all. Embryos that grow in the laboratory through IVF are transferred to hired women who have been given hormone treatments to prepare them for pregnancy.

The situation in which the birth mother acts as "incubator" for the product of other people is still very new, and the consequences for the children are not known. How will they feel about having grown inside a stranger's body, about being birthed by a woman who saw herself as only a carrier? Perhaps they will feel less compelled to search for the "host mother" if there is no genetic connection to her. We think not. Just as these women often grieve for the babies as much as birth mothers who have a genetic tie, the children are as likely to be interested in knowing who it was that carried them and delivered them into the world.

There is no one best model for how these complex relationships should work. Every family must resolve the dilemmas in its own way.

What is most difficult is that the interests of those involved may conflict with each other. The parents, the donors, and the children may all need, or want, something very different from one another.

Telling the Child

Aware of the possibility of problems, many parents wonder if they should tell a child about his or her origins at all. Their decision depends a great deal on the particular method involved.

For people trying IVF, for instance, secrecy is not much of an issue. Everyone we surveyed who has or is trying to have a child through IVF intends to tell the child. They generally want the children to know how special they are. But they must proceed with some caution, as this mother of a child born after IVF points out:

> I want her to know what we went through so she will understand how special she is to us. But I think you can get into a bind—you don't want it to be something she has to live up to.

Couples who hired surrogate mothers were a little less sure, but they generally planned to treat the subject openly. Surrogacy is similar to adoption because of the existence of a birth mother who relinquishes the child to a couple through a legal adoptive process. Not surprisingly, most parents expect to tell their children about their birth mother in the same way professionals now advise parents to talk about adoption—gradually, openly, and early in the child's life.

The parents of children born after AIH and AID, in contast, are divided and uncertain about what to do. Couples who use AIH may feel that there is no reason to talk about the conception with a child, although one could say the same is true for IVF. For couples who use AID, telling presents the most difficult dilemma. Of all the methods, donor insemination is the only one that has been treated with so much secrecy. Hardly anyone suggests that other procedures be kept secret. Instead we hear that the child *should* know how much he or she was wanted.[20]

Why the tremendous difference in attitude? Logically, the child is *least* likely to need to know about an IVF conception where there was no donor involved, and yet this is the situation in which parents are most likely to plan to tell. The key difference seems to be that artificial insemination usually involves male infertility and that other methods usually treat female infertility. AIH, which can be used for either partner's problem, is more likely to be kept secret when used for male than for female infertility. It appears that the couples, and society as a whole, consider male infertility a much more serious stigma than female infertility. Men judge themselves and are judged by others by their ability to "perform," whether it be at work, in bed, or in producing offspring. A man who is lacking in any one of these domains feels deficient in all areas of life. This can be seen in one father's comments:

> When I told my son about his AID origins, I also said that I still have an erection, so he would know that infertility is one thing and potency something else.

Infertile mothers rarely feel compelled to explain to their adopted children that they can have orgasms. It appears that secrecy is more for the protection of the husband than for the benefit of the child. This may not even be recognized by the couple, who focus their concerns on what they judge to be the child's welfare.

It is much easier to keep AID secret than other forms of conception, and certainly easier than adoption. There is no legal transaction, and the mother has an apparently normal pregnancy and birth. The father's name is on the birth certificate, and often the attending obstetrician or midwife is unaware of the origin of the pregnancy. In addition, most physicians who offer AID and therapists who counsel prospective parents about donor insemination strongly advise the couples to maintain secrecy, never to tell the child or anyone else.[21]

The reality, however, is that many children do suspect something and are troubled by their suspicions. They notice that they have genetic characteristics that are improbable, or they observe strange glances between their parents at odd moments. They may overhear comments from others, since most couples do tell a few friends or family members. In addition, the mother's medical records may include information about AID. The potential for divulging the secret is always present. If they do find out from others, the children will learn that their parents can deceive them about something so central to their identities. If they do not find out, they will assume a medical history that is false and risk marrying incestuously.

Studies of adopted people suggest that the child's knowledge of his or her origins may indeed create problems, even turmoil. Yet they also show that a lack of complete information and understanding is even more harmful.[22] This is a harsh dilemma for parents who are committed to openness in their families yet fear the consequences of telling. One man wrote to us describing his ambivalent feelings about this question:

> Ideally, I don't want to lie to my child or deceive her by failing to tell her the whole truth. It doesn't seem right for me to decide that she doesn't need to know the truth about her conception. Yet, if I do tell her about it when she's old enough to understand, it could be too upsetting for her. After all, she

would never be able to trace the donor if she wanted to. Why cause problems unnecessarily?

Jim is a father who resolved these questions by deciding to tell his son, Michael, even though he worried about what the news would do to their relationship. He described to us his reasons for telling his son about AID and the "momentous day" when he did finally share with Michael the story of his conception:

> It was too stressful keeping this information from my boy. I don't think my wife and I ever sat down and said "We need to tell Michael. When should we tell him?" I think it was understood that it was my job, since I'm not the biological parent.
>
> I knew in his earlier years that he was too young to understand; he didn't have enough information to process what I was going to tell him. But on the other hand, I wasn't going to wait until adolescence, because then, with whatever else was going on between us, this would just be thrown in the hopper. It would be a terrible betrayal. He's ten now, and I knew it would have to happen soon. I wasn't nervous because I hadn't planned it out; it happened really spontaneously, and I will just never forget it.
>
> I was jogging in the morning and he was riding his bike along with me, and we saw a dog go by and I said, "You know, I'm really afraid of dogs." I told him there was a runner who got his testicle ripped by a dog, and Michael said, "Oh really, can that man still have children?" And I thought Okay, he knows, he's got that information. So I said, "Michael, there's something I've got to tell you." And I told him. I was running, and he was riding his bike. He wanted to know whose sperm it was. I said, "We don't know who it was, but we know that it was a medical student in New York." And we ran on a little bit, and he said, "You know, maybe that's why I want to be a doctor." And my heart leaped, because I thought that he had accepted this information in such a positive way. In a sense he was saying that he accepts the fatherhood of this other person, this abstract kind of thing.
>
> And that's how it happened. He didn't seem shocked. We've mentioned it to each other a few times since. I want to make sure he heard it. I will bring it up, not anything dramatic, from time to time, to make it regular, something reinforced, since I guess he could repress it. He doesn't say much, but he knows that on his father's side that's where he's from.
>
> I just felt so good after, I had not realized how much it took

out of me to be keeping it from him. I felt like I had completed something, I had ended a travail. I really felt a burden lifted from me. It may be one thing to say they don't need to know, but it's another to say that you as a parent don't need to share it.

More parents are beginning to share Jim's view about AID. Our study showed that somewhat more people (48%) intended to tell their child about AID than did not (39%). The remaining 13 percent were unsure, hoping to find an answer as the child grew older. Our sample is an unusual one, since most of the people are members of the RESOLVE support organization. They are people who are willing to talk about infertility. But they are likely to represent a growing trend toward more openness about infertility.

Other studies have shown that the great majority of parents do not tell their children about AID. When they have told, it has often been due to special circumstances, such as a later divorce and custody battle or when the children faced infertility themselves as adults. An important follow-up study by Snowden, Mitchell, and Snowden of English families who had used AID found only a few who had told their offspring of the AID origins, and only as adults. In each case, the mother had wanted her son to know he was not genetically related to his father. The husbands in these families were disabled, immoral, or economic failures, and the mother's revealing the AID could be seen as an act of hostility. In fact it is likely that AID information, kept secret for so many years, may be revealed in an angry environment. Dissatisfied fathers may blurt out to an unruly child, "You're not mine anyway." Studies of adoptees have found that many also were told in an angry way or at an inappropriate time, with damaging results.[23]

On the other hand, Snowden and colleagues also interviewed adults who had been told of their AID origins. They all said that they had suspected something all along, and that the telling had been a relief. They also said they felt especially important, and that their relationship to their father was enhanced by realizing what he had been through.[24]

The difficult task in telling for all parents is to make it seem natural and normal. Parents may emphasize that there are other children born in the same way. As one mother wisely commented, "The way you say it is important. You can convince a child that there is a problem if he has five toes on his foot—if you present it like it's a problem."

Psychiatrist Robert Abramovitz agrees. Speaking at a conference of the American Society of Law and Medicine, he said, "Children can handle almost any kind of information. The issue is not whether or not we tell them, but how we tell them and when we tell them." He urges that children born through AID be told because of the potential harm of family secrets. He suggests that the telling should be a part of good basic sex education:

> Telling a child "I'm not your parent" is harmful. Start with "I'm your parent," and then explain that there is more than one way to become a parent.[25]

Telling children about AID as they learn about sexuality and "the facts of life" is a reasonable approach. It is likely to avoid the confusion of a child told at a very young age and the anger of those who are not told until adolescence or adulthood. Ultimately, however, without good studies on the effects of telling and not telling, every family is left to decide for itself what is best for them.

Single Heterosexual and Gay Parents

The majority of single heterosexual and lesbian women who use AID do not keep the information secret. They would rather that others—and the child—realize that the conception was planned and wanted, not the accidental result of a casual affair. Secrecy, then, is usually not a problem, nor is the issue of genetic inequality between parents. The mothers are not worried about protecting men.

A lesbian mother of an AID baby described the relaxed attitude she intended to take in telling the child.

> I'll tell her the truth. Some women have relationships with men, and some women want to have babies and they don't want to have relations with men. Real basic terminology—the sperm and the egg story is still valid. And she'll know other children whose mothers were inseminated. We have lesbian couple friends that are having babies by insemination. So we can say, "Johnny was inseminated, too."

Many people object to AID for single or lesbian women because they believe a child born into such a situation will suffer. Yet such children are more likely to suffer from the attitudes of others than from the family environment. Existing studies do not show a negative effect on children.

Elaine Bleckman reviewed the studies of one-parent families and concluded that there are so many flaws in the studies' design that it is impossible to say that children are hurt by single parenthood. If they are, it is likely to be a result of poverty or the child's experiencing the loss of one parent through divorce or death. These problems are much less likely to exist where single women seek out AID.[26]

A positive view has also emerged from studies of children living with a gay parent or parents. They are apparently no different nor any more likely to become homosexual than other children.[27] The reality is that the "family" can have many faces, and no particular structure is inherently healthy or unhealthy for the children.

The Family

When we asked parents if they feel any differently toward their child because he or she was born from an alternative method, the great majority answered with a resounding no. They often qualified the answers, however. For example, they emphasized that AID children are really *theirs* (often underlined). They also expressed an overwhelming gratitude for the children, as seen in this mother's comment:

> I do not feel that a child conceived by IVF is different from any other baby born in this world. However, at his birth we realized how much responsibility we'd taken for his conception and after waiting for him for so long, he certainly is *very* special to us. He certainly can't be taken for granted.

Dutch researcher Levie asked fathers to describe their feelings about their children who were born after donor insemination. Their responses suggest the ambivalence—the satisfaction as well as the regrets—that many men experience:

> Fatherhood does not cause me any conflicts, although I do wonder sometimes what the child would have been like if it had been my own. The only thing that troubled me terribly was the idea of failing as a man. . . . This obsession has completely gone now that we have this child. I feel rich![28]

One father told us he had a great deal of difficulty accepting the daughter born of AID, and he sought psychiatric help. At about the same time, the girl became very ill and had to be hospitalized. It took this crisis for the father to realize how much he loved the child and how deep was his emotional commitment to her.

However they deal with the unusual origins of their children, most parents try hard to minimize the effects. They want it to be "no big deal," an incidental piece of information. For some parents, this is not difficult, as seen in this woman's comment:

> A child is a child and the outcome is always going to be the same—someone to love and cherish. When I look at her now, I don't even think that she's a product of *in vitro*. She's just our daughter.

Because they were conceived in an unusual way, there may be some advantages for the children. For example, the fathers of children conceived through donor insemination are often more involved in the pregnancy and birth than the average father. This is confirmed by a study carried out in Australia, which found 94 percent of the fathers attending the delivery, considerably higher than average.[29] Wives sometimes make a special effort to involve their husbands in parenting, to make sure they feel part of the child's life.

Despite all of the potential difficulties, the adoption literature is reassuring. The great majority of adoptees are as well adjusted as any comparable group of nonadoptees, and the chances are good that the same will be true of the children born of the alternative technologies. These children, similar to adoptees, are much more likely than most children to have parents who are more educated and well-off and who, most importantly, want them very much. Their parents are likely to be older and therefore more mature, more confident. And they will have the advantages experienced by only children or those with few siblings.[30]

Additionally, greater openness about a child's origins and a chance to meet with others in similar situations is expected to help children. As the number of children born through IVF and the other methods continues to grow, a child will not have to feel that he or she is so unusual. Parents who have become friends through RESOLVE or infertility clinics are likely to bring their children together as they meet to talk through the problems they face and to celebrate the growth of their children.

Although there are risks in being a child who has answered parents' years of anguished prayers, there may be a special dimension to the relationship, as pointed out by a sixteen-year-old adopted girl:

> Mother's Day is a kind of wonderful day in our house—between my mother and myself. We've got a different relationship than most people because I'm adopted. If I do something special for her on that day, it makes her more happy than most mothers since, I guess, there's always a fear on her part that I'm not going to think of her as my mother. But I do, because she's the one who raised me and because she's such a terrific person. I never think of my natural mother on Mother's Day.[31]

One woman who found out at the age of twenty-one that her genetic father had been an anonymous donor wrote in *The New York Times*:

> Knowing about my AID origin did nothing to alter my feelings for my family. Instead, I felt grateful for the trouble they had taken to give me life. And they had given me a strong set of roots, a rich and colorful cultural heritage, a sense of being loved.[32]

Troubles and dilemmas. It is hard enough to be a parent under the most "normal" of circumstances, and the introduction of conception in a petri dish or of another person who made this life possible, adds to the issues that prospective parents must resolve. They and those who care about them come to understand that there are many kinds of healthy and loving families and that social biases which demand that everyone fit a mold are only harmful to children. But we must also pay much greater attention to the wide variety of possible physical, social, and psychological consequences of all these methods for the children who are born. We should not allow them and their families to continue to be guinea pigs for fertility doctors unless we can be more confident that they are not hurt by the needs and ambitions of others.

CHAPTER 11

Reactions of Others

It's one thing when people watch Phil Donahue's show and hear about bizarre new ways of making babies. It's another thing when somebody they know walks up to them with his own kid who was born that way. After all is said and done, a child is still a child, and people know with their heart that this couldn't be bad.
—John, father of child born to surrogate mother

There is a great deal of controversy over the new methods of conception. Organized political, medical, and religious groups have taken strong positions for and against these technologies. Friends and relatives of infertile people, as well as the general public, may also object to the methods when they hear about them in the news. Yet, as John said, it is harder for people to disapprove when someone they care about wants so much to have a child.

Responses of Friends and Family

Those who share their struggles and experiences with others are often surprised at the positive reactions. They find people curious, interested, excited for them. Many of those we interviewed said their friends and relatives were very understanding and supportive. One woman said:

> All my friends were very excited when we decided to try IVF. They didn't see this as some weird thing to do. We were afraid to tell my parents until after the baby was born. When we did, my mother said, "You know, after all you've been through, this is certainly a miracle for you. She's all the more special."

One surrogate mother was worried about telling her grandparents, because they were in their late seventies and she considered them very old-fashioned in their ideas and beliefs. She said:

165

When I told my grandmother, she surprised the heck out of me because she said, "Kathy, I think that is the most wonderful thing you could do for somebody." It really floored me there for a minute because it wasn't the reaction that I was expecting at all.

Not everyone is so positive, however. People who are trying to conceive have heard plenty of hurtful reactions. "The world is already over-populated—you should adopt." "You don't know how lucky you are not having kids." "Adopt and you'll get pregnant." "Just be glad you have one child." A surprising negative reaction sometimes comes from people one might think would be understanding and sympathetic. As one woman said:

A couple of friends who were infertile and were going through the adoption process were very nasty about our finding a surrogate. I thought they of all people would understand. I think they were very jealous.

When negative comments are made by friends or relatives, the relationship often changes. As one man said, "When you've had an argument like that with someone, you're never quite the same kind of friends."

It is hard not to be angry with others when they oppose something that looks as though it might help. One man said:

There is a lot of controversy around, a lot of people with religious and legal ideals of how the world should be, with their own axes to grind, and they are trying to impose them on other people.

It is hard enough to be infertile. It is painful and difficult to choose a new route to pregnancy and go through all the arrangements and procedures. The attitudes of others—the misunderstandings and the disapproval—sometimes make it even harder. But public discussion of the implications of these new methods is essential for establishing policies to protect people from the worst aspects of unregulated medical experimentation.

Public Responses

When IVF programs first began, there was vocal opposition for a short while from pro-life groups. They picketed the Norfolk Clinic and staged a hunger strike in an Australian clinic. The director of the program at Yale devoted much of his energy at the beginning to speaking to church groups to try to ease their fears. Now, the programs report, the opposition is less visible. According to Linda Lynch, who was coordinator in the early years of the Norfolk program:

> I don't hear that much controversy anymore, not like in the
> beginning. The right-to-life people used to really get on us all the
> time, but not anymore. The Catholic Church doesn't recognize
> it, but the general public must be accepting it.

The general public's attitudes toward the new methods vary tremendously depending on the particular alternative in question. This is seen both in the media response and in public opinion polls.

The media, for example, have been most positive about IVF. Reporters followed the first IVF experiences with the same interest and enthusiasm they give to stories of children receiving organ transplants or premature babies saved by intensive care nurseries. Each new development results in photographs of healthy IVF babies and their glowing parents appearing in newspaper and magazine articles. IVF programs seek out such publicity in their competition for clients.

In contrast, surrogacy arrangements have often been sensationalized by the media, treated with distaste and fascination. It is true that surrogacy programs also seek publicity as a way to recruit women. But they may endure criticism from the media in the process.

Donor insemination is rarely mentioned in the news at all. The program as well as the patients are committed to secrecy, and the method makes it easy to keep it secret. It is also not new and does not involve interesting technology. Except when controversial cases arise—such as a couple's charge that they were given semen from the wrong donor, or the conviction of a physician for inseminating women with his own semen without telling them—the media are apparently not interested.

The public is also most accepting of IVF, as seen in a variety of polls. Even in 1978, when only one baby had been born from the *in vitro* method, a *Parents* magazine poll of 1,500 women found that 85 percent of them would approve of IVF for married couples who could not have children any other way.[1] Studies carried out in the mid to late 1980s of a variety of groups, including students in different parts of the country, infertile people, and *Psychology Today* readers, show continued support for IVF. Surrogacy is much less acceptable to most people than IVF or AIH, with donor insemination in between but still quite low. For example, in our study of mostly middle-class white students in two Pennsylvania colleges, 60 percent of the students would use IVF themselves if needed, but only 16 percent would turn to AID and 8 percent to surrogacy if they were the only ways for them to conceive a child. In a study of students at two universities in the Southeast, 57 percent of white students and 51 percent of black students found IVF acceptable, but only 23 percent of the whites and 14 percent of blacks approved of donor insemination.[2]

The students' opinions are similar to those of the infertile people we surveyed. For them as well, surrogacy programs are the least popular of all alternatives. Of the eighty-five people who responded to our question-naire, only thirteen had even considered hiring a surrogate mother, and almost every one of them rejected the idea.

The programs that involve a third parent—a donor or a surrogate mother—are the ones that arouse the most disapproval. The greater ac-ceptance of IVF is largely due to the fact that, in most cases, both parents are genetically related to the child. Adoption still receives the highest rating of all alternatives in every survey. There is no scientific interven-tion in the conception, and the parents are equal in being genetically unrelated to the child.

Psychology Today readers who responded to a survey printed in the magazine in 1984 also agreed that adoption would be their preferred choice and surrogate motherhood their last option. Although 84 percent would consider adopting if they could not have children, only 14 percent thought they might try surrogacy. AID and IVF were both approved by 48 percent of the people who responded.[3]

The students we surveyed were much more approving of the use of the methods by others who could not conceive than by themselves. Although only 8 percent would use surrogacy themselves, for example, 39 percent would approve of others hiring surrogate mothers. They ex-plained that they did not want to tell other people what they should or should not do.

There are limits to this laissez-faire position, however. There is a strik-ingly lower approval rate (25%) for the use of alternative methods by gay people. In addition, for some people in our sample, these methods are unacceptable under any circumstance. For example, students who call themselves "very religious" and attend religious services often are much more likely than other students to object to anyone using the methods. They were more likely to call them "immoral" or "unnatural."

Ultimately, public opposition to alternative methods of conception does not affect people personally as much as do their friends' negative comments. Most people, both providers and their clients, told us that the ethical and legal controversies surrounding reproductive technologies simply do not affect them. They find it hard to believe that anyone could object to what they are doing.

Yet public opinion and organized opposition do influence decisions regarding what will be researched, who is eligible for services, and what procedures can be reimbursed by insurance. Public opinion also affects laws governing the status of children born from donor insemination and the legality of surrogacy contracts. A single woman who wants a baby through AID, for example, may have great support from her family, but she is also likely to discover tremendous obstacles in seeking a facility to help her because fertility centers are afraid of negative publicity. A couple who thinks they might be helped by IVF is likely to be deterred more by their insurance company's decision not to reimburse their costs than by any negative reaction from their friends.

Reasons for Disapproval

Why is there so much controversy about these methods, especially when a third person is involved? Why does the idea of mixing the sperm and egg of a man and woman who are not married to each other make so many people uneasy? The reasons for opposition have not changed much since 1969, when Lou Harris polled 1,600 American adults for *LIFE* magazine about ideas such as the artificial womb, egg implants, and donor insemination. More than half agreed with statements that the new methods would mean the end of babies born through love, that they are against God's will, and that they would encourage promiscuity. Many people in the sample had experienced problems having children and welcomed help for infertility, but at the same time they feared the takeover of the family by science and the potential for creating a superrace. Harris quotes some of the reservations:

> We should not mess around with the laws of nature. Someone would have to play God, and who's to decide who is the chosen select?
>
> I think I kind of detest the scientific world. It leaves no room for enjoyment. Don't systematize babies.[4]

Part of the negative response is due to ignorance. Although most people have heard of the new methods through the media, they often do not realize what is involved. In a 1978 Gallup Poll, for instance, 93 percent said they had heard of IVF, but only 42 percent could describe it correctly.[5] IVF has become much more common since 1978, yet the mistaken ideas persist. One woman told us she heard the strangest remarks after telling everyone at work she had tried IVF but had not gotten pregnant. People asked if the baby was growing in a test tube in the lab and did they have to change tubes as the baby got larger.

Even the relatively educated group of college students who we surveyed displayed considerable ignorance about the new methods. The questions that asked for their opinions about each method provided some description. Yet, when asked to explain how the alternatives work, fewer than half of the students answered accurately. Most surprising were the health professionals we met in the course of speaking about this research who also did not understand how any of the methods work.

Because people do not always understand the methods, many believe that sexual activity is involved with donor insemination or surrogacy. Surrogate mothers are sometimes thought to be prostitutes, and a few men have called surrogacy programs asking where these women were that they could sleep with. AID is considered by many people to be adultery.

Ironically, sexual fantasies exist about these methods despite the fact that none of them involves sexual intercourse. But that fact is precisely the reason for many people's opposition to these alternatives. They see the separation of conception from sex as the beginning of the end of marriage and the family.

As with the controversies over birth control and abortion, the idea that technology would allow reproduction to be placed under human control is frightening to many. Some people fear that such methods will undermine the traditional basis of the family. There is irony here since those who use the methods are desperately committed to family. They have worked hard at maintaining a marriage under extreme stress. Whether married or not, they have invested tremendous energy in having children, something most people don't even have to think about. As Gary Hodgen of the Norfolk IVF program commented:

> Pro-life people do not support this, and yet this is the most pro-life thing that you can possibly have. How can they not see the value of giving this little baby, which is just like every other little baby when it's born, to a man and woman who so desperately want it?

As the general public becomes more familiar with these methods, and as people think about alternatives less in the abstract than in relationship to specific situations, their opposition declines. For example, in 1978, when the first IVF baby, Louise Brown, was born, Harris's survey of 1,500 women for *Parents* magazine revealed a 49 percent approval of IVF in general. After the procedure was explained, however, and the women were asked if it should be available to married couples who could not have children otherwise, approval rose to 85 percent.[6]

Another reason for negative attitudes toward those methods is seen in the attitude that considers infertility a minor problem. "It's not a major disease," people say. "It's not going to kill you." A survey of readers of *U.S. Catholic* revealed that 74 percent agreed with the statement, "Infertility should not be treated as a major illness", and 54 percent agreed that all money spent on fertility research and treatment should be redirected toward conditions such as cancer and heart disease.[7]

A common reaction is that if a woman cannot have children, then she was not meant to, and it is wrong to try to change that. Some believe that relaxation or adoption will solve infertility and cannot understand why a couple would waste their time with doctors.

People who do not understand infertility or who believe it just could not happen to them seem to be less sympathetic to alternatives. We were surprised, for example, to see that the female students in our study were less likely to approve of each of the alternative methods than the males, particularly opposing surrogates and ovum transfer. When asked, the students explained that the women are more idealistic than the men, that they have grown up thinking about having their own baby, and still hold on to that idea. Their problem was not so much with technology per se, but with the idea of relying on another woman's egg or body in order to have a child.

These are young people, of course, and they have never had to face the reality of infertility. A study that appeared in the *Journal of Social Psychology* in 1977 and included both married and unmarried students found the married women (who were also older) to be more accepting of alternative methods. Infertile people are, not surprisingly, much more positive abut the alternatives. In Charlene Miall's study of 71 infertile Canadian women who had adopted or were waiting to adopt children, 90 percent approved of the practice of donor insemination and 70 percent of surrogacy.[8]

Many of the young women students will one day, unfortunately, experience the shock of learning they cannot have babies. At that point, if they are like many of the women we interviewed, they are likely to feel very differently. They will have a long difficult path, a great deal to give up, as they move from this earlier idealism to the later reality.

Groups in Opposition

The most committed opposition to alternative methods of conception comes primarily from conservative religious groups, particularly the Catholic Church, fundamentalist Christians, and some representatives of Orthodox Judaism. Some feminists are equally fervent in their opposition to these alternatives. Both groups acknowledge that the children conceived by these methods can bring great happiness to their parents, but they conclude that the drawbacks involved are just too great. It is ironic that the religious right and the feminist left, which disagree on just about everything else, should appear to agree in their desire to eliminate or sharply limit artificial procreation.[9]

Their reasons, however, are fundamentally different. For the religious groups, most or all of the alternatives are "moral abominations," violating the sacred marital relationship, interfering with God's control over nature, challenging patriarchal rules of procreation, and increasing the likelihood of abortion. As Rev. Theodore Hall, a Catholic theologian wrote, "The child's existence does not justify morally evil means or techniques used in its origin."[10] And a surrogate mother spoke to us of her cousin who is a devout Catholic and who said to her, "It's morally wrong. First of all the masturbation is wrong, the artificial insemination is wrong, giving the baby away is wrong."

Feminist authors and leaders who are outspoken and articulate in their opposition to these methods have entirely different reasons, which focus on the many ways in which they can be harmful for women. They see artificial reproduction as a means for increasing male control over pregnancy and birth, over women's and children's lives. They believe that women are being used as guinea pigs in massive uncontrolled experiments that have serious risks and whose goals are only in part to help women. In addition, the increasing use of prenatal sex selection allows parents to have more boys, especially firstborns who tend to be more successful. The availability of the technologies makes it harder for women to say no to bearing children, and poor women are being used as reproductive vessels for the well-off.[11]

The religious objections focus on both the techniques and the possible negative consequences for families. According to Hall:

> Masturbatory methods of obtaining semen must be outrightly condemned as objectively immoral, since it is the church's official, constant (and therefore irreversible) teaching that such acts are "intrinsically and seriously disordered."[12]

Since all the methods require masturbation to obtain semen, this alone is enough to make them unacceptable to the Catholic Church and to many Catholics. In addition, the church condemns any procreation that is not a result of sexual relations within a marriage. In 1987, the Vatican issued a statement against IVF as well as most other methods. One of the chief concerns of fundamentalist Christians as well as of the Catholic Church, is that embryos, which are considered to be living beings, become objects of production, and some are likely to be destroyed in the process of implantation or freezing.[13]

Not all religious leaders agree with this total opposition. Orthodox Jewish rabbis, for instance, find no basis in Jewish law for opposing AIH or IVF, but most of them do object to AID and many also oppose surrogacy. Religious commentators who express reservations are most likely to object to those methods that involve a donor. The Christian Medical and Dental Society, for example, approved a statement favoring reproductive alternatives as long as both sperm and egg come from a married heterosexual couple trying to have a child together.[14]

More liberal Jewish and Protestant leaders tend to be supportive of IVF and AID, although some question them on social and economic grounds. For example, the World Council of Churches does not object to IVF but would prefer to see the money spent on prevention and cure of blocked tubes and on meeting the health needs of the poor. Similarly, an editorial in *Christianity Today* discouraged Christian couples from using IVF because its great expense excludes racial minorities and needlessly adds to the cost of medical care, and also because there are already so many children in need of loving families but unwanted due to age, race, or disability.[15] This idea is echoed in *U.S. Catholic* magazine:

> The claim that people have the right to reproductive technologies in order to secure their "right" to have children is a violation of distributive justice—the principle of justice for all, not for a few. The high cost of establishing and operating fertility centers that offer a relatively small number of people an exceedingly small chance of having their own children is inconsistent with society's more general obligation to provide all of its citizens with basic health care.[16]

Protestant theologians differ widely in their views. Jack Moore, a professor of philosophy and religion, outlines two major views of theology, one in which humans must not tamper with God's creation, the other in which people are partners with God in improving nature. Those who endorse the second view, he says, are more likely to see the alternatives as acceptable for couples seeking to overcome infertility. Michael Gold, a Conservative rabbi, agrees with the second view; he points to the many cases of infertility in the Bible and describes the Jewish response as an activist one.[17]

One minister told us of his own ambivalence when first asked for advice, and then the change in his views:

> A couple came to me to talk about their plan to hire a surrogate mother to have a baby for them. They explained how much they wanted to have a family and that it was their only option. I can't say I was happy about the idea, but I also felt I was not in a position to judge them or to tell them not to do this. Now when I see them with the results—a gorgeous little boy—I am totally delighted.

Not all feminists oppose the methods either. Even among those who see grave dangers in the new alternatives, there are many, such as ourselves, who are torn by sympathy for infertile women and men, and who would defend the right of single women, heterosexual and lesbian, to have children without sexual involvement with a man.

Ethicists and legal experts offer widely varying views, from full acceptance to total rejection. An important concern that emerges from their many discussions is the "slippery slope" problem—the idea that one action may open the door to others that will be much worse. They wonder, for instance, if technologies that currently are designed to help the infertile will ultimately lead to life being treated as a commodity. Attorney George Annas, speaking at a conference of the American Society of Law and Medicine, vividly described one scenario. He worried that we will one day soon have embryo stores, with catalogs describing the sex, characteristics, and merits of each embryo offered for sale.[18]

Some authors also worry that the combining of IVF with surrogacy will lead wealthy women to hire poor women to carry a couple's embryo for convenience. Motherhood would be degraded into a totally commercial activity.[19]

Coping with Disapproval

There is no doubt that the new technologies raise serious concerns about the future of motherhood. For people struggling with infertility, the desire to conceive and bear a child often overrides any concern for the objections of others. On the other hand, ignoring one's church or going against public opinion and the attitudes of family and peers may be difficult and troubling. Choosing an alternative often means having to deal with being "deviant," doing something unusual and not always approved of.

The people who try the alternatives rely on a number of different strategies for coping with their "deviance." Some try to educate the public or their friends to change their minds; others resort to secrecy. For some, the idea of being different and doing something unusual has its own attraction. On the other hand, some people have become so used to the insensitivity of others to their infertility that they have already developed thick skins, screening out negative comments. They already know who understands and who will object, and they may choose their friends and tailor their conversations accordingly. As one man said, "Some people are really negative, but we just say 'the hell with them.'"

Some who become involved with alternatives respond to the objections of others by trying to change their opinions with information. The director of the Norfolk IVF program even went to the Vatican to try to influence the Catholic Church's position. On a more personal level, a woman who had recently applied to be a surrogate mother told us:

> I was so excited, I told my friends what I was doing. Then someone would say, "How much money are you getting for that?" and I'd get mad and say, "What do you mean, how much money am I getting?" That's not the important thing. They didn't understand at first, but when I finished with them they understood and were supportive.

Some take their educational efforts beyond their immediate acquaintances. They go on television shows, speak to reporters, or write up their experiences for magazine articles. They may enjoy the excitement of the publicity, but they also want the public to understand what they are doing. They hope that by presenting their experiences they will be able to lessen the opposition. One man reported:

> This might come off real corny, but we're a reasonably intelligent couple and we want to portray surrogate mothering for all the benefits and all the positive things that it's done. That's why we agreed to do the media thing.

Many people wrote to us at length about their experiences because they wanted to communicate their views and feelings to the public. Their plea was voiced by one woman who ended a long letter with, "Please tell people about us!"

Total secrecy—not telling anyone what they are doing—is the opposite strategy employed by some of those who are concerned with the negative views of others. It is used most often by those who try AID and sometimes by people involved with surrogacy. Some couples who hire surrogate mothers either fake a pregnancy or tell friends that they adopted the child. One woman explained:

> We live in a rural area and people have very, very, conservative values, not necessarily consistent with our own, and it's not our desire to be on the front page of a two-bit newspaper. We don't want our child talked about or teased by the other kids. We knew we were doing something different and some people might frown upon it.

When we requested through RESOLVE newsletters that people who had tried the alternatives contact us, we discovered a striking difference between letters from women who had used AID and everyone else. Many of the letters about AID mentioned the desire for secrecy—"Please leave a discreet message when you call." "Please don't use our names." "My husband doesn't want to discuss this." RESOLVE has even set up a separate information network just for AID that allows people to exchange letters with each other in total anonymity.

Associating with other infertile people, especially through RESOLVE, is a helpful strategy for many. A woman who tried AID said:

> It's not something we discuss with the man on the street or with casual acquaintances. In fact, we didn't even tell our family. But we have talked about it with a few people from our RESOLVE group who have become our closest friends now.

Many people who turn to these methods are unaware of the objections to them or are simply unconcerned. Most ignore the religious prohibitions and do not think about what they are doing as related to male exploitation of women. They are not worried about cloning or artificial wombs or any of the visions of the future. They are not looking for an easy way to avoid pregnancy. In fact, they would much rather have a natural pregnancy. All they want is a baby, a healthy baby as close to them genetically as possible. As one woman said:

> I think all the controversies are media hype, because when you are in the middle of it—all you want is a baby and all that other stuff is just superfluous; it really is.

Some people who consider using the alternatives are devoutly religious, yet they often make their decisions without consulting religious authorities. For example, an Orthodox Jewish man whose wife was artificially inseminated with a donor's sperm (a method opposed by most Orthodox rabbis) commented, "I never asked the rabbi if it was okay or not. I guess I just didn't want to hear what his answer might be." A Catholic woman who tried IVF said, "I never talked to my priest about it. The way I figured, it was none of his business."

By avoiding the people who are likely to disapprove and explaining their situation to others who might be sympathetic, most people manage not to hear many open objections. One man said he believes a lot of people are against his hiring a surrogate mother, but they do not voice their opinion directly to him: "I think if people think it is kind of strange and awkward, they just don't say anything."

There is another reason most people do not respond negatively, despite the reservations they may have. It may be easy to discuss the dangers and problems of these methods in theory, but it is another matter to object to the creation of a real family. For others, just as for the parents, when they see and come to love the children, they are no longer test-tube babies or AID children, they are simply "our kids," "Joe's baby," "Cousin Tammy." This idea was expressed by a respondent in the 1969 *LIFE* poll: "When you hold a baby who depends on you in your arms, you don't worry where the egg came from."[20]

Conclusion

In 1977 Russell Baker wrote in his *New York Times* column:

> Until a few years ago, people just happened. As a result, most of them were hodgepodges, like London and Rome, which also just happened.
>
> Occasionally you might run into somebody who had been planned, like Washington, D.C. These planned people were the product of Planned Parenthood. Their parents had sat down with architects. The architects had shown them blueprints of beautiful families in which all the siblings would be as neatly spaced as the oaks on a Washington boulevard. . . .
>
> It would be interesting to know what it feels like to be a fully planned person. Having your sex determined by your parents, of course, is surely only a primitive beginning on the intricate architecture which biology will make possible in another generation or so. Before the century is out, science will probably enable parents to decide not only what size and shape their productions will take, but also how bright they will be and what careers they will pursue. . . .[1]

This vision is already a lot closer to reality than even Baker could have imagined at the time he wrote this column. The methods for conceiving that we have described in this book are just the beginning. Scientists have been working on variations that are making it more and more possible to create human beings to the designer's specifications in a laboratory. There are many examples of this: the successful cloning of human embryos; the greater use of sperm banks, with the father's characteristics to be chosen by the buyers of the sperm; and the expanding use of genetic analysis of embryos in the laboratory. Indeed, the explosion of knowledge about the genetic code made possible through the multibillion-dollar federal funding of the Genome Project has opened the door for incredible changes in embryonic design, prenatal diagnosis, and genetic modification. The changes this new knowledge and technology will create for women, for children, for society as a whole, can be frightening to consider.

The newer infertility treatments, including the most controversial developments, such as experiments with cloning and the use of aborted fetuses for obtaining ova for IVF, are defended by their proponents as offering more hope to infertile women. We have also felt the agony of those who want to have children and cannot. For them we want technologies for enhancing conception to work. We want the procedures to be easier, safer, cheaper, and more successful. We want them to be available to poor women, who are most likely to be affected by infertility but have almost no access to treatment. We do not want to see more grief and desperation for people who feel deprived of the chance to be parents.

Yet we are still very troubled. Our research into the personal experiences of people who consider or try the methods has uncovered a great deal of trauma and uncertainty. We are troubled and worried about the personal dilemmas, the emotional upheavals, the physical risks, the lack of control, and the unanswered questions about long-term effects.

We are also very troubled by the growing role of profit-making in baby making, currently estimated to be a $2 billion industry. No one should make a great deal of money from the anguish and desperation of infertile couples and from the financial and emotional neediness of donor women. When powerful men, whether they be lawyers, doctors, or financiers, make large profits from linking two vulnerable women, as is the case with surrogacy and potentially with ovum donation, we must worry about the consequences.

There is more. Thoughtful observers remind us of past medical discoveries that were supposed to be good for women. DES (diethylstilbestrol) was offered as a cure for miscarriages, a guarantee of healthier pregnancies. Instead it caused cancer in women and in their children and is the source of many of the infertility problems being experienced today by the children of women given DES. The Dalkon Shield IUD was inserted in millions of women to give them control over conception. Instead, it caused massive infections, infertility, and even death for untold numbers of these women. Silicone breast implants, unnecessary hysterectomies, forced cesareans—the history of women's health care is full of accounts of women being convinced that they must have procedures or products that it turned out were useless or harmful.[2]

DES, Dalkon Shield, and silicone implants are only a few examples of products that were heavily marketed to physicians and the public without adequate testing and continued to be sold even after proof of their harmfulness was established. Given this history, and the more recent revelations that many Americans were unknowingly exposed by physicians to high levels of radiation during the cold war, many women are asking, "Why should we trust that newer technologies will be any more safe or beneficial?"

Biologist Ruth Hubbard worries, along with many others, about the long-term effects of interfering with natural reproductive processes by using a technique such as IVF:

> After all, embryonic development is the most complicated of biological processes, one in which an infinite number of re-actions are taking place in intricate interrelationships, where timing and all kinds of factors in the chemical environment are fantastically important and split seconds or tiny changes in con-centration can make a difference. So, coming from this perspec-tive I frankly view with incredibility and horror the notion that one can "simply" remove an egg from a woman's ovary, put it in a culture medium in a dish, and then "simply" pick it up and reinsert it in a uterus that is at the proper stage of prepared-ness, and have it implant and go through development, without these many manipulations having some effect on the process of development. I cannot believe that there is no effect.[3]

It will be many years before the risks of these methods become known. In the meantime, women and children are once again the guinea pigs in a massive, and potentially dangerous, experiment.

Scenarios for the Future

The commentators are not only worried about the possible physi-cal damage, they also see the shift of conception into the laboratory as another step toward male control over the conditions of motherhood. It is the fear of what may happen with the use of these methods that is most troubling.

It is possible that not so far in the future a young woman will make a trip to the bank after graduating from high school. She will not be deposit-ing her graduation checks, but rather some of her own eggs. In the bank they will be frozen, presumably protected from any future exposure to hazards in the air or at work. She can now be sterilized and never have to worry again about the dangers and uncertainty of birth control. When she is ready to become a mother, she can return to the bank for a withdrawal. A few eggs will be thawed and mixed with the semen (also newly thawed) of her husband, lover, or donor. Scientists will inspect the embryos for ge-netic characteristics, "defects," and for sex. They will eliminate unwanted characteristics and add those most desired by the parents if they are miss-ing. The future mother can then choose which embryo she or a surrogate mother or the artificial womb will receive to start growing this "ideal" baby. She can also have it cloned so that if the "product" turns out well, she can produce another perfect specimen in the future.

Some people are horrified by such a scenario. It gives control over the creation of babies almost completely into the hands of the scientists. It makes imperfection, however that is defined, unacceptable. Yet we have described such a scene to women, and they have responded laughingly that much of it sounds very attractive. "Wouldn't that be wonderful if it really worked?" they say. "No worries about birth control, no worries about waiting too long to get pregnant and then being infertile, no worries about genetic defects. We wouldn't have to finish childbearing by age forty. We could really control when and if we want to have children."

Some feminists such as Shulamith Firestone have claimed that women will be truly liberated only when they are free of pregnancy, when completely artificial reproduction is developed in a postrevolutionary society.[4] Freedom from pregnancy, both wanted and unwanted, does have its appeal for many women, especially if they can still become parents.

Many feminists today fear that such liberation will ultimately become enslaving. As professionals come to control the "banks" and the technology for conception, they are also able to dictate the terms. They decide whose genes should be reproduced, what defects are unacceptable, which embryos should be discarded. It is already clear from most fertility clinic policies that married heterosexual couples with money are the ideal, indeed the only, acceptable candidates for having children. In Huxley's *Brave New World*, among the most powerful members of society are the ones who make such decisions, the "Directors of Hatcheries and Conditioning."[5]

Social class will be more important than ever as poor women are hired to carry embryos for the rich under carefully controlled conditions. Sociologist Barbara Katz Rothman described to us her fear of how this will work:

> I'm convinced that there will be "farms" for surrogates. Once it's possible to implant an embryo created from a man's sperm and a woman's egg into another woman, Third World and poor women will be hired for a low fee and kept on the farms to produce highly valued white babies. These women will be carefully watched to make sure they eat right and don't smoke, and people will say it's good for them.

Gena Corea, author of *The Mother Machine*, calls such farms "breeding brothels." She reminds us that control over women—such as black slave women—for use as breeders of children or wet nurses for the wealthy is nothing new in our society.[6]

The most extreme versions of such scenarios appear in novels such as Huxley's *Brave New World* or Atwood's *The Handmaid's Tale*.[7] In these fictional accounts, reproduction is rigidly controlled by totalitarian rulers in order to perpetuate caste divisions in society. Even these visions, however, are not totally divorced from reality. The Nazis, Corea writes, kidnapped young girls, branded them, and gave them hormones, with the intention that they breed Aryan children and then be killed.[8]

Of course it doesn't *have* to go that far. Most professionals who work in IVF and surrogate programs are interested only in helping infertile people, not in changing the way everyone reproduces. They would be horrified to consider the work that they do, mostly with dedication and care for patients, could be connected in any way to maniacal population schemes. "Just because you wouldn't want to use a hammer to kill someone," they say, "doesn't mean you should abolish hammers and lose their benefits."

This is a compelling argument. But the question remains: Who decides which benefits are worth preserving? For now it is primarily the scientists, for whom the excitement of the research and the prestige of breaking through new scientific frontiers is the foremost goal. They are looking for ways to gain greater control over reproduction in general and ultimately to cure diseases in adults. Through genetic engineering, tissue grafts from embryos, and other experiments, a whole host of other "problems" will be "solved." Some scientists envision the creation of fetuses solely for their use in harvesting tissues or organs, a sort of "spare parts" resource. Aborted animal fetuses have already been used experimentally in Scotland as a source for "donated" ova in IVF. Whatever happened to this being done soley for the sake of infertile people?

Many infertility specialists agree with the director of Columbia University's IVF program when she speaks of responsible scientists who "live in fear of abuse of the new technology." As physician Kurt Hirschhorn wrote, "It is a general rule that whatever is scientifically feasible will be attempted."[9]

Some of the scientists and entrepreneurs are cautious not to move faster than public opinion permits. They are carefully attuned to what will be acceptable to most people, at the same time offering new options that stretch the limits of acceptability. And they are ready to take advantage of society's growing willingness to allow interventions in reproduction. As James Twerdahl, formerly chief executive officer of Fertility and Genetics Research, said about the ovum transfer program:

> We will never do it for eugenics or sex selection. The smart clinics will follow trends, not lead them; but, if in twenty years society says eugenics is good, then we might consider it. If

society decides it wants diagnosis of embryos, then we have the delivery system that can do it.

We know that medical products can create new uses and needs where none existed before. As competition grows and products are perfected, new markets must be found. For example, technologies such as fetal monitoring, developed for high-risk deliveries, moved quickly to routine use in almost all deliveries, where they are unnecessary and may actually cause problems.[10] The wide dissemination of new technologies is often justified on the grounds of patient demand for them. Yet as Corea aptly points out:

> A pattern emerges in the development of many new reproductive technologies. . . . Experimentation on women is presented through the media as a "medical breakthrough." There is much hoopla and many cries of "new hope for the infertile." Infertile women begin clamoring for what they think of as a "new" rather than "experimental" procedure. The demand for the procedure created by the researchers through the media is then used to justify further experimentation on women.[11]

Sociologist Elisabeth Beck-Gernsheim, using reproductive technologies as an example, describes a four-step process in the introduction of new technologies. Starting with small-scale and mostly unpublicized exploration, scientists proceed to widespread experimental introduction of a procedure or product, then define a much larger population as the clientele; ultimately, in the fourth stage, social expectations develop that people *should* use the technology, changing it from an option to an obligation. She describes this process:

> With the arrival of new options and opportunities, standards of behavior gradually begin to change. The same act that once seemed totally impossible, and later possible but taboo, may appear today as an interesting novelty and tomorrow perhaps as routine. Eventually, it may become *the* legally sanctioned course of action.[12]

Is "forced implementation," the name Beck-Gernsheim gives to the final stage in her model, really likely to happen with the new methods of conception? We have seen this happen with many other interventions. For example, prenatal diagnosis such as amniocentesis was originally introduced on a very limited basis for women considered at high risk of delivering a baby with genetic problems. Over time the targeted clientele has expanded greatly, prenatal testing through blood analyses has become more routine, and women who choose not to have amniocentesis may be condemned as immoral if they give birth to a child with a genetic defect. As Beck-Gernsheim says, choice turns into pressure, promise into threat.

In less than a decade, IVF expanded from being an experimental treatment for women with blocked fallopian tubes offered in a few research centers to being the routine "solution" offered in many hundreds of locations around the world for endometriosis, low sperm count, premature menopause, and unexplained infertility. Women in their fifties and occasionally sixties are now trying IVF with the use of younger women's eggs. We are already in the third stage, where more and more people are defined as "needing" these technologies.

But aren't these still the choices of women who want to have children; how could it be seen as becoming coercive? Already many women who, a dozen years ago, might have resolved to be satisfied with no children or whatever number they already had, now feel compelled to at least attempt IVF. Infertile people who do not want to endure further procedures, or women with children who have a new partner who wants to have "his own" kids, have so far been able to beg off on the grounds of cost, risk, distance, or their experimental nature. But the programs are quickly becoming more accessible, more routine, and less invasive. Insurance is covering more of the costs. Older women can start childbearing all over again with a new partner, even well beyond menopause. It will be increasingly difficult to say no to IVF and related technologies.

More and more women feel compelled by social pressures to use the new technologies, and the reasons for using them continue to expand. Older women (maybe even over thirty-five), overweight women, women who are working, women who have had cesareans, women under stress, women on medications, smokers, will all certainly "need" other women to carry their embryos—created through IVF—in a healthier "environment." We will be told that it is better to have a controlled setting—a supervised surrogate or ultimately an artificial womb.

These are not only fears for the future. In 1989, Dr. Eugene Sandberg, in his presidential address to the Pacific Coast Obstetrical and Gynecological Society, was already speaking in such terms, extolling the potential of "reproductive surrogacy" for a long list of possible indications. He concludes:

> An ability to grow healthy, fat, bubbly babies is aspired to by all would-be mothers, but it is not an ability they all possess. Why should any woman be consigned to childlessness for lack of that ability? Even worse, why should a woman be consigned to the abusive production of a thin, pathetically damaged infant when a superbly healthy gestational specialist of proved ability is at hand and wants to market her talent? *To the contrary, should*

not that woman be held criminally accountable who know-
ingly permits herself to produce a sickly child whose entire
life will be encumbered by imperfections of health and struc-
ture when the prevention of such was possible and available?
(emphasis added)[13]

As sociologist Barbara Katz Rothman points out, all of the new choices offered to women in the area of reproduction can be limiting as well as liberating. A woman does not have a free choice to use a technology if a physician tells her that it is for the good of her baby and she would be irresponsible—indeed, "criminally accountable"—not to use it. It will not be a choice whether or not to have our embryos or fetuses checked for abnormalities if society condemns women as irresponsible if they give birth to handicapped children. This is what Beck-Gernsheim means by "forced implementation," and its presence is already being felt.

Another example: In the past, some employers convinced women to be sterilized before they could work in a hazardous setting.[14] Some women resisted that pressure, but new technologies could be used to overcome the reluctance. Someday soon companies may require prospective women workers to have eggs retrieved and stored, and then be sterilized before they are hired. Rather than make the work environment safe, they could protect themselves against possible lawsuits by children born with birth defects and by women deprived of fertility.

Many of the elements of the futuristic vision are already with us. Hired women are carrying embryos that are genetically unrelated to them. Eggs and embryos are being "harvested," in the terminology commonly used, then frozen and stored. IVF and sex selection clinics exist in franchise operations all over the world.

Another type of selection—for intelligence—is already going on with donor insemination. In 1982, the first two children were born to mothers who were inseminated with sperm from the Repository for Germinal Choice in California, better known as the Nobel sperm bank. Although not all donors are Nobel Prize winners, they must be exceptionally accomplished scientists—outstanding artists are not acceptable. The purpose of the Repository is to "breed more intelligent human beings," as stated by its medical director in a letter to *The New York Times*.[15]

This Nobel sperm bank has been widely criticized for its philosophy. What is usually not recognized, however, is that almost all donor insemination is based on some form of selection, and intelligence is a key criterion. Physicians claim that they usually select medical residents because they are most accessible, but there are certainly other men who work in hospitals who are not approached. Sperm banks turn away 80 percent of donor applicants, and one of their criteria is university education. At least one sperm bank includes the donor's grade point average in the profiles they send physicians, and their preference for A students is obvious.

Despite this long-standing practice, many people were dismayed by reports in 1994 that two black women, one in England and the other in Italy, had chosen to become pregnant with ova from white women so that their children would more closely resemble their lighter-skinned husbands. Public officials and physicians in those countries condemned the idea of choosing one's offspring's characteristics in this way, but surely this is one more of the many bumps along the road toward increasing public acceptance of these practices.

What Should Be Done?

Because the present and future dangers of the new methods can be so frightening, many opponents urge that we just stop using them. But what about the real, legitimate needs of infertile people? Is it fair to deprive them of the technology that might help them have children?

Some writers, such as biologist Ruth Hubbard, respond that the need for children is socially created. It would be better if infertile women overcame the social pressures to have children. She says that some good consciousness-raising to understand that society wants women to think their primary role is breeder of children would be more beneficial than risky technological interventions.[16]

Others add that there are plenty of children available who could be adopted. Since many of these children are members of minority groups, the infertile are accused of racism for not wanting them.

Yes, women need to understand the pressures and to realize that we have other fulfilling roles to play beside that of being a mother. Childlessness needs to be a much more acceptable solution for those who have not been able to succeed.

We believe that it is simply not fair, however, to tell infertile people that they must raise their consciousness or overcome their racism in order to give up the goal of having their genetic child or one that would come close. We all need to have our consciousness raised, and we all need to eliminate racism. There is no logical reason that the infertile, who have already suffered social stigma and personal loss, should have to bear these important burdens more than others. Were they somehow designated, because of their biological handicap, to be more virtuous, more selfless, more liberated than people who can bear genetic children?

Because women have been and are oppressed through motherhood does not make motherhood in itself necessarily oppressive. To want to raise children who do not suffer handicaps, who have not been given up by a grieving birth mother, who bear some resemblance to oneself, who will not have to struggle with the difficulties of being a different race from their parents—for a white couple to desire a healthy white infant is not necessarily racism.

Being a parent is an extraordinarily difficult job under any circumstances, and much more difficult if the child is handicapped, more complicated if the child is from a different racial background. These "special needs children" need to be adopted by especially committed and capable parents. Infertility is simply not a qualification for being such a parent.

Having a child may not be a right, as some are arguing. It may not be an entitlement that comes with citizenship, that should be provided by society. Yet to create life, to see oneself in one's children, is to participate in a miracle. It is this miracle that so many people are trying for, one that technology makes possible for some of them.

Again, the counterargument: The alleviation of some people's pain, the satisfaction of some people's desires, does not outweigh the potential harm caused to the majority. Freedom of choice is less important than the welfare of society, of women as a whole. This is the heart of the most difficult dilemma posed by the new technologies—how to balance the needs, desires, rights of some against the possible risks for the many.[17]

It is imperative that, at the very least, controls be exercised over the use of the technology. Gena Corea proposes a federal regulatory agency on the model of the Environmental Protection Agency.[18] Although such agencies are notoriously poor at regulating industry effectively, often being controlled by the industries themselves, some systematic review may be much better than what exists today, which is essentially nothing. Many other countries have established national panels to set policy with regard to reproductive technology. Thus far the United States has done very little, leaving decisions almost entirely up to the practitioners and scientists.[19]

If such bodies are to be established, it is clearly essential that they not be controlled by the scientists, whose priorities and concerns are often very different from those of the women and the society who are affected most by these decisions. The people who make policy should include representatives of infertile people and of the women's health movement, which has done so much to monitor the effects of medical decisions on women. There are extraordinarily difficult decisions that need to be made about what technologies can be developed and used and under what circumstances. These issues deserve very careful consideration and full exploration of the short- and long-term effects of the methods.

———— • ————

Between us we have four young daughters. In ten or more years, they will probably be thinking about becoming mothers. We worry about the kinds of pressures and technologies that will shape their choices, or how much choice they will have at all.

What will it be like to become grandmothers then? Will we visit our grandchildren embryos in laboratories and watch them developing as fetuses in their artificial wombs from behind a window, as many grandparents now get their first glimpse of newborns?

Will our daughters be able to accept any hint of imperfection? Will they feel they have to make sure they have a boy first and then a girl, further increasing the male advantage by adding the advantage of being firstborn? Will they select only children who are clones of Barbie and Ken dolls, or whatever the ideal model is at the time?

As we worry about their future, we take comfort from the awareness that people can and do resist the pressures of science and medicine. Women have organized to promote more natural births and succeeded in making very important changes in childbirth practices. Consumer pressures have led to the removal of dangerous drugs and products from the market. Many women refused to believe that formula was really healthier for babies, and they succeeded in convincing mothers and pediatricians alike of the values of breast-feeding. Some couples do decide not to try a method for conception they are offered, or to stop after one or two tries.

With all of the dramatic social changes of the past decades, almost all women and men still prefer to make babies the "old-fashioned" way. We hope that better prevention of infertility and better treatments will allow infertile people to do just that, reducing the demand for these other methods. We can work for a society in which women and men can have enough time with young children and still succeed professionally, allowing those who would prefer to have children earlier not to feel they must postpone parenthood or lose out in their careers. And we hope as well that an active informed public will resist the pressures toward conformity and control. We hope our daughters will also know how to resist these pressures, and how to balance their own desires with the welfare of their communities.

Notes

Introduction

1. Susan Borg and Judith Lasker, *When Pregnancy Fails: Families Coping with Miscarriage, Ectopic Pregnancy, Stillbirth and Infant Death* (New York: Bantam, 1989).
2. Merle J. Berger and Donald P. Goldstein, "Infertility Related to Exposure to DES *in utero:* Reproductive Problems in the Female," in Miriam D. Mazor and Harriet F. Simons, eds., *Infertility: Medical, Emotional, and Social Considerations* (New York: Human Sciences Press, 1984), 157–68; Daniel Cramer et al., "Tubal Infertility and the Intrauterine Device," *New England Journal of Medicine,* 312 (1985), 941; Elina Hemminki, B. I. Graubard, H. J. Hoffman, W. D. Mosher, and K. Fetterly, "Cesarean Section and Subsequent Fertility: Results from the 1982 National Survey of Family Growth," *Fertility and Sterility* 43 (1985): 520–28; Gerry Hendershot, "Maternal Age and Overdue Conceptions," *American Journal of Public Health* 74 (1984): 35–37; Jane Menken, J. Trussel, and U. Larsen, "Age and Infertility," *Science,* 233, September 26, 1986, 1389–94; William D. Mosher and Sevgi O. Aral, "Factors Related to Infertility in the United States, 1965–1976," *Sexually Transmitted Diseases,* 12 (1985): 117–23; Alan B. Retik and Stuart B. Bauer, "Infertility Related to DES Exposure *In Utero:* Reproductive Problems in the Male," in Mazor and Simons, *Infertility,* 169–79; Constance Matthiessen and David Weir, "The Forest of Sterility," *Hispanic* (July 1990): 48.
3. Stanley K. Henshaw and Susheela Singh, "Sterilization Regret Among U.S. Couples," *Family Planning Perspectives* 18, 1986: 238–40; William D. Mosher and William D. Pratt, "Fecundity and Infertility in the United States, 1965–88," National Center for Health Statistics, Advance Data, Vol. 92, Dec. 4, 1990.
4. William Mosher, "Reproductive Impairments in the United States, 1965– 1982," *Demography* 22 (1985): 415–29; Sevgi O. Aral and William Cates, "The Increasing Concern with Infertility—Why Now?" *Journal of the American Medical Association,* 250, November 4, 1983, 2327–31; Mosher and Pratt, "Fecundity and Infertility in the United States."
5. Mosher and Pratt, "Fecundity and Infertility in the United States"; Marilyn B. Hirsch and William D. Mosher, "Characteristics of Infertile Women in the United States and Their Use of Infertility Services," *Fertility & Sterility* 47 (1987): 618–25.
6. "When Baby's Mother Is Also Grandma—and Sister," Case Studies, *Hastings Center Report* 15 (1985): 29–31; Barbara Katz Rothman, "How Science Is Redefining Parenthood," *Ms.,* August 1982, 154–58.

Chapter 1: The Drive to Have Children

1. Lesley Brown and John Brown, with Sue Freeman, *Our Miracle Called Louise: A Parents' Story* (New York and London: Paddington Press, 1979).

189

2. Edward O. Wilson, *Sociobiology: The New Synthesis* (Cambridge: Harvard University Press, 1975); Jessie Bernard, *The Future of Motherhood* (New York: Penguin, 1974); Betty Friedan, *The Feminine Mystique: Twentieth Anniversary Edition* (New York: Norton, 1983); Charlene Miall, "The Stigma of Involuntary Childlessness," *Social Problems* 33 (1986): 268–82; J. Richard Udry, "The Effect of Normative Pressures on Fertility," *Population and Environment: Behavioral and Social Issues* 5 (Summer 1982): 109–22; Jean Veevers, "Voluntary Childlessness: A Review of Issues and Evidence," *Marriage and Family Review* 2 (1979): 1–26; Sarah Franklin, "Deconstructing Desperateness: The Social Construction of Infertility in Popular Representations of New Reproductive Technologies," in Maureen McNeal, Ian Varcoe and Steven Yearly, eds., *The New Reproductive Technologies* (New York: St. Martin's Press, 1990).

3. P. H. Jamison, Louis R. Franzini, and Robert M. Kaplan, "Some Assumed Characteristics of Voluntarily Childfree Women and Men," *Psychology of Women Quarterly* 4 (1979): 266–73; Charlene Miall, "Perceptions of Informal Sanctioning and the Stigma of Involuntary Childlessness," *Deviant Behavior* 6 (1985): 383–403; Marcia Ory, "The Decision to Parent or Not: Normative and Structural Components," *Journal of Marriage and the Family* 40 (Aug. 1978): 531–39.

4. Charles Westoff, "Fertility in the United States," *Science,* 233, October 31, 1986, 554–59; Barbara Vobejda, "U.S. Childbirths Booming; Experts Wondering Why," *The Morning Call,* Allentown, PA, Jan. 20, 1991, p. A22; Judith D. Schwartz, "Will I Be Able to Have a Baby?" *Glamour* 88 (Dec. 1990): 223, 256–59.

5. Judy Klemesrud, "Single Mothers by Choice: Perils and Joys," *New York Times,* May 2, 1983, 35; Maureen McGuire and Nancy Alexander, "Artificial Insemination of Single Women," *Fertility and Sterility* 43 (Feb. 1985): 182–84.

6. Nancy Felipe Russo, "The Motherhood Mandate," *Journal of Social Issues* 32 (1976): 143–53.

7. Norval Glenn and Sara McLanahan, "Children and Marital Happiness: A Further Specification of the Relationship," *Journal of Marriage and the Family* 44 (Feb. 1982):63–72; Sharon Houseknecht, "Childlessness and Marital Adjustment," *Journal of Marriage and the Family* 41 (May 1979):259–65; Richard Lerner and Spanier Graham, eds., *Child Influences on Marital and Family Interaction* (New York: Academic Press, 1978); Elaine Hilberman Carmen, N. F. Russo, and J. B. Miller, "Inequality and Women's Mental Health: An Overview," *American Journal of Psychiatry* 138 (Oct. 1981): 1319–30; Walter Gove and J. F. Tudor, "Adult Sex Roles and Mental Illness," *American Journal of Sociology* 78 (1973): 50–73; Holly Waldron and Donald Routh, "The Effect of the First Child on the Marital Relationship," *Journal of Marriage and the Family* 43 (Nov. 1981): 785–88; Sara McLanahan and Julia Adams, "Parenthood and Psychological Well-Being," *Annual Review of Sociology* 13 (1987): 237–57.

8. Erving Goffman, *Stigma* (Englewood Cliffs, NJ: Prentice Hall, 1963); Charlene Miall, "The Stigma of Involuntary Childlessness," *Social Problems* 33 (1986):

268–82; Jean Veevers, "The Violation of Fertility Mores: Voluntary Childlessness as Deviant Behavior," in Craig Boydell, Craig F. Grindstaff, and Paul C. Whitehead, eds., *Deviant Behavior and Societal Reaction* (New York: Holt Rinehart and Winston, 1973).

9. Edmond J. Farris and Mortimer Garrison, "Emotional Impact of Successful Donor Insemination," *Obstetrics and Gynecology* 3 (1954): 19–20; Charlene Miall, "Reproductive Technology vs. the Stigma of Involuntary Childlessness," *Social Casework,* 70 (1989): 43–50; Linda Williams, "Adoption Actions and Attitudes of Couples Seeking In Vitro Fertilization: An Exploratory Study," *Journal of Family Issues* 13 (1992): 99–113.

10. Linda Williams, "Adoption Actions and Attitudes of Couples Seeking *In Vitro* Fertilization."

11. Margarete Sandelowski, "Compelled to Try: The Never Enough Quality of Conceptive Technology," *Medical Anthropology Quarterly* 5 (1991):29–49; Arthur L. Greil and Karen L. Porter, "Couple Infertility as a Social Disability," pp. 17–38 in *Advances in Medical Sociology,* Vol. 2, eds. Gary Albrecht and Judith Levy. (JAI Press, 1991); Barbara Katz Rothman, *Recreating Motherhood; Ideology and Technology in a Patriarchal Society* (New York: W.W. Norton, 1989); Paul Lauritzen, "What Price Parenthood," *Hastings Center Report* 20 (1990): 38–46.

12. Debra Kalmuss, "The Use of Infertility Services Among Fertility Impaired Couples," *Demography* 24, (1987): 575–85; Marilyn B. Hirsch and William D. Mosher, "Characteristics of Infertile Women in the United States and Their Use of Infertility Services," *Fertility and Sterility* 47 (1987): 618–25; E. Bostofte, J. Semp, N. Bischoff, and H. Rebbe, "Socio-economic Status and Fertility of Couples Examined for Infertility; Social Status and Fertility," *Androlgia* 17 (1985): 564–69; Jeannette E. Given, G. S. Jones, and D. L. McMillen, "A Comparison of Personality Characteristics Between In Vitro Fertilization Patients and Other Infertile Patients," *Journal of In Vitro Fertilization Embryo Transfer* 2 (1985): 49–54.

Chapter 2: Feelings of Grief

1. Kathleen McGinnis-Craft, "Once Again," *RESOLVE Newsletter,* September 1985, 5.

2. Jill Woodcliff, "Changing," *RESOLVE Newsletter,* April 1985, 8.

3. Erich Lindemann, "Symptomatology and Management of Acute Grief," *American Journal of Psychiatry* 101 (1944): 141–48; Anne Martin Matthews and Ralph Matthews, "Beyond the Mechanics of Infertility: Perspectives on the Social Psychology of Infertility and Involuntary Childlessness," *Family Relations* 35 (Oct. 1986): 479–87; Barbara Eck Menning, "The Emotional Needs of Infertile Couples," *Fertility and Sterility* 34 (Oct. 1980): 313–19; Ann Lalos, Othon Lalos, Lars Jacobsson, and B. Von Schoultz, "Depression, Guilt and Isolation Among Infertile Women and their Partners," *Journal of Psychosomatic Obstetrics and Gynecology* 5 (1986): 197–206.

4. Patricia Mahlstedt, "The Psychological Component of Infertility," *Fertility and Sterility* 43 (March 1985): 341.
5. Janet Daling et al., "Tubal Infertility in Relation to Prior Induced Abortion," *Fertility and Sterility* 43 (March 1985): 389–94.
6. Miriam Mazor, "Emotional Reactions to Infertility," in *Infertility: Medical Emotional and Social Considerations* (New York: Human Science Press, 1984), 23–35; Helene Deutsch, *The Psychology of Women* (New York: Grune and Stratton, 1945); F. M. Mai, "The Diagnosis and Treatment of Psychogenic Infertility," *Infertility* 1 (1978): 109; Philip Sarrel and Alan H. DeCherney, "Psychotherapeutic Intervention for Treatment of Couples with Secondary Infertility," *Fertility and Sterility* 43 (June 1985): 897–900; Alice D. Domar, Machelle M. Seibel, and Herbert Benson, "The Mind/Body Program for Infertility: A New Behavioral Treatment Approach for Women with Infertility," *Fertility and Sterility* 53 (1990): 246–49.
7. Mazor, "Emotional Reactions to Infertility."
8. William D. Mosher and William F. Pratt, "Fecundity and Infertility in the United States, 1965–1988." National Center for Health Statistics, Advance Data, Vol. 92, December 4, 1990.
9. Gjerde Dausch, "Secondary Infertility: A Personal Experience," *RESOLVE Newsletter,* April 1982, 5.
10. Susan Borg and Judith Lasker, *When Pregnancy Fails: Families Coping with Miscarriage, Ectopic Pregnancy, Stillbirth, and Infant Death* (New York: Bantam, 1989); Lori Miller Kase, "Mixed Blessings", *Health* 22 (Nov. 1990): 64–67, 83–86.
11. Regina Furlong Lind, Rebecca L. Pruitt, and Dorothy Greenfield, "Previously Infertile Couples and the Newborn Intensive Care Unit," *Health and Social Work* 14, (1989): 127–33; Australian In Vitro Collaborative Group, "High Incidence of Preterm Births and Early Losses in Pregnancy after In Vitro Fertilization," *British Medical Journal* 291, (1985): 1160–63.

Chapter 3: Artificial Insemination

1. In 1987, a government survey of physicians' practices in the United States led to the estimate that 35,000 babies are born each year from AIH and 30,000 from AID. Baran and Pannor point out that, due to the secrecy that has surrounded AID, it is impossible to know how widespread the practice is. Annette Baran and Reuben Pannor, *Lethal Secrets: The Shocking Consequences and Unsolved Problems of Artificial Insemination* (New York: Warner Books, 1989); U.S. Congress, Office of Technology Assessment, *Artificial Insemination: Practice in the U.S.: Summary of a 1987 Survey* (Washington, DC: U.S. Government Printing Office): 1988.
2. Lori Andrews, *New Conceptions: A Consumer's Guide to the Newest Infertility Treatments* (New York: Ballantine, 1985); Erik Bostofte, Jorgen Serup, and Heinrich Rebbe, "Has the Fertility of Danish Men Declined through the Years in Terms of Semen Quality?" *International Journal of Fertility* 28 (1983): 91–95; Jane E. Brody, "Sperm Found Especially Vulnerable to

Environment," *New York Times,* March 10, 1981; Cynthia Cooke and Susan Dworkin, "It's Time to Take Male Infertility Seriously," *Ms.* March 1981, 89–91; Katherine Bouton, "Fighting Male Infertility," *The New York Times Magazine,* June 13, 1982, 86–91; Hiroshi Takihara, Jisaburo Sakatoku, and Abraham T. K. Crockett, "The Pathophysiology of Varicocele in Male Infertility," *Fertility and Sterility* 55 (1991): 861–68.

3. Stephen Corson and Frances F. Batzer, "Homologous Artificial Insemination," *Journal of Reproductive Medicine* 26 (May 1981): 909–15; Michael Diamond, G. Lavy, and A. H. DeCherney, "Pregnancy Following Use of the Cervical Cup for Home Artificial Insemination Utilizing Homologous Semen," *Fertility and Sterility* 39 (Apr. 1983): 480–84; Claude Gernignon and Jean-Marie Kunstmann, "AIH for Semen Insufficiency: 119 Cases," in G. David and W. Price, eds., *Human Artificial Insemination and Semen Preservation* (New York: Plenum Press, 1980); M. Usherwood, "AIH for Cases of Spermatozoa Antibodies and Oligo-zoospermia, *in* David and Price, *Human Artificial Insemination.*

4. Ethics Committee of the American Fertility Society, "Ethical Considerations of the New Reproductive Technologies," *Fertility and Sterility Supplement* 46 (Sep. 1986): 15–925; Jonathan Hewitt, "Treatment of Idiopathic Infertility, Cervical Mucus Hostility, and Male Infertility: Artificial Insemination with Husband's Semen or In-Vitro Fertilization," *Fertility and Sterility* 44 (Sep. 1985): 350–55; Andrew J. Friedman, Mary Juneau-Norcross, Beverly Sedensky, Nina Andrews, Jayne Dorfman, Daniel W. Cramer, "Life Table Analysis of Intrauterine Insemination Pregnancy Rate for Couples with Cervical Factor, Male Factor and Idiopathic Infertility," *Fertility and Sterility* 55 (1991): 1005–07.

5. Nancy Allen et al., "Intrauterine Insemination: A Critical Review," *Fertility and Sterility* 44 (Nov. 1985): 569–80; Roger Toffle et al., "Intrauterine Insemination: The University of Minnesota Experience," *Fertility and Sterility* 43 (May 1985): 743–47.

6. Vinay Sharma, Julian S. Pampiglione, Bridgett A. Mason, Stuart Campbell, and Andrew Riddle, "Experience with Peritoneal Oocyte and Sperm Transfer as an Outpatient-Based Treatment for Infertility," *Fertility and Sterility* 55 (1991): 579–82; Oute Hovatta, Henri Kurunmaki, Aila Tiitinen, Pekka Lahteenmaki, and Aarne I. Koskimies, "Direct Intraperitoneal or Intrauterine Insemination and Superovulation in Infertility Treatment: A Randomized Study," *Fertility and Sterility* 54 (1990): 339–41; William C. Dodson and A. F. Haney, "Controlled Ovarian Hyperstimulation and Intrauterine Insemination for Treatment of Infertility," *Fertility and Sterility* 55 (1991): 457–67.

7. Diane Clapp, "Artificial Insemination by Husband or Donor Sperm," publication of RESOLVE, n.d.; Martin Curie-Cohen, L. Luttrell, and S. Shapiro, "Current Practice of Artificial Insemination by Donor in the United States," *New England Journal of Medicine,* 300, March 15, 1979, 585–90; U.S. Congress, Office of Technology Assessment, *Artificial Insemination: Practice in the U.S.*

8. David Berger, "Couples' Reactions to Male Infertility and Donor Insemina-

tion," *American Journal of Psychiatry* 137 (September 1980): 1047–49; Laurence Karp, "Artificial Insemination: A Need for Caution," *American Journal of Medical Genetics* 9 (1981): 179–81; W. Thompson and D. D. Boyle, "Counselling Patients for Artificial Insemination and Subsequent Pregnancy," *Clinics in Obstetrics and Gynaecology* 9 (Apr. 1982): 211–25; A. Blaser, B. Maloigne-Katz, and U. Gigon, "Effects of Artificial Insemination with Donor Semen on the Psychology of the Husband," *Psychotherapy and Psychosomatics* 49, 1988: 17–21; Annette Baran and Reuben Pannor, *Lethal Secrets: The Shocking Consequences and Unsolved Problems of Artificial Insemination* (New York: Warner Books, 1989).

9. "More Childless Wives Conceive through Use of Frozen Sperm," *New York Times,* January 8, 1979, 19; U.S. Congress, Office of Technology Assessment, *Artificial Insemination: Practices in the U.S.;* Morbidity and Mortality Weekly Report, "Semen Banking, Organ and Tissue Transplantation, and HIV Antibody Testing," *JAMA* 259 (1988): 1301; Jon H. Alfredsson, S. P. Gudmundsson, and G. Snaedal, "Artificial Insemination by Donor with Frozen Sperm," *Obstetrical and Gynecological Survey* 38 (1983): 305–12.

10. Katrine Ames, "Savings Plan for a Generation," *Newsweek* 117 (February 18, 1991): 71.

11. G. L. Foss, "Artificial Insemination by Donor: A Review of 12 Years' Experience," *Journal of Biosocial Science* 14 (1982): 253–62; Michael Richter, Ray Haning, and Sanders Shapiro, "AID, Fresh vs Frozen," abstract, *Fertility and Sterility* 39 (March 1983): 397; William P. Hummel and Luther M. Talbert, "Current Management of a Donor Insemination Program," *Fertility and Sterility* 51, 1989: 919–30; Mari Schroeder-Jenkins and Susan A. Rothmann, "Causes of Donor Rejection in a Sperm Banking Program," *Fertility and Sterility* 51, 1989: 903–06.

12. Andrews, *New Conceptions,* 172; Charles Marwick, "Artificial Insemination Faces Regulation, Testing of Donor Semen, Other Measures," *JAMA* 260 (1988): 1339–40; Judith Gaines, "A Scandal of Artificial Insemination," *The New York Times Magazine,* 140 (Oct. 7, 1990): 523, 528–29.

13. Bernard Rubin, "Psychological Aspects of Human Artificial Insemination," *Archives of General Psychiatry* 13 (August 1965): 121–32.

14. George J. Annas, "Fathers Anonymous; Beyond the Best Interests of the Sperm Donor," *in* Aubrey Milunskey and G. Annas, *Genetics and the Law II* (New York: Plenum, 1979); Annette Baran and Reuben Pannor, *Lethal Secrets: The Shocking Consequences and Unsolved Problems of Artificial Insemination.*

15. Curie-Cohen, Luttrell, and Shapiro, "Current Practice of Artificial Insemination"; U.S. Congress, Office of Technology Assessment, *Artificial Insemination: Practice in the U.S.:* Summary of a 1987 survey. (Washington, DC: U.S. Government Office): 1988; J. Lasker and S. Borg, "Secrecy and the New Reproductive Technologies," in *New Approaches to Human Reproduction: Social and Ethical Dimensions,* eds. Linda Whiteford and Marilyn Poland (Westview Press, 1989).

16. "Barn Genom Insemination," (Children through Insemination) *Sou* 42 (1983): 201–19 (English summary); Kurt Back and Robert Snowden, "The

Anonymity of the Gamete Donor," *Journal of Psychosomatic Obstetrics and Gynecology* 9 (1988): 191–98; Judith Gaines, "A Scandal of Artificial Insemination," *The New York Times Magazine,* 140 (Oct. 7, 1990): 523, 528–29; Purdie, A., J. C. Peek, R. Irwin, J. Ellis, F. M. Graham, P. R. Fisher, "Identifiable Semen Donors—Attitude of Donors and Recipient Couples," *New Zealand Medical Journal* 105 (1992): 27–8; Ken Daniels and Karyn Taylor, "Secrecy and Openness in Donor Insemination," *Politics and The Life Sciences* (Aug. 1993).

17. Andrews, *New Conceptions.*

18. G. L. Foss, "Artificial Insemination by Donor"; Stephen Corson, F. R. Batzer, and M. M. Baylson, "Donor Insemination, "*Obstetrics and Gynecology Annual* 12 (1983): 283–309; Curie-Cohen, Luttrell, and Shapiro, "Current Practice of Artificial Insemination."

19. U.S. Congress, Office of Technology Assessment, *Artificial Insemination: Practice in the U.S.*

20. Rubin, "Psychological Aspects."

21. Alan F. Guttmacher, "The Role of Artificial Insemination in the Treatment of Sterility," *Obstetric and Gynecologic Survey* 15 (1960): 761–85.

22. B. I. Somfai and A. Lynch, "A Judeo-Christian Evaluation of Artificial Insemination and Its Implication to Embryo Transfer," *Archives of Andrology* 5 (1980): 50; J. Lasker and H. Parmet, "Rabbinic and Feminist Responses to Reproductive Technology," *Journal of Feminist Studies in Religion* 6 (1990): 117–30.

23. R. Snowden, G. D. Mitchell, and E. M. Snowden, *Artificial Reproduction: A Social Investigation* (London: George Allen and Unwin, 1983).

24. J. C. Czyba and M. Chevret, "Psychological Reactions of Couples to Artificial Insemination with Donor Sperm," *International Journal of Fertility* 24 (1979): 240–45; R.S. Ledward, E. M. Symonds, and S. Eynon, "Social and Environmental Factors as Criteria for Success in Artificial Insemination by Donor," *Journal of Biosocial Science* 14 (1982): 263–75; Leslie R. Schover, Robert L. Collins, Susan Richards, "Psychological Aspects of Donor Insemination: Evaluation and Follow-Up of Recipient Couples," *Fertility and Sterility* 57 (1992): 583–90.

25. Aphrodite Clamar, "Psychological Implications of Donor Insemination," *American Journal of Psychoanalysis* 40 (1980): 176; Baran and Pannor, pp. 13, 152.

26. Maureen McGuire and Nancy Alexander, "Artificial Insemination of Single Women," *Fertility and Sterility* 43 (February 1985): 182–84; Cheri A. Pies, "Lesbians and the Choice to Parent," *Marriage and Family Review* 14, 1989: 137–54; Ann E. Potter and Patricia K. Knaub, "Single Motherhood by Choice: A Parenting Alternative," *Lifestyles: Family and Economic Issues* 9, 1988: 240–49; Carson Strong and Jay Schinfeld, "The Single Woman and Artificial Insemination by Donor," *Journal of Reproductive Medicine* 29 (May 1984): 293–99.

27. William P. Hummel and Luther M. Talbert, "Current Management of a Donor Insemination Program," *Fertility and Sterility* 51, 1989: 919–30.

28. Leslie Dreyfous, "Gay Couples Are Redefining Parenthood," *The Morning Call* April 21, 1991, p. A4.
29. Patricia St. Clair Stephenson and Marsden G. Wagner, "Turkey—Baster Babies: A View from Europe," *The Milbank Quarterly* 69, 1991: 45–50.
30. Ian Milsom and Per Bergman, "A Study of Parental Attitudes after Donor Insemination," *Acta Obstetrica et Gynecologica Scandinavica* (1982): 125–28; Michael Humphrey and Heather Humphrey, "Marital Relationships in Couples Seeking Donor Insemination," *Journal of Biosocial Science* 19 (1987): 209–19.

Chapter 4: In Vitro *Fertilization*

1. Carolyn M. Mazure and Dorothy A. Greenfield, "Psychological Studies of In-Vitro Fertilization/Embryo Transfer Patients," *Journal of In-Vitro Fertilization and Embryo Transfer* 6 (1989): 242–56; David Baram, Ellen Tourtelot, Eberhard Muechler, and Ko-En Huang, "Psychosocial Adjustment Following Unsuccessful in Vitro Fertilization," *Journal of Psychosomatic Obstetrics and Gynecology* 9 (1988): 181–90; Dorothy Greenfield, M. P. Dramond, and Alan H. DeCherney, "Grief Reactions Following a Failed Cycle of In-Vitro Fertilization," *Journal of Psychosomatic Obstetrics and Gynecology* 8 (1988): 169–74; M. Seibel and S. Levin, "A New Era in Reproductive Technologies: The Emotional Stages of In-Vitro Fertilization," *Journal of In-Vitro Fertilization and Embryo Transfer* 4 (1987): 135; Christopher R. Newton, Margaret T. Hearn, and Albert A. Yuzpe, "Psychological Assessment and Follow-Up after In-Vitro Fertilization: Assessing the Impact of Failure," *Fertility and Sterility* 54 (1990): 879–86; Anthony E. Reading, Li C Chang, and John F. Klein, "Psychological State and Coping Styles Across an In-Vitro Fertilization Treatment Cycle," *Journal of Reproductive and Infant Psychology* 7 (1989): 95–103; Ken Daniels, "Psychosocial Factors for Couples Awaiting In Vitro Fertilization," *Social Work in Health Care* 14 (1989): 81–98; Aila Collins, Ellen W. Freeman, Andrea S. Boxer, Richard Tureck, "Perceptions of Infertility and Treatment of Stress in Females as Compared with Males Entering In Vitro Fertilization Treatment," *Fertility and Sterility* 57 (1992): 350–56.
2. C. Campagnoli, A. DiGregorio, R. Arisio, and L. Fessia, "Patient Selection for In Vitro Fertilization and Embryo Transfer," *Experientia*, 41, December 15, 1985, 1491–93; Claudio Chillik, "The Role of In Vitro Fertilization in Infertile Patients with Endometriosis," *Fertility and Sterility* 44 (July 1985): 56–61; Jacques Cohen et al., "In Vitro Fertilization: A Treatment for Male Infertility," *Fertility and Sterility* 43 (March 1985): 422–32; Patrick Steptoe, "The Selection of Couples for In Vitro Fertilization and Embryo Replacement," *Annals New York Academy of Sciences* 442 (1985): 487–89.
3. Medical Research International, Society for Assisted Reproductive Technology, American Fertility Society, "In Vitro Fertilization—Embryo Transfer in the U.S.: 1990 results from the IVF-ET Registry," *Fertility and Sterility* 57 (1992): 15–24; Jose P. Balmaceda, Veronica Alam, Daniel Roszjtein, Teri Ord, Kellie Snell, Ricardo H. Asch, "Embryo Implantation Rates in Oocyte Dona-

tion: A Prospective Comparison of Tubal Versus Uterine Transfers," *Fertility and Sterility* 57 (1992): 362–65; Thomas Toth, Sergio Oehninger, James P. Toner, Robert G. Brzyski, Anibal A. Acosta, Suheil J. Muasher, "Embryo Transfer to the Uterus or the Fallopian Tube after in vitro Fertilization Yields Similar Results," *Fertility and Sterility* 57 (1992): 1110–13; Sheldon J. Silber, *How to Get Pregnant with the New Technology* (New York: Warner Books, 1991).

4. Jacques Cohen et al., "In Vitro Fertilization Using Cryopreserved Donor Semen in Cases Where Both Partners Are Infertile," *Fertility and Sterility* 43 (Apr. 1985): 570–74; Maha Mahadeven, A. D. Trounson, and J. F. Leeton, "Successful Use of Human Semen Cryobanking for In Vitro Fertilization," *Fertility and Sterility* 40 (Sep. 1983): 340–43; Thomas B. Pool, Joseph E. Martinez, Linda R. Ellsworth, Janette B. Perez, and Suzanne H. Atiel, "Zygote Intrafallopian Transfer with Donor Rescue: A New Option for Severe Male Factor Infertility," *Fertility and Sterility* 54 (1990): 166–68; Mark V. Sauer, Richard J. Paulson, and Rogerio A. Lobo, "A Preliminary Report on Oocyte Donation Extending Reproduction Potential to Women Over 40," *New England Journal of Medicine* 323 (1990): 1157–60; Alan Trounson, J. Leeton, M. Besanko, C. Wood, and A. Conti, "Pregnancy Established in an Infertile Patient after Transfer of a Donated Embryo Fertilized In Vitro," *British Medical Journal* 286 (1983): 835–38; Simon Fishel, Peter Jackson, Severino Antinore, Joanne Johnson, Stefano Grossi, and Caterina Versaci, "Subzonal Insemination for the Alleviation of Infertility," *Fertility and Sterility* 54 (1990): 828–35.

5. Michael R. Soules, "The In Vitro Fertilization Pregnancy Rate: Let's Be Honest with One Another," *Fertility and Sterility* 43 (Apr. 1985): 511–13; Sherman J. Silber, *How to Get Pregnant With the New Technology* (New York: Warner Books, 1991); Medical Research International, Society for Assisted Reproductive Technology, American Fertility Society, "In Vitro Fertilization—Embryo Transfer in the United States: 1990 Results from the IVF-ET Registry."

6. Committee on Small Business, House of Representatives, *Consumer Protection Issues Involving In Vitro Fertilization Clinics*, U.S. Government Printing Office, Washington, DC 1989; MRI, SART and AFS, "In Vitro Fertilization—Embryo Transfer in the U.S."

7. Howard H. Jones et al., "What Is a Pregnancy? A Question for Programs of In Vitro Fertilization," *Fertility and Sterility* 40 (Dec. 1983): 728–33; Medical Research International, Society for Assisted Reproductive Technology, American Fertility Society, "In Vitro Fertilization and Embryo Transfer in the U.S."

8. MRI, SART and AFS, *Ibid.*

9. *Ibid.*

10. Ellen Freeman, A. S. Boxer, K. Rickels, R. Tureck, and L. Mastroianni, Jr., "Psychological Evaluation and Support in Program of In Vitro Fertilization and Embryo Transfer, *Fertility and Sterility* 43 (Jan. 1985): 48–53; F. P. Haseltine, C. Mazure, W. de L'Aune, D. Greenfeld, N. Laufer, B. Tarlatzis, M. L. Polan, E. E. Jones, R. Graebe, F. Nero, A. D'lugi, D. Fazio, J. Masters, A. H. DeCherney, "Psychological Interviews in Screening Couples Undergoing In Vitro Fertilization," *Annals New York Academy of Sciences* 442 (1985): 504–22.

11. Some states have passed legislation requiring insurance companies to cover in vitro fertilization and some countries offer reimbursement under their national health programs; Phillip Godwin, "The High Cost of Fighting Infertility," *Changing Times* 45 (March 1989): 73–78.

12. Ken Mao and Carl Wood, "Barriers to Treatment of Infertility by In Vitro Fertilization and Embryo Transfer," *Medical Journal of Australia* 140 (Apr. 1984): 532–33; S. R. Leiblum, E. Kemmann, D. Colburn, S. Pasquale, A. DeLisi, "Unsuccessful In Vitro Fertilization: A Follow-Up Study," *Journal of In Vitro Fertilization and Embryo Transfer* 4 (1987): 46.

13. Margaret Sandelowski, "Compelled to Try: The Never Enough Quality of Conceptive Technology," *Med Anthro Quarterly* 5 (1991): 29–47; Linda Williams, "It's Going to Work for Me: Responses to Failures of In Vitro Fertilization," *Birth* 15 (1988): 153–56.

14. Australian In Vitro Collaborative Group, "High Incidence of Preterm Births and Early Losses in Pregnancy after In Vitro Fertilization," *British Medical Journal,* 291 (1985): 1160–63; John Yovich, "Embryo Transfer Technique as a Cause of Ectopic Pregnancies in In Vitro Fertilization," *Fertility and Sterility* 44 (Sep. 1985): 318.

15. A. Demoulin, R. Bologne, J. Hustin, and R. Lambotte, "Is Ultrasound Monitoring of Follicular Growth Harmless?" *Annals of New York Academy of Sciences* 442 (1985): 146–52; Melvin Stratmeyer and Christopher Christman, "Biological Effects of Ultrasound," *Women and Health* 7 (1982): 65–81; Gregory Corsan and Ekkehard Kemmann, "The Role of Superovulation with Monotropins in Ovulatory Infertility: A Review," *Fertility and Sterility* 55 (1991): 468–77; Alison Solomon, "Sometimes Perganol Kills" *in* Renate D. Klein, ed., *Infertility: Women Speak Out About Their Experiences of Reproduction* (London: Pandora Press, 1989): 46–50; Marian E. Carter and David N. Joyce, "Ovarian Carcinoma in a Patient Hyperstimulated by Gonadotropin Therapy for In Vitro Fertilization: A Case Report," *Journal of In Vitro Fertilization and Embryo Transfer* 2 (1987): 126–28; Patricia A. Stephenson, "Ovulation Induction in Infertility Treatment: An Assessment of the Risks", pp. 97–121 *in Tough Choices: In Vitro Fertilization and The Reproductive Technologies: A Health Services Perspective,* eds. Patricia A. Stephenson and Marsden G. Wagner (Philadelphia: Temple University Press, 1993); Renate D. Klein, "The Making of This Book" and "Resistance: From the Exploitation of Infertility to an Exploration of In-Fertility," *in Infertility: Women Speak Out,* pp. 1–7, 229–95.

16. Susan Lenz and Jorgen Lauritsen, "Ultrasonically Guided Percutaneous Aspiration of Human Follicles under Local Anesthesia: A New Method of Collecting Oocytes for In Vitro Fertilization," *Fertility and Sterility* 38 (December 1982): 673–77; Matts Wikland, L. Enk, and L. Hamberger, "Transvesical and Transvaginal Approaches for the Aspiration of Follicles by Use of Ultrasound," *Annals of New York Academy of Sciences* 442 (1985): 146–52.

17. John Biggers, "Risks of In Vitro Fertilization and Embryo Transfer in Humans," *In Vitro Fertilization and Embryo Transfer,* 1983, 393; John Henahan, "Fertilization, Embryo Transfer Procedures Raise Many Questions," *Journal of American Medical Association,* August 17, 1984, 877–82; James Schlessel-

man, "How Does One Assess the Risk of Abnormalities from Human In Vitro Fertilization?" *American Journal of Obstetrics and Gynecology,* 135 (1979): 135–48; J. P. Relier, M. Couchard, C. Huon, "Risks of IVF—The Neonatologist's Experience," *in* Stephenson and Wagner, *In Vitro Fertilization and the New Reproductive Technologies.*

18. Nico Bollen, Michael Camus, Caterina Staessen, Herman Tournaye, Paul Devroey, and Andre C. Van Steirteghem, "The Incidence of Multiple Pregnancy after In Vitro Fertilization and Embryo Transfer, Gamete or Zygote Intrafallopian Transfer, *Fertility and Sterility* 55 (1991): 314–18.

19. Lori Miller Kase, "Mixed Blessings," *Health* 22 (Nov. 1990): 64–67, 83–86; Khalil M. A. Tabsh, "Transabdominal Multifetal Pregnancy Reduction: Report of 40 Cases," *Obstetrics and Gynecology* 75 (1990): 739–41; Lauren Lynch, Richard Berkowitz, Usha Chitkara, and Manuel Alvarez, "First-Trimester Transabdominal Multifetal Pregnancy Reduction: A Report of 85 Cases," *Obstetrics and Gynecology,* 75 (1990): 735–38.

20. Constance Holden, "Two Fertilized Eggs Stir Global Fervor," *Science,* 225, July 6, 1984, 35; Alan Trounson, "In Vitro Fertilization, Problems of the Future," *British Journal of Hospital Medicine* 31 (Feb. 1984): 104–06; David Levran, Jehoshua Dor, Edwina Rudak, Laslo Nebel, Izhar Ben-Shlomo, Zion Ben-Rafael, and Shlomo Mashiach, "Pregnancy Potential of Human Oocytes— The Effect of Cryopreservation," *New England Journal of Medicine* 323 (1990): 1153–56.

21. Ethics Advisory Board, *Report and Conclusions: HEW Support of Research Involving Human In Vitro Fertilization and Embryo Transfer* (Washington, DC: HEW, 1979); Peter Singer and Diane Wells, "In Vitro Fertilization: The Major Issues," *Journal of Medical Ethics* 9 (1983): 192–95.

Chapter 5: Surrogacy

1. Cynthia Gorney, "For Love and Money," *California,* October 1983, 91.

2. Gena Corea, *The Mother Machine: Reproductive Technologies from Artificial Insemination to Artificial Wombs* (New York: Harper and Row, 1985); Ethics Committee of the American Fertility Society, "Ethical Considerations of the New Reproductive Technologies," *Fertility and Sterility Supplement* 46 (Sep. 1985): 15–925; Dianne Bartels, *Beyond Baby M: Ethical Issues in New Reproductive Techniques* (Clifton, NJ: Humana Press, 1990); Karen H. Rothenberg, "Baby M, The Surrogacy Contract and The Health Care Professional," *Law, Medicine, and Health Care* 16 (1988): 113–20.

3. See text and footnotes to chapter 11.

4. Lea Stewart, "The Discourse of Reproductive Technology: The Ethical Implications of Surrogate Motherhood" in J. Jaksa and M. Pritchard, eds., *Communication Ethics,* 2nd ed. (Belmont, CA: Wadsworth, 1994).

5. Lisa Belkin, "Childless Couples Hang on to Last Hope, Despite Law," *New York Times* July 28, 1992, A1, B2.

6. *Ibid.*

7. "Women Who Experienced Surrogacy Speak Out," Patricia Foster in Renate D.

Klein, ed., *Infertility; Women Speak Out About Their Experiences of Repro-ductive Medicine.* (London: Pandora Press, 1989): 151–52.

8. "Women Who Experienced Surrogacy Speak Out," Mary Beth Whitehead, *in* Klein, *ibid.,* pp. 140, 142.

9. Noel Keane, with Dennis Breo, *The Surrogate Mother* (New York: Everest House, 1981).

10. Phyllis Chesler, *Sacred Bond: Motherhood Under Siege;* Andrews, Lori, *Be-tween Strangers; Surrogate Mothers, Expectant Fathers, and Brave New Babies* (New York: Harper and Row, 1989); "Contract Enforced in Child's 'Best Interests'" (Baby M decision by Judge Harvey R. Sorkow), 119 *New Jersey Law Journal* (Apr. 16, 1987): 29–41.

11. Walter Wadlington, "Baby M: Catalyst for Reform?" *Journal of Contemporary Health Law and Policy* 5 (1989): 1–20.

12. Phyllis Chesler, *Sacred Bond: Motherhood Under Siege;* Andrews, Lori, *Be-tween Strangers;* Mahoney, Joan, "An Essay on Surrogacy and Feminist Thought," *Law, Medicine and Health Care* 16 (1988): 81–88; Auyela R. Holder, "Surrogate Motherhood and the Best Interest of Children," *Law, Medicine, and Health Care* 16 (1988): 51–56.

13. Gena Corea, *The Mother Machine;* Anita Allen, "The Black Surrogate Mother," *Harvard Black Letter Journal* 8 (1991): 17–31; Kathy Pollitt, "When is a Mother not a Mother?" *The Nation,* December 31, 1990, 825, 840–46.

14. Lori Andrews, "Surrogate Motherhood: The Challenge for Feminists," *Law, Medicine, and Health Care* 16 (1988): 72–80; Mahoney, "An Essay on Surro-gacy and Feminist Thought."

15. Lisa Belkin, "Childless Couples Hang on to Last Hope, Despite Law"; David Bauder, "New York Gets Law Banning Surrogate Parenting For Pay," *Morning Call,* Allentown, PA, July 23, 1992.

16. *Ibid.*

Chapter 6: The Rise and Fall of Ovum Transfer: A Cautionary Tale

1. Information about possible reasons for using OT and about the research on OT is derived from the following sources: Harris Brotman, "Human Embryo Transplants," *The New York Times Magazine,* January 8, 1984; John E. Buster and Mark V. Sauer, "Nonsurgical Donor Ovum Transfer: New Option for Infer-tile Couples," *Contemporary OB/GYN,* August 1986, 39–48; John E. Buster, Maria Bustillo et al., "Biologic and Morphologic Development of Donated Human Ova Recovered by Nonsurgical Uterine Lavage," *American Journal of Obstetrics and Gynecology,* 153, September 15, 1985, 211–17; Maria Bustillo, John E. Buster et al., "Nonsurgical Ovum Transfer as a Treatment in Infer-tile Women," *Journal of the American Medical Association,* 251, March 2, 1984, 1171–73; FGR Information Packet, Fertility and Genetics Research, Inc., Los Angeles, CA; Grace Ganz Blumberg, "Legal Issues in Nonsurgical Human Ovum Transfer," *Journal of the American Medical Association,* 251, March 2, 1984, 1178–81; Transcript #08223, "Donahue Show," Multimedia Entertainment, Inc., Syndication Services, Cincinnati, OH.

2. Fern Chapman, "Going for Gold in the Baby Business," *Fortune,* September 17, 1984, 41–77; Hal Lancaster, "Firm Offering Human Embryo Transfers for Profit Stirs Legal and Ethical Debates," *Wall Street Journal,* March 7, 1984, 33; Martin Stuart-Harle, "Making a Buck on Babies," *Globe and Mail,* Toronto, April 19, 1984, L1.

3. "Breeding Bonanza: Embroy Swaps Yield Cows Many Calves Each Year," *Wall Street Journal,* May 9, 1979, 1, 39.

4. Anne Marie C. Kelly, "Psychological Interviews with Ovum Transfer Candidates," typescript, paper presented at the American Psychological Association meetings, Anaheim, CA, 1983; David J. Martin, "MMPI Profiles of Ovum Transfer Donors and Recipients," paper presented at the American Psychological Association meetings, Anaheim, CA, 1983.

5. George J. Annas, "Surrogate Embryo Transfer: The Perils of Parenting," *Hastings Center Report,* June 1984, 25–26; Brotman, "Human Embryo Transplants."

6. John Jenkins, "Fertility Rights," *TWA Ambassador,* January 1985, 60–62.

7. Glenn Kramon, "Infertility Chain: The Good and Bad in Medicine," *New York Times,* June 19, 1992, D1; Alison Leigh Cowan, "Market Place; Can a Baby-Making Venture Deliver?" *New York Times,* June 1, 1992, D1.

8. Mona Field, "On the Demise of a Research Project: A Case Study," Glendale Community College, Glendale, CA.

9. *Ibid.*

10. Buster and Sauer, "Nonsurgical Donor Ovum Transfer: New Option for Infertile Couples"; Buster et al., "Biologic and Morphologic Development of Donated Human Ova Recovered by Nonsurgical Uterine Lavage"; Bustillo et al., "Nonsurgical Ovum Transfer as a Treatment in Infertile Women."

11. Brotman, "Human Embryo Transplants"; Buster and Sauer, "Nonsurgical Donor Ovum Transfer"; Buster et al., "Biologic and Morphologic Development Development of Donated Human Ova Recovered by Nonsurgical Uterine Lavage"; Bustillo et al., "Non-surgical Ovum Transfer as a Treatment in Infertile Women"; FGR Information Packet.

12. Leonardo Formigli, Graziella Formigli, Carlo Roccio, "Donation of Fertilized Uterine Ova to Infertile Women," *Fertility and Sterility* 47 (Jan. 1987): 162–65.

13. Mark V. Sauer, M. Jan Gorrill, John R. Marshall, and John E. Buster, "An Instrument for the Recovery of Preimplantation Uterine Ova," *Obstetrics & Gynecology* 71 (1988): 804–06.

14. Mark V. Sauer, Robert E. Anderson, Richard J. Paulson, "A Trial of Superovulation in Ovum Donors Undergoing Uterine Lavage," *Fertility and Sterility* 51 (Jan. 1989): 131–34.

15. Mark V. Sauer, and Richard J. Paulson, "Human Oocyte and Preembryo Donation: An Evolving Method for the Treatment of Infertility 163 (Nov. 1990): 1421–24.

16. Ethics Committee of the American Fertility Society, "Ethical Considerations of the New Reproductive Technologies," *Fertility and Sterility Supplement* 46 (Sep. 1986): 15–92.

17. John E. Buster and Sandra A. Carson, "Genetic Diagnosis of the Preimplan-

tation Embryo," *American Journal of Medical Genetics* 34 (1989): 211–16; Ronald Kotulak and Peter Gorner, "Babies By Design," *Chicago Tribune*, March 3, 1991, Sunday Magazine, 14.
18. Stuart-Harle, "Making a Buck on Babies."

Chapter 7: Donors and Surrogate Mothers

1. D. Franks, "Psychiatric Evaluation of Women in a Surrogate Mother Program," *American Journal of Psychiatry* 138 (1981): 1378–79; Hilary Hanafin, "The Surrogate Mother: An Exploratory Study," Ph.D. diss., California School of Professional Psychology, Los Angeles, 1984; Philip J. Parker, "Motivation of Surrogate Mothers: Initial Findings," *American Journal of Psychiatry* 140 (Jan. 1983): 117–18.
2. An exception is Annette Baran and Reuben Pannor, *Lethal Secrets: The Shocking Consequences and Unsolved Problems of Artificial Insemination* (New York: Warner Books, 1989).
3. David J. Handelman, S. M. Dunn, A. J. Conway, L. M. Boylan, and R. P. Jansen, "Psychological and Attitudinal Profiles in Donors for Artificial Insemination," *Fertility and Sterility* 43 (January 1985): 95–101; Patrick Huerre, "Psychological Aspects of Sperm Donation," *in* G. David and W. S. Price, eds., *Human Artificial Insemination and Semen Preservation* (New York: Plenum Press, 1980), 461–65; Gabor T. Kovacs, C. E. Clayton, and P. McGowan, "The Attitudes of Semen Donors," *Clinical Reproduction and Fertility* 2 (1983): 73–75; Piet Nijs, O. Steeno, and A. Steppe, "Evaluation of AID Donors: Medical and Psychological Aspects," *in* David and Price, *Human Artificial Insemination* 453–59; Ken R. Daniels, "Semen Donors: Their Motivations and Attitudes to Their Offspring," *Journal of Reproductive and Infant Psychology* 7 (1989): 121–27.
4. Martin Curie-Cohen, L. Luttrell, and S. Shapiro, "Current Pratice of Artificial Insemination by Donor in the United States," *New England Journal of Medicine*, 300, March 15, 1979, 585–90.
5. See above, note 3.
6. Huerre, "Psychological Aspects"; Kovacs, Clayton, and McGowan, "The Attitudes of Semen Donors"; Lynn Snowden, "Sperm and The Single Girl," *Elle*, Nov. 1991, 180–84.
7. Robyn Rowland, "Attitudes and Opinions of Donors on Artificial Insemination by Donor (AID) Programme," *Clinical Reproduction and Fertility* 2 (1983): 249–59.
8. Nancy Reame, "Stress and Obstetrical Complications of Pregnancy, Labor, and Delivery with Emphasis on a Surrogate Mother Population," paper presented at American Orthopsychiatric Association, Toronto, April, 1984.
9. Tamar Kaufman, "With Her Ova, She Helps Replenish Jewish People," *Jewish Exponent*, June 5, 1992, 2X, 3X; Jacqueline A. Bartlett, "Psychiatric Issues in Non-Anonymous Oocyte Donation," *Psychosomatics* 32 (1991): 433–37; Barbara Nevins, "The $2000 Egg," *Redbook* (Nov. 1992): 119–26.
10. J. Leeton, C. Caro, D. Howlett, and J. Harman, "The Search for Donor Eggs:

A Problem of Supply and Demand," *Clinical Reproduction and Fertility* 4 (1986): 337–40.

11. Snowden, "Sperm and the Single Girl."

12. Nijs, Steeno, and Steppe, "Evaluation of AIDS Donors."

13. Sandra R. Leiblum and Christopher Barbrack, "AID: A Survey of Attitudes and Knowledge in Medical Students and Infertile Couples," *Journal of Biosocial Science* 15 (1983): 165–72.

14. Bartlett, "Psychiatric Issues in Non-Anonymous Oocyte Donation"; Cheri A. Pies, "Lesbians and the Choice to Parent," *Marriage and Family Review* 14 (1989): 137–54; Gena Corea, *The Mother Machine: Reproductive Technologies from Artificial Insemination to Artificial Wombs* (New York: Harper and Row, 1985); Ann Snitow, "The Paradox of Birth Technology: Exploring the Good, the Bad, and the Scary," *Ms.,* December 1986, 42–46, 76–77. "Sperm Donor May Seek Rights to the Lesbian Couple's Baby," *Morning Call,* Allentown, PA, July 25, 1991; James M. Treppa, "In Vitro Fertilization Through Egg Donation: A Prospective View of Legal Issues," *Golden Gate University Law Review* 22 (1992): 777–95; "Court Denies Visitation Rights to Lesbian Parent in New York," *Morning Call,* Allentown, PA, May 5, 1991.

15. John A. Robertson, "Ethical and Legal Issues in Human Egg Donation," *Fertility and Sterility* 52 (1989): 353–63.

16. Rita Arditti, "Surrogate Mothering Exploits Women," *Science for the People* (May/June 1987): 22–23.

17. Philip J. Parker, "The Psychology of the Pregnant Surrogate Mother: A Newly Updated Report of a Longitudinal Pilot Sutdy," paper presented at American Orthopsychiatric Association, Toronto, April 1984; Elizabeth Kane, *Birth Mother* (So. Melbourne: Sun Books, 1990).

18. Leverett Millen and Samuel Roll, "Solomon's Mothers: A Special Case of Pathological Bereavement," *American Journal of Orthopsychiatry* 55 (1985): 411–18; Eva Y. Deykin, Lee Campbell, and Patricia Patti, "The Postadoption Experience of Surrendering Parents," *American Journal of Orthopsychiatry* 54 (1984): 271–80; Phyllis Silverman, *Helping Women Cope with Grief* (Beverly Hills: Sage, 1981).

19. Rowland, "Attitudes and Opinions of Donors"; Daniels, "Semen Donors: Their Motivations and Attitudes to their Offspring."

20. Judith Lasker and Susan Borg, "Secrecy and the New Reproductive Technologies," in *New Approaches to Human Reproduction: Social and Ethical Dimensions,* eds. Linda Whiteford and Marilyn Poland (Westview Press, 1989); Kurt W. Back and Robert Snowden, "The Anonymity of the Gamete Donor," *Journal of Psychosomatic Obstetrics and Gynaecology* 9 (1988): 191–98.

21. George Annas, "Fathers Anonymous: Beyond the Best Interest of the Sperm Donor," *Family Law Quarterly* 14 (1980): 1–13.

22. Richard Titmuss, *The Gift Relationship* (London: Allen and Unwin, 1971).

Chapter 8: The Professionals

1. Alan H. DeCherney, "Doctored Babies," *Fertility and Sterility* 40 (Dec. 1983): 724–27.

2. House of Representatives, Committee on Small Business, "Consumer Protection Issues Involving *In Vitro* Fertilization Clinics," March 9, 1989; Richard E. Blackwell, Bruce R. Carr, R. Jeffrey Chang, Alan H. DeCherney, Arthur F. Haney, William R. Keye, Jr., Robert W. Rebar, John A. Rock, Zev Rosenwaks, Machelle M. Seibel, Michael R. Soules, "Are We Exploiting the Infertile Couple," *Fertility and Sterility* 48 (1987): 735–39.

3. C. R. Stewart, K. R. Daniels, and J. D. H. Boulnois, "The Development of a Psychosocial Approach to Artificial Insemination of Donor Sperm," *New Zealand Medical Journal,* December 8, 1982, 853–55.

4. Patricia St. Clair Stephenson and Marsden G. Wagner, "Turkey-Baster Babies: A View From Europe," *The Milbank Quarterly* 69 (1991): 45–50.

5. F. P. Haseltine, C. Mazure, W. de L'Aune, D. Greenfeld, N. Laufer, B. Tarlatzis, M. L. Polan, E. E. Jones, R. Graebe, F. Nero, A. D'lugi, D. Fazio, J. Masters, A. H. DeCherney, "Psychological Interviews in Screening Couples Undergoing In Vitro Fertilization," *Annals of New York Academy of Sciences* 442 (1985) 504–22; W. I. H. Johnston et al., "Patient Selection for In Vitro Fertilization: Physical and Psychological Aspects," *Annals of New York Academy of Sciences* 442 (1985): 490–503.

6. Marcia Millman, *The Unkindest Cut: Life in the Backrooms of Medicine* (New York: Morrow, 1977).

7. Howard Jones, "In Vitro Fertilization: Past, Present, and Future," presentation at Lehigh University, October 14, 1986.

8. Merle A. Bombardieri and Diane Clapp, "Easing Stress for IVF Patients and Staff," *Comtemporary OB/GYN,* October 1984, 91–97; Susan Anderson, Filomena Nero, Judith Rodin, Michael Diamond, and Alan DeCherney, "Coping Patterns of In Vitro Fertilization Nurse Coordinators: Strategies for Combating Low Outcome Effectance," *Psychology and Health* 3 (1989): 221–32.

Chapter 9: The Couple

1. Arthur L. Greil, Thomas A. Leitko, Karen L. Porter, "Infertility: His and Hers," *Gender and Society* 2 (1988): 172–99; H. J. Brand, "The Influence of Sex Differences on the Acceptance of Infertility": *Journal of Reproductive and Infant Psychology* 7 (1989): 127–31; Frank M. Andrews, Antonia Abbey, and L. Jill Halman, "Stress From Infertility, Marriage Factors, and Subjective Well-Being of Wives and Husbands," *Journal of Health and Social Behavior* 32 (1991): 238–53; John Wright, Claude Duchesne, Stephane Sabourin, Francois Bissonnette, Johanne Benoit, Yvan Girard, "Psychosocial Distress and Infertility; Men and Women Respond Differently," *Fertility and Sterility* 55 (1991): 100–08; Ann Lalos, Othon Lalos, Lars Jacobsson, Bo Von Schoultz, "Depression, Guilt, and Isolation Among Infertile Women and Their Partners," *Journal of Psychosomatic Obstetrics and Gynecology* 5 (1986): 197–206; Robert D. Nachtigall, Gay Becker, Mark Wozny, "The Effects of Gender-Specific Diagnosis on Men's and Women's Response to Infertility," *Fertility and Sterility* 57 (1992): 113–21; Kandi Stinson, Judith Lasker, Janet Lohmann, and Lori Toedter, Parents' Grief Following Pregnancy Loss; A Comparison of Mothers and Fathers," *Family Relations* 41 (1992): 218–223.

2. Judith Lasker and Susan Borg, "Secrecy and the New Reproductive Technologies," in *New Approaches to Human Reproduction: Social and Ethical Dimensions,* eds. Linda Whiteford and Marilyn Poland (Westview Press, 1989); Kurt W. Back and Robert Snowden, "The Anonymity of the Gamete Donor," *Journal of Psychosomatic Obstetrics and Gynecology* 9 (1988): 191–98.

3. Judith Lorber, "Gender Politics and In Vitro Fertilization Use," paper presented at the Emergency Conference of the Feminist International Network on the New Reproductive Technologies, Sweden, July 3–8, 1985.

4. Lili Hartman, "Thoughts from the Fertile Partner," *RESOLVE Newsletter,* September 1985, 3.

5. Anonymous, "AID Doubts and Feelings," *RESOLVE Newsletter,* December 1985, 2.

6. Giuseppe d'Elicio, Aldo Campana, and L. Mornaghini, "Psychodynamic Discussions with Couples Requesting AID," *in* G. David and W. Price, eds., *Human Artificial Insemination and Semen Preservation* (New York: Plenum Press, 1980), 409–10.

7. Barbara Katz Rothman, *Recreating Motherhood: Ideology and Technology in a Patriarchal Society* (New York: Norton, 1989).

8. Adrienne Rich, *Of Woman Born: Motherhood as Experience and Institution* (New York: Norton, 1976); Gena Corea, *The Mother Machine* (New York: Harper and Row, 1985); Simone De Beauvoir, *The Second Sex* (New York: Vintage, 1974).

9. Betty Friedan, *The Second Stage* (New York: Summit Books, 1982); Phyllis Chesler, *With Child* (New York: Berkeley Publishing, 1981).

10. "Requests for Contact," *RESOLVE Newsletter,* December 1985, 7.

11. Wulf Utian, James Goldfarb, and Miriam Rosenthal, "Psychological Aspects of Infertility," *in* L. Dennerstein and G. D. Burrows, eds., *Handbook of Psychosomatic Obstetrics and Gynecology* (New York: Elsevier Biomedical, 1983), 234; Arthur L. Greil, Karen L. Porter, Thomas A. Leitke, "Sex and Intimacy Among Infertile Couples," *Journal of Psychology and Human Sexuality* 2 (1989): 117–38; Sandra R. Leiblum, "Intimacy and the New Reproductive Options," *Women and Therapy* 7 (1988): 131–43; Rachel Code, John Parsons, Bridgett Mason, Susan Golombok, "Emotional, Marital, and Sexual Functioning in Patients Embarking Upon IVF and AID Treatment for Infertility," *Journal of Reproductive and Infant Psychology* 7 (1989): 87–93.

12. David Berger, "Couples' Reactions to Male Infertility and Donor Insemination," *American Journal of Psychiatry* 137 (Sept. 1980): 1047–49.

13. Rosa Salter, "Make a Baby, Break a Marriage," *Morning Call,* Allentown, PA, May 15, 1986, D-1.

Chapter 10: High-Tech Children

1. James Schlesselman, "How Does One Assess the Risks of Abnormalities from Human In Vitro Fertilization?" *American Journal of Obstetrics and Gynecology* 135 (1979): 135–48; J. F. Mattei and B. LeMarec, "Genetic Aspects of Artificial Insemination by Donor (AID): Indications, Surveillance and Results," *Clinical Genetics* 23 (1983): 132–38; Gabriele Semenov, Roger Mises,

and Jacqueline Bissery, "Attempt at Follow-up of Children Born through AID," *in* David and Price, eds., *Human Artificial Insemination,* 475–77. See also Chapter 4, note 15.

2. David M. Brodzinsky and Loreen Huffman, "Transition to Adoptive Parenthood," *Marriage and Family Review* 13 (1988): 267–86.

3. Arthur Sorosky, Annette Baran, and Reuben Pannor, *The Adoption Triangle* (Garden City, NY: Doubleday, 1984).

4. Sorosky, Baran, and Pannor, *Adoption Triangle,* 102–03.

5. Betty Jean Lifton, *Lost and Found: The Adoption Experience* (New York: Dial Press, 1979), 23.

6. Jerome Smith and Franklin Miroff, *You're Our Child: A Social Psychological Approach to Adoption* (Lanham, MD: University Press of America, 1987), 30; Christine Manuel and Jean-Claude Czyba, "Follow-up Study on Children Born through AID," *in* G. David and W. S. Price, eds., *Human Artificial Insemination and Semen Preservation* (New York: Plenum Press, 1980), 467–73.

7. Sorosky, Baran, and Pannor, *Adoption Triangle,* chapter 8.

8. Joseph Davis and Dirck Brown, "Artificial Insemination by Donor and the Use of Surrogate Mothers," *Western Journal of Medicine* 141 (July 1984): 128.

9. Jill Krementz, *How It Feels to Be Adopted* (New York: Alfred A. Knopf, 1983), 67.

10. Charlene Miall, "The Stigma of Adoptive Parent States: Perceptions of Community Attitudes Toward Adoption and the Experience of Informal Social Sanctioning," *Family Relations* 36 (1987): 34–39.

11. Jean Pierce, "Misconceptions about Adoptive Families," *Early Child Development and Care* 13 (1984): 365–76; Brodzinsky and Huffman, "Transition to Adoptive Parenthood."

12. Krementz, *How It Feels,* 29.

13. Sorosky, Baran, and Pannor, *The Adoption Triangle,* 92.

14. *Ibid.,* chapters 11 and 12; Lee Campbell, Phyllis Silverman, Patricia B. Patti, "Reunions between Adoptees and Birth Parents: The Adoptees' Experience," *Social Work* 36 (1991): 329–35.

15. Sue Aumend and Marjie Barrett, "Searching and Non-Searching Adoptees," *Adoption and Fostering* (1983): 37–42; idem, "Self-concept and Attitudes toward Adoption: A Comparison of Searching and Nonsearching Adult Adoptees," *Child Welfare* 63 (May–June 1984): 251–59.

16. George Annas, "Artificial Insemination: Beyond the Best Interests of the Donor," *Hastings Center Report* 9 (Aug. 1979): 14–43; Annette Baran and Reuben Pannor, *Lethal Secrets: The Shocking Consequences and Unsolved Problems of Artificial Insemination* (New York: Warner Books, 1989).

17. Sorosky, Baran, and Pannor, *The Adoption Triangle,* 157.

18. Carol Amadio and Stuart Deutsch, "Open Adoption: Allowing Adopted Children to 'Stay in Touch' with Blood Relatives," *Journal of Family Law* 22 (1983/84): 59–93; Reuben Pannor and Annette Baran, "Open Adoption as Standard Practice," *Child Welfare* 63 (May–June 1984): 245–50; Michael Vitez, "Adoption Without Secrets," *Philadelphia Inquirer Magazine* March 4, 1990, 12–20, 26, 36, 43.

19. Krementz, *How It Feels,* 52.
20. Judith Lasker and Susan Borg, "Secrecy and The New Reproductive Technologies" in *New Approaches to Human Reproduction: Social and Ethical Dimensions,* eds. Linda Whiteford and Marilyn Poland (Westview Press, 1989).
21. Herbert Waltzer, "Psychological and Legal Aspects of Artificial Insemination (A.I.D.): An Overview," *American Journal of Psychotherapy* 36 (Jan. 1982): 91–102.
22. Lifton, *Lost and Found;* H. D. Kirk, *Shared Fate* (New York: Free Press, 1964).
23. P. K. Snowden, G. D. Mitchell, and E. M. Snowden, *Artificial Reproduction: A Social Investigation* (London: George Allen and Urwin, 1983); Lifton, *Lost and Found;* Baran and Pannor, *Lethal Secrets.*
24. Snowden, Mitchell, and Snowden, *Artificial Reproduction.*
25. Robert Abramovitz, "Psychological Factors for Children with 'Multiple Parentage,'" paper presented at American Society of Law and Medicine, Cambridge, Massachusetts, October 1984.
26. Elaine Bleckman, "Are Children with One Parent at Psychological Risk? A Methodological Review," *Journal of Marriage and the Family* 44 (1982): 179–95; Barbara Kritchevsky, "The Unmarried Woman's Right to Artificial Insemination: A Call for an Expanded Definition of Family," *Harvard Women's Law Journal* 4 (1981): 1–4; Carson Strong and Jay Schinfeld, "The Single Woman and Artificial Insemination by Donor," *Journal of Reproductive Medicine* 29 (May 1984): 293–99.
27. S. Golombok, H. Spencer, and M. Rutter, "Children in Lesbian and Single-Parent Households: Psychosexual and Psychiatric Appraisal," *Journal of Child Psychology and Psychiatry* 24 (1983): 551; R. Green, "Sexual Identity of 37 Children Raised by Homosexual or Transsexual Parents," *American Journal of Psychiatry* 135 (1978): 692; Brenda Maddox, "Homo-sexual Parents," *Psychology Today,* February 1982, 62–69; Margaret Somerville, "Birth Technology, Parenting and 'Deviance,'" *International Journal of Law and Psychiatry* 5 (1982): 123–53.
28. L. H. Levie, "An Inquiry into the Psychological Effects on Parents of Artificial Insemination with Donor Semen," *Eugenics Review* 59 (1967): 103.
29. John Leeton and June Backwell, "A Preliminary Psychosocial Follow-up of Parents and Their Children Conceived by Artificial Insemination by Donor," *Clinical Reproduction and Fertility* 1 (1982): 307–10; Ian Milsom and Per Bergman, "A Study of Parental Attitudes after Donor Insemination," *Acta Obstetrica et Gynecologica Scandinavica* 16 (1982): 125–28.
30. Brodzinsky and Huffman, "Transition to Adoptive Parenthood"; Christine A. Bachrach, "Children in Families: Characteristics of Biological, Step-, and Adopted Children," *Journal of Marriage and The Family* 45 (1983): 171–79.
31. Krementz, *How It Feels,* 37.
32. Lillian Atallah, "Report from a Test-Tube Baby," *The New York Times Magazine,* April 18, 1976, 52.

Chapter 11: Reactions of Others

1. "What Do You Think about Test-Tube Babies?" *Parents,* November 1978, 148–50.

2. Annette Brodsky, David Martin, Anne Marie Kelly, and Karen Bierman, "Survey of Attitudes about Reproductive Technologies," paper presented at American Psychological Association meetings, Anaheim, CA, 1983; Robyn Rowland and Coral Ruffin, "Community Attitudes to Artificial Insemination by Husband or Donor, *In Vitro* Fertilization and Adoption," *Clinical Reproduction and Fertility* 21 (1983): 195–206; E.S., "A Womb of One's Own," *Psychology Today,* January 1985, 11; Patricia C. Dunn, Ione J. Ryan, and Kevin O'Brien, "College Students' Acceptance of Adoption and Five Alternative Fertilization Techniques," *Journal of Sex Research* 24 (1988): 282–87; Harriet L. Parmet and Judith N. Lasker, "Religion and Views on Reproductive Technologies: A Comparative Study of Jews and Non-Jews," *Shofar* 10 (1991): 57–71; Sandra R. Leiblum and Christopher Barbrack, "Artificial Insemination by Donor: A Survey of Attitudes and Knowledge in Medical Students and Infertile Couples," *Journal of Biosocial Science* 15 (1983): 165–72.

3. E.S., "A Womb of One's Own."

4. Louis Harris, "The Life Poll," *Life* magazine, June 13, 1969, 52–55.

5. Lori Andrews, *New Conceptions: A Consumer's Guide to the Newest Infertility Treatment* (New York: Ballantine, 1985).

6. "What Do You Think about Test-Tube Babies?" *Parents,* November 1978, 148–50.

7. "Feedback," *U.S. Catholic* 54 (1989): 15.

8. Richard L. Matteson and Gerald Terranova, "Social Acceptance of New Techniques of Child Conception," *Journal of Social Psychology* 10 (1977): 255–29; Charlene E. Miall, "Reproductive Technology vs. The Stigma of Involuntary Childlessness," *Social Casework* 70 (1989): 43–50.

9. William Tucker, "In Vitro Veritas," *New Republic,* October 28, 1981, 14–16; Judith N. Lasker and Harriet Parmet, "Rabbinic and Feminist Responses to Reproductive Technology," *Journal of Feminist Studies in Religion* 6 (1990): 117–30.

10. Theodore Hall, "Test Tube Babies and Beyond: Moral Considerations," *Homiletic and Pastoral Review* 79 (Feb. 1979): 25–32, 47–49; Arthur L. Greil, "The Technology of Reproduction: Religious Responses," *The Christian Century* 106 (1989): 11–14.

11. Rita Arditti, Renata Duelli Klein, and Shelly Minden, eds., *Test Tube Women: What Future for Motherhood* (Boston: Pandora Press, 1984); Gena Corea, *The Mother Machine: Reproductive Technologies from Artificial Insemination to Artificial Wombs* (New York: Harper and Row, 1985); Renate Klein, ed., *Infertility: Women Speak Out About Their Experiences of Reproduction* (London: Pandora Press, 1989); G. Corea, R. Duelli Klein, J. Hanmer, H. B. Holmes, B. Hoskins, M. Kishwar, J. Raymond, R. Rowland, R. Steinbacher, *Man-Made Women: How New Reproductive Technologies Affect Women* (Bloomington: Indiana University Press, 1987); Patricia Spallone and Deborah Lynn

Steinberg, *Made to Order: The Myth of Reproductive and Genetic Progress* (Oxford: Pergamom Press, 1987).

12. Hall, "Test Tube Babies," 27.
13. Philip Boyle, "Solutions to Infertility: Even the Simplest Medical Answer Raises Troubling Ethical Questions for Catholics," *Counseling and Values* 33 (1989): 234–39.
14. Immanuel Jakobovits, "Artificial Insemination," *in Jewish Medical Ethics* (New York: Bloch Publishers, 1975); Fred Rosner, "In Vitro Fertilization and Surrogate Motherhood: The Jewish View," *Journal of Religion and Health* 22 (Summer 1983): 139–60; Beth Spring, "Christian Doctors Approve In Vitro Fertilization," *Christianity Today,* June 18, 1990, 56–57.
15. David Neff, "Test-Tube Tangle," *Christianity Today,* October 20, 1989, 15; J. Robert Nelson, ". . . And Keeps Rebounding/Dilemmas of Conception and Birth," in *Science and Our Troubled Conscience* (Philadelphia: Fortress Press, 1980).
16. "Feedback," *U.S. Catholic* 54 (1989): 15.
17. Jack Moore, "Human In Vitro Fertilization: Can We Support It?" *Christian Century* 98 (1981): 442–46; Michael Gold, *And Hannah Wept; Infertility, Adoption, and the Jewish Couple* (Philadelphia: The Jewish Publication Society, 1988).
18. George Annas and Sherman Elias, "Social Policy Implications of Noncoital Reproduction," paper presented at American Society of Law and Medicine, Cambridge, MA, October 1984.
19. Corea, *The Mother Machine.*
20. Harris, "Life Poll," 52.

Conclusion

1. Russell Baker, "Tinker People," *New York Times,* May 24, 1977, 35.
2. Karen M. Hicks, *Surviving The Dalkon Shield IUD: Women v. The Pharmaceutical Industry* (New York: Teachers College Press, 1994); Merle J. Berger and Donald P. Goldstein, "Infertility Related to Exposure to DES *in utero:* Reproductive Problems in the Female," in Miriam D. Mazor and Harriet F. Simons, eds., *Infertility: Medical, Emotional, and Social Considerations* (New York: Human Sciences Press, 1984), 157–68; Alan B. Retik and Stuart B. Bauer, "Infertility Related to DES Exposure *in utero:* Reproductive Problems in the Male," *in* Mazor and Simons, *Infertility,* 169–79; Daniel Cramer et al., "Tubal Infertility and the Intrauterine Device," *New England Journal of Medicine* 312 (1985): 941.
3. Ruth Hubbard, "The Case against In Vitro Fertilization and Implantation," in Helen Holmes, Betty Hoskins, and Michael Gross, *The Custom-Made Child: Woman-Centered Perspectives* (Englewood Cliffs, NJ: Humana Press, 1981), 259–60.
4. Shulamith Firestone, *The Dialectic of Sex* (New York: Bantam, 1971).
5. Aldous Huxley, *Brave New World* (New York: Harper and Row, 1979).
6. Gena Corea, *The Mother Machine: Reproductive Technologies from Artificial*

Insemination to Artificial Wombs (New York: Harper and Row, 1985); Rita Arditti, "Surrogate Mothering Exploits Women," *Science for the People* (May/June 1987): 22–31.

7. Aldous Huxley, *Brave New World;* Margaret Atwood, *The Handmaid's Tale* (New York: Houghton Mifflin, 1986).

8. Corea, *The Mother Machine.*

9. Meg Dooley, "Helping Mother Nature," *Columbia,* October 1985, 26; Kurt Hirschhorn, "Practical and Ethical Problems in Human Genetics," *Birth Defects* 8 (July 1972): 30.

10. Albert Havercamp and Miriam Orleans, "An Assessment of Electronic Fetal Monitoring," *Women and Health* 7 (1982): 115–34; David Banta, "Benefits and Risks of Electronic Fetal Monitoring," *in* Helen B. Holmes, Betty B. Hoskins, and Michael Gross, eds., *Birth Control and Controlling Birth* (Clifton, NJ: Humana Press, 1980), 183–91.

11. Corea, *The Mother Machine,* 97.

12. Elizabeth Beck-Gernsheim, "From the Pill to Test Tube Babies: New Options, New Pressures in Reproductive Behavior," *in* Kathryn S. Ratcliff, ed., *Healing Technology: Feminist Perspectives* (Ann Arbor: University of Michigan Press, 1989), 28.

13. Eugene Sandburg, "Only an Attitude Away: The Potential for Reproductive Surrogacy," *American Journal of Obstetrics and Gynecology* (1989): 1441–46.

14. Gail Robinson, "The New Discrimination," *Environmental Action* 10 (March 1979): 4–9; Ronald Bayer, "Women, Work, and Reproductive Hazards," *Hastings Center Report* 12 (Oct. 1982): 14–19; "Four Women Assert Jobs Were Linked to Sterilization," *New York Times,* January 5, 1979, 21.

15. Sherry Wieder, Letter to the Editor, *New York Times,* July 9, 1982.

16. Hubbard, "The Case against In Vitro Fertilization and Implantation."

17. Robyn Rowland, "Technology and Motherhood: Reproductive Choice Reconsidered," *Signs* 12 (1987): 512–29.

18. Corea, *The Mother Machine.*

19. Alexander Morgan Capron, "The New Reproductive Possibilities: Seeking a Moral Basis for Concerted Action in a Pluralistic Society," *Law, Medicine and Health Care,* October 1984; "Position Paper: Issues Arising from In Vitro Fertilization, Artificial Insemination by Donor, and Related Problems in Biotechnology," *New Zealand Medical Journal* 22 (May 1985): 396–98; Peter Singer, "Making Laws on Making Babies, *Hastings Center Report,* August 1985, 5–6; Warnock Committee of Inquiry, "Recommendations," *British Medical Journal,* July 1984, 289.

Index

Deleted

Aug 16/96